Islamophobia in the West

Since the late 1980s, growing migration from countries with a Muslim cultural background, and increasing Islamic fundamentalism related to terrorist attacks in Western Europe and the US, have created a new research field investigating the way states and ordinary citizens react to these new phenomena. However, while we already know much about how Islam finds its place in Western Europe and North America, and how states react to Muslim migration, we know surprisingly little about the attitudes of ordinary citizens toward Muslim migrants and Islam. Islamophobia has only recently started to be addressed by social scientists.

With contributions by leading researchers from many countries in Western Europe and North America, this book brings a new, transatlantic perspective to this growing field and establishes an important basis for further research in the area. It addresses several essential questions about Islamophobia, including:

- What exactly is Islamophobia and how can we measure it?
- How is it related to similar social phenomena, such as xenophobia?
- How widespread are Islamophobic attitudes, and how can they be explained?
- How are Muslims different from other outgroups and what role does terrorism and 9/11 play?

Islamophobia in the West will be of interest to students and scholars of sociology, religious studies, social psychology, political science, ethnology, and legal science.

Marc Helbling is Head of the research group 'Immigration Policies in Comparison' (IMPIC) at the Social Science Research Centre Berlin (WZB), Germany. His recent publications include *Restructuring Political Conflict in Western Europe* (Cambridge University Press, 2012, with Hanspeter Kriesi, Edgar Grande *et al.*) and *Practising Citizenship and Heterogeneous Nationhood: Naturalisations in Swiss Municipalities* (Amsterdam University Press, 2008). He has also published articles in journals such as the *European Journal of Political Research*, *Ethnic and Racial Studies*, and the *Journal of Ethnic and Migration Studies*.

Routledge Advances in Sociology

Islamophobia in the West

Measuring and explaining individual attitudes

Edited by Marc Helbling

Routledge
Taylor & Francis Group

LONDON AND NEW YORK

First published 2012
by Routledge
2 Park Square, Milton Park, Abingdon, Oxon OX14 4RN

Simultaneously published in the USA and Canada
by Routledge
711 Third Avenue, New York, NY 10017

Routledge is an imprint of the Taylor & Francis Group, an informa business

British Library Cataloguing in Publication Data
A catalogue record for this book is available from the British Library

Library of Congress Cataloging-in-Publication Data
Islamophobia in the West : measuring and explaining individual attitudes / edited by Marc Helbling.
    p. cm. -- (Routledge advances in sociology)
    1. Islam--Public opinion. 2. Muslims--Public opinion.
    3. Islamophobia--Europe. 4. Islam in mass media.
    5. Europe--Ethnic relations. I. Helbling, Marc.
    BP52.I8545 2012   305.6'97--dc23
    2011036005

ISBN: 978-0-415-59444-8 (hbk)
ISBN: 978-0-203-84173-0 (ebk)

Typeset in Bembo
by Bookcraft Ltd, Stroud, Gloucestershire

MIX
Paper from
responsible sources
FSC
www.fsc.org   FSC® C004839

Printed and bound in Great Britain by the MPG Books Group

Contents

List of figures

List of tables

List of contributors

Pieter Bevelander, Malmö University

Erik Bleich, Middlebury College

Brian H. Bornstein, University of Nebraska

Marco Cinnirella, Royal Holloway, University of London

Henk Dekker, Leiden University

Juan Díez-Nicolás, Universidad Complutense Madrid

Donald Ernst, Hillsdale College

Joel S. Fetzer, Pepperdine University

Clive D. Field, Universities of Birmingham and Manchester

Marc Helbling, Social Science Research Center Berlin (WZB)

Kerem Ozan Kalkan, Middle East Technical University Ankara

Rahsaan Maxwell, University of Massachusetts Amherst

Jonas Otterbeck, Lund University

Edwin Poppe, Utrecht University

J. Christopher Soper, Pepperdine University

Zan Strabac, Trondheim Business School (TØH)

Eric M. Uslaner, University of Maryland

Marko Valenta, Norwegian University of Science and Technology (NTNU)

Jolanda van der Noll, Bremen International Graduate School of Social Sciences (BIGSSS)

Maykel Verkuyten, Utrecht University

Ricard Zapata-Barrero, Universitat Pompeu Fabra

1 Islamophobia in the West

An introduction

Marc Helbling

When asked what comes to mind upon hearing the words 'Islam' and 'Muslims', many people answer with names like Osama bin Laden, events such as 9/11 and other terrorist attacks, sources of terrorist violence such as Palestinian suicide bombers, and ideas and practices related to oppression, including *jihad*, veiling, Islamic law, and the like (Park *et al.* 2007; Gottschalk and Greenberg 2008: 3).

The term 'Islamophobia' is often invoked to label such negative connotations and associations, and the word has enjoyed an extraordinary vogue over the past decade; indeed, it has come to appear regularly in both academic and political debates. Its success, however, is not free of problems. The term has been used by a considerable variety of people and in remarkably different ways, leading to controversy over what it really means, and whether it is useful. As Cesari (2006: 6) has noted, the term is 'imprecisely applied to very diverse phenomena, ranging from xenophobia to anti-terrorism.'

In a similar vein, Maussen (2006: 100) argues that: '"Islamophobia" is a reductive "catchall" – pulling together diverse forms of discourse, speech and acts, and suggesting that they all emanate from an identical core (in this case, a "fear" or a "phobia" of Islam)'. He is right to suggest that a distinction should be made between different kinds of discourses – differentiating, for instance, between academic discussions on the relations between Islam and modernity, public discussions on whether Islam recognizes the principle of separation of state and church, and public exclamations about Islam being 'a backward religion' or a 'violent religion'. For this reason, it is important to clarify straight away what is understood by Islamophobia as we are discussing it, and thus what this book is about.

Maussen's statement remarks upon Islamophobia's frequent conceptual applications – how it is used to investigate public and media debates, political discourses and policy decisions. In such use, it refers to the general social climate and the positions of political actors. It certainly goes without saying that Islamophobia can also be found at the micro level among ordinary citizens. However – even though these two levels are highly interconnected – the attitudes of ordinary citizens have not been investigated as thoroughly as social debates and policies have been, so far.

With this in mind, this volume reunites a group of researchers who have been working on ordinary Western Europeans' and North Americans' attitudes toward Muslim immigrants and Islam, by means of survey data. The main goals of the various chapters include studying how pervasive Islamophobic attitudes are and deducing how best we can measure and explain them. The goal of this introduction is to clarify and discuss why we should study Islamophobia and how we can define and measure it.

Why study Islamophobic attitudes of ordinary citizens?

Since the beginning of the twenty-first century, Islam has become an increasingly important religion in Europe, with growing immigration from Muslim countries. Depending on which estimation one uses, between 10 and 15 million Muslims now live in Western Europe (Modood 2003; Fetzer and Soper 2005). According to Cesari (2010b: 10), approximately 5 per cent of the European Union's 425 million inhabitants are Muslims. Smith (2010: 29) considers four to seven million Muslims living in the US to be a reasonable estimate.

In many West European countries Islam has become the third largest religion (Hollifield 1992; Nielsen 1992, 1999). Islam's growing presence has also led to new conflicts. While in the past, guestworkers typically formulated claims that were predominantly social and political in nature, some Muslim immigrants are now demanding religious and cultural rights as a consequence of their permanent settlement. Western societies must now deal with religious rules and customs – something that can be very difficult for parties that perceive such rules and customs as at odds with the norms of a secular liberal state. As Cesari (2010b: 17) and many others have pointed out, Western European states tend to consider faith as misplaced and illegitimate in secular societies. This kind of conflict is perhaps best summarized in the provoking title of Sniderman and Hagendoorn's (2007) book, *When Ways of Life Collide* – a volume that investigates attitudes toward Muslims in the Netherlands, and also Muslims' perceptions of Western Europeans. In the US, by contrast, religion is often seen as a bridge rather than a barrier (Clark *et al.* 2010: 19; Foner and Alba 2008).

Demands for the construction of mosques, Islamic religious education and gender-separated sports lessons – as well as provisions for the protection of cultural practices, such as forced marriages and female circumcision (which are also heavily disputed within Islam) – pose new challenges to some actors and groups in the host societies (for example, Cesari 2005b; Koopmans *et al.* 2005: 149; Wohlrab-Sahr and Tezcan 2007). The headscarf affair in France is probably the most prominent issue in this context, since it sparked heated political debates in France and other countries, and also led to academic debates on the limits of liberalism (Thomas 2006; Bowen 2007; Joppke 2007; 2009a). As much as the issue of wearing of the veil can be debated, it also remains an open discussion as to whether critical views on Islam – for example, those expressed in the Danish newspaper cartoons featuring the prophet Mohammed – should be allowed in the name of freedom of speech (Levey and Modood 2009).

Unfortunately, as relevant as these debates on normative issues may be, we cannot address them here. Following Sniderman and Hagendoorn (2007: 29), the real problem at the core of this volume is not that certain cultures might not be compatible with each other – or that one group misunderstands the culture of another – but, rather, that 'it is a misunderstanding to suppose that there is a culture, a definite set of beliefs and values to be understood'.

Since the terrorist attacks of 9/11, debates on Muslim integration have often been linked to questions of public security (Bleich 2009a; Cesari 2010b). One would do well not to forget, however, that even before 9/11 Islam had often been regarded as a particularly violent religion. Events such as the Iranian revolution and the occupation of the American embassy in Tehran, the Salman Rushdie *fatwa* and the Palestinian suicide bombings in Israel have shaped the picture of Muslims for many West Europeans and North Americans.

That fact that Muslim issues have become more controversial, taking 'centre stage' over the past two decades, is also due to political mobilization by populist and radical right parties. Concerns over Islam and Muslim migration have had an important impact on the success of populist and radical right parties in Western Europe (Allen 2006: 72; Skenderovic 2006; Mudde 2007: 84–6; Shooman and Spielhaus 2010: 203–4). Many parties have profited from increasing fear of Islam and have mobilized to exploit this issue. Shooman and Spielhaus (2010: 204) have even argued that Islam has allowed various national populist and radical right parties to establish contacts with each other and to cooperate at the European level; in sum, they suggest that Islam serves as a unifying topic and a common enemy.

As one might expect, these developments have led to extensive research on Islam and Muslim migration in Western Europe, and – to a lesser extent – in North America (see Buijs and Rath 2002 as well as Maussen 2007 for extensive overviews). Maussen (2007: 4) identifies two broad fields of study. The first field has dealt predominantly with the dynamics of Islamic beliefs, values, everyday religiosity and practice. These studies focus on types of religious belongings, differences between generations or the emergence of a 'European Islam' (for an overview see Peter 2006). There is already a series of excellent books and edited volumes on the topic of Muslims in Western countries (Haddad 2002; Haddad and Smith 2002; Hunter 2002; Cesari 2004; Klausen 2005; Modood 2005; Abdo 2006).

The second strand of this literature is concerned with various aspects of the regulation of Islam – or, 'the way in which societies create opportunities for the development of Islam, or oppose them' (Buijs and Rath 2002: 9, quoted in Maussen 2007: 4). These, mostly comparative, studies are interested in how West European states react to Muslim migration and accommodate Islam (Pauly 2004; Fetzer and Soper 2005; Koopmans *et al.* 2005: ch. 4; Joppke 2007; 2009a; Dolezal *et al.* 2010; Cesari 2010a; Triandafyllidou 2010).

While we know quite a bit about how Islam finds its place in Western Europe and North America, and about how states react to Muslim migration, we know surprisingly little about the attitudes of ordinary citizens toward Islam and Muslim migrants. Research on individual attitudes has been neglected for a long time and remains scarce today. Only recently, and in the context of the events and developments mentioned above, have social scientists begun to describe and analyze Islamophobic attitudes. Most of these initial papers were not published until the second half of the 2000s (Leibold and Kühnel 2003; 2006; Stolz 2005; Dekker and Van der Noll 2007; Kühnel and Leibold 2007; Strabac and Listhaug 2008; Velasco González *et al.* 2008; Bevelander and Otterbeck 2010; Helbling 2010).

This is not to say that Islamophobia did not exist in earlier periods, naturally. Anti-Muslim or anti-Islamic phenomena have existed at various points in time in European history. Since we lack the space to expand on this aspect of Islamophobia in our current project, I must make do with a reference to Edward Said's (1978) seminal study on Orientalism – which brought into focus how, over the past several centuries, western cultural, academic and imperial projects have created a negative and stereotypical representation of an exotic and barbarous Orient that exists in opposition to the enlightened Occident. Cesari (2010a: 1) refers to Mamdani's (2004) concept of 'cultural talk' to describe how Muslims have been 'petrified' in history and occupy a mould from which they cannot escape (see also Love 2009).

The recent increase in studies on Islamophobic attitudes can be explained by two related reasons: first, Muslim migrants have been present in West European and North American societies for almost half a century now, and second, Muslim issues have been on the political agendas of Western states since the 1980s. Muslims have seldom been defined by their religion, however (Bleich 2009a: 353). Rather, they were more often considered an ethnic or economic group – seen as 'guest-workers', 'Turks' or 'blacks'. In the aftermath of 9/11, however, the category of 'Muslim' has become much more relevant in political and academic debates. As a result, data availability has also undergone a change. Until recently, most surveys on attitudes toward immigrants typically included only general questions on respondents' perceptions of immigrants, with other categories deemed irrelevant. Today, however, there are more and more surveys that include specific questions on attitudes toward Muslims. Data from some of the first studies – focusing exclusively on attitudes toward Muslims and Islam – are presented in this volume.

Defining Islamophobia

While the term 'Islamophobia' had appeared as early as the 1920s, it became extremely popular in the 1990s (Allen 2006: 68–71). According to Otterbeck and Bevelander (2006) the term appeared for the first time in 1918 in French. Until the 1990s, however, it was used in a very general way without a clear definition. The Runnymede Trust report on Islamophobia – published in 1997 in Great Britain – now stands as one of the first major contributions in this field, and one that has proven extremely influential on subsequent works (Runnymede Trust 1997). Allen (2010: 3) speaks of the 'first decade of Islamophobia' that began with the publication of this report. According to Allen (2004: 71), it has been the most often cited source on Islamophobia since its publication. In it, Islamophobia is defined as the fear of or aversion to Islam and Muslims. It also differentiates between a narrow and open view on Islam. The former view, it holds, considers Islam either to be monolithic and static, or to be aggressive and ideological. The latter view, by contrast, recognizes that Islam – as much as Christianity – is dynamic and consists of various aspects and ideologies. Accordingly, attitudes toward 'Islam' and 'Muslims' can be attuned to different aspects. This is one reason why research on Islamophobia has started to differentiate between attitudes toward different immigration groups from Muslim countries, and between general attitudes concerning groups of migrants and their cultural practices (see below).

As Bleich (2011) has noticed, many scholars deploy the term Islamophobia without explicitly defining it (MacMaster 2003; Kaplan 2006; Bunzl 2007; Poynting and Mason 2007; Cole 2009; Halliday 1999) or by using rather vague, narrow and generic definitions, such as 'fear of Muslims and Islam', 'rejection of the Muslim religion' or 'a form of differentialist racism' (Geisser 2003:10; Werbner 2005: 8; Gottschalk and Greenberg 2008: 5). The absence of a more thorough discussion on how to define and conceptualize Islamophobia is even more problematic in the light of the fact that it refers to very different social phenomena, as we have seen above.

Shyrock (2010: 4–8) even speaks of a 'troubling term'. For some people it is not even clear whether it is rather 'good' or 'bad' to be Islamophobic. Islamophobia can stand for a justified criticism of Islamic fundamentalism, or just certain aspects of Islam. Bleich (2011) presents examples of writers and newspaper columnists who publicly declare that they are proud to be Islamophobic. For them, Islamophobia means distrust of Islam as a doctrine, rather than hostility toward Muslims. Thus, it is unclear whether Islamophobia stands for negative attitudes toward a group of people – and thus a concept comparable to those of prejudice and xenophobia – or reflects a critical and reflexive position toward Islam.

One could also argue that the term is completely useless and even dangerous as there is no new social phenomenon, and thus no need for a new term to describe one. Quite the opposite, in fact: the term 'Islamophobia' is sometimes politically loaded, serving only to stigmatize a certain group instead of describing a social reality. Thus, the term might create a social reality that had not existed before. Proponents of this view feel there is nothing particular about Muslim immigrants; hostilities against them can be described using existing terms, such as prejudice and xenophobia. More generally, it is unclear whether Islamophobic attitudes – if they exist at all – are turned toward Muslims as immigrants and an ethnic group, or Muslims as a religious group, or Islam in general, or specific aspects of Islam or Muslim cultural and religious practice, and so on.

As Gottschalk and Greenberg (2008: 3) also show, most peoples' geographic reference frames are limited to the Middle East when they hear the words 'Muslims' or 'Islam'. As a matter of fact, however, more Muslims live east of Afghanistan, in countries such as Indonesia, Pakistan and India. Thus, it is unclear whether Islamophobia is about Islam and Muslims in general, or about immigrants from Arabic countries.

In contrast to the many vague, narrow and generic definitions, some authors employ rather precise definitions. According to Stolz (2005: 548), for example, a good definition of Islamophobia should be attuned to already-existing definitions from research in the field of racism and xenophobia, in order to enable a comparison between Islamophobia and other outgroup phobias. Furthermore, the definition has to be encompassing enough to include all phenomena meant by the term – for example, not just attitudes toward Islam, but also toward Muslim groups. Finally, he maintains, the definition should be devoid of any theoretical explanations of the phenomenon, as these must be tested empirically. On the basis of these criteria, for Stolz, 'Islamophobia is a rejection of Islam, Muslim groups and Muslim individuals on the basis of prejudice and stereotypes. It may have emotional, cognitive, evaluative as well as action-oriented elements (e.g. discrimination, violence)' (2005: 548).

Despite these various controversies, I believe Islamophobia is a useful concept. By this, I do not suggest that it is an indispensable term or a widespread social phenomenon, however. We might very well come to the conclusion that other concepts – such as prejudice and xenophobia – already adequately describe what Islamophobia is intended to describe, or that Islamophobia – if it is clearly distinguishable from concepts such as prejudice and xenophobia – is ultimately a rather minor social phenomenon. All these questions remain open for research, and the aim of this volume is to consider them in greater detail.

I decided to use the term Islamophobia mainly because it has already taken root in public, political and academic discourses. Ignoring a widely used term would only cause confusion, after all. At a roundtable of the 2006 World Convention of the Association for the Study of Nationalities, Charles Tilly –in his comments on Brubaker's book, *Ethnicity without Groups* (2004) – voiced serious doubts about Brubaker's suggestions to completely abolish terms such as 'identity' and 'nation.' While Tilly agreed that the use of such terms might create a certain (false) reality – as they are often linked to certain understandings of how the social world works – he prefers to define these concepts more comprehensively. This comes close to Spillman's (1995: 144) argument concerning the limits that may be reached in questioning profound categories such as gender: '[I]t is much more possible to challenge meanings and values associated with gender than to constitute for oneself a genderless identity.' I do not claim that Islamophobia is as established a concept as nation or gender. I am convinced, however, that, instead of abolishing a widely used term, supplying a definition upfront – one that makes clear what we are measuring form the beginning – is much more fruitful.

As a guiding definition, I like to invoke Erik Bleich's (2011) definition of Islamophobia. I call it a guiding definition as each chapter will use its own. It was not possible to use exactly the same definition for all the studies presented here, for a simple pragmatic reason. Although all of the chapters present original work, the various analyses are based on surveys that were designed a long time before this book project was started. In spite of the number of studies that used the same or very similar questions, we cannot be sure whether they measure the exact same concept. Since we have no means of undertaking the necessary validation tests, we make do with a guiding definition, allowing each chapter to adapt it to its own needs and purposes.

Bleich (2011) defines Islamophobia as 'indiscriminate negative attitudes or emotions directed at Islam or Muslims'. This definition consists of four key elements: First, Islamophobia is about *attitudes or emotions* and can therefore clearly be distinguished from behavior. While Islamophobic behavior can likely be explained to a large extent by Islamophobic attitudes, various other factors – such as opportunity structures and social control mechanisms – are crucial for explaining why and when attitudes lead to a specific behavior (Dahl 1956; Ajzen and Fishbein 1980; Offe and Preuss 1991). It has also been shown that even *positive* attitudes can sometimes lead to discriminative behavior (Sniderman and Hagendoorn 2007; Van der Noll *et al.* 2010). These studies show that there is a relatively large minority of people with positive attitudes who are nonetheless unwilling to attribute the same rights and liberties to certain outgroups.

Under Bleich's definition, these attitudes and emotions must be *indiscriminately* directed at Islam and Muslims. This is a second crucial element in the definitions of parallel concepts, such as homophobia and xenophobia. It means that people make generalizations about a group of people on the basis of traits that can be ascribed to a minority of its members at best. Many people fear Islam, for example, considering Muslims to be religious fundamentalists or even terrorists. As a matter of fact, some Muslims interpret the *Qur'an* in a very fundamentalist way, and al-Qaida has been responsible for many terrorist attacks. On the other hand, we also know that the very large majority of Muslims – living in the West or in Muslim countries – condemn these acts and ideas. While people might be justified in fearing terrorist attacks, it is a sign of Islamophobia for one to consider all Muslims to be terrorists. Thus, the true problem of Islamophobia lies in its essentializing and universalizing quality.

It might go without saying that Islamophobia is about *negative* indiscriminate attitudes or emotions. I still like to emphasize this aspect, however, since it makes it clear that we are not simply speaking about stereotypes that are indiscriminate and simplifying, but that can also be positive or negative. As Shryock (2010) convincingly points out, Islamo*philia*, the selective construction of a positive image of Islam, can be as problematic as Islamophobia since it might lead to bizarre 'good-Muslim/bad-Muslim' binaries, 'in which the good Muslim (the friend) is the real Muslim, and the bad Muslim (the enemy) is a creature who violates the good Muslim code' (Shryock 2010: 9–10). The 'good' Muslim – peaceful, politically moderated, pluralist, in favor of equality between men and women, highly educated, etc. – is as much a stereotype as a 'bad' Muslim. Even if many Muslims correspond to the image of the good Muslim, such generalizations are scarcely helpful to understanding the social world. Indeed, as Cesari (2010b: 14) points out, 'the fact that Muslims must be named as good or law-abiding means that there is an underlying assumption that Islam is a potential menace to society.'

What finally distinguishes Islamophobia from other similar concepts is that, in the case of Islamophobia, indiscriminate negative attitudes or emotions are directed at *Islam or Muslims* – not just at outgroups in general. Again, there might be some dispute as to whether it makes sense to include both terms, Islam and Muslims, especially in the light of the fact that some people differentiate between Muslims as a group and Muslim practices (Sniderman and Hagendoorn 2007). Some people may have negative attitudes toward Islam but neutral or positive attitudes toward Muslims, for instance (for similar arguments about anti-Americanism, see Chiozza 2007 and Isernia 2007). Halliday (1999: 898), however, notes that current circumstances in Western Europe and North America suggest prejudices against *Muslims*, rather than fear of Islam. There is no fear of Islam in the narrow sense, he argues, since Islam is not threatening to win primary controlling influence in large segments of the Western world. For Halliday (1999: 898) 'the enemy is not a faith or a culture, but a people. Hence the more accurate term is not "Islamophobia" but "Anti-Muslimism".' As Bleich (2011) rightly emphasizes, though, it should nevertheless be an open empirical question, as to the extent to which these two components are intertwined or need to be separated especially in the light of more recent conspiracy theories according to which Europe is taken over by Islam (see Bat Ye'or 2005).

Measuring Islamophobia

Once we have defined our central concept, we need to find ways to measure it. So far, most research on Islamophobia has relied on rather crude and simple indicators. Strabac and Listahaug (2008) and Helbling (2010), for example, used the World Values Survey question, which asked respondents whether or not they would like to have Muslims as neighbors. Clearly, such an indicator runs the risk of oversimplifying the underlying theoretical concept; indeed, it is hard to imagine that such a question encompasses all aspects of Islamophobia and/or that no other factors than Islamophobia might influence the answer.

The problem, however, is that there are hardly any surveys that have been conceptualized to study Islamophobia. Especially in the matter of country comparisons, there are no data available that might allow us to create more sophisticated indicators. Thus, researchers remain dependent on single questions that have been included in the questionnaires of international surveys. Even at the national level, relatively few surveys have been designed to analyze attitudes toward Muslims and Islam. The few that do exist are presented and discussed in this volume. One of the many innovative aspects of this volume is that many of the chapters collected here base their analyses on specifically designed surveys, and use indicators that are based on a series of questions that delineate different aspects of Islamophobia.

While most work on Islamophobia focuses on the extent and the causes of this social phenomenon, some scholars have made the *construction* of Islamophobia indicators the focus of their work (Echebarria-Echabe and Fernandez Guede 2007; Lee *et al.* 2009). While Lee *et al.* explicitly speak of an Islamophobia scale, Echebarria-Echabe and Fernandez Guede prefer to call their indicator an 'anti-Arab prejudice measure' – though many of their items refer to Islam. When it comes to attitudes toward the people who have been linked to Islam, Echebarria-Echabe and Fernandez Guede (2007) speak of Arabs, Arab immigrants, and sometimes of Muslims – whereas Lee *et al.* (2009) prefer the term 'Muslims'.

This raises again the question of whether or not these terms refer to different groups, and whether or not respondents might make a difference between these groups. This question needs to be investigated through qualitative research, in which people are asked what they understand by the terms 'Islam' and 'Muslims.' To prepare the questionnaire for the Dutch study they present in this volume, Dekker and Van der Noll have held focus group discussions that have revealed, for example, that Muslims are almost always linked to the nationalities of the major Muslim groups in the Netherlands, that is Turks and Moroccans. At the same time, they observed that the participants *did not* make a difference between various Muslim groups, such as Sunnites and Shiites. Whether we would observe similar discussions about Islam and Muslims in other contexts cannot be answered here. It appears, however, that it is extremely useful to combine different methods when creating valid indicators.

Quantitative validation tests represent another means of putting indicators in perspective – a means of relating the indicators under investigation to indicators that are supposed to measure or explain similar social phenomena. Generally speaking, 'validity is concerned with whether a variable measures what it is supposed to measure' (Bollen 1989: 194). Indicators can be assessed in terms of their convergent validity, which concerns the comparison of alternative measures of the same concept. Valid measures of the same underlying construct are empirically associated, and therefore similar and 'convergent'. Two common instruments for assessing convergent validity are correlation tests and exploratory factor analyses. While correlation tests enable us to observe whether indicators converge or not, factor analysis allows us the additional ability to discriminate among different underlying dimensions and to show which dimension an indicator belongs to and how strongly it correlates with that respective dimension. Another way to evaluate whether or not an indicator measures what it is supposed to measure concerns *construct validity* – that is, 'whether a measure relates to other observed variables in a way that is consistent with theoretically derived predictions' (Bollen 1989: 188). In other words, an indicator is considered to be valid if it behaves in a manner consistent with theoretical expectations.

In the studies by Echebarria-Echabe and Fernandez Guede (2007) and Lee *et al.* (2009), exploratory factor analyses produced very meaningful factors that tap specific aspects of Islamophobia. Correlation tests revealed that these respective indicators were related to other prejudicial attitude scales – such as racism and anti-Semitism – as well as to indicators including authoritarianism, conservatism and cultural desirability bias, which the authors argue are causally related to Islamophobia and other forms of prejudice.

In this volume, Ernst and Bornstein present yet another indicator that they call the Anti-Muslim Prejudice Scale (AMP). They claim that their indicator taps a broader range of negative attitudes toward Muslims than already existing scales. In contrast to nearly every other study measuring broad prejudice against Muslims, they provide data on the internal consistency, the test-retest reliability and the concurrent and discriminant validity of their indicator.

With three different indicators at hand already – whose validity and reliability have been found to be very satisfactory – we must consider how these indicators relate to one another, whether they measure all the same phenomenon, and how useful it really is to have different indicators. In a young research field, it is not uncommon for similar ideas to be pursued in parallel. In a next step, however, it will be necessary to compare the different indicators and to specify when each one should be used. Moreover, these indicators need to be put into practice. The data in all three studies are solely descriptive and correlational in nature. To investigate the causes and effects of Islamophobia, more sophisticated multivariate tests will be needed.

Islamophobia and other phobias

The validation tests of the three studies briefly presented in the previous part reveal that respective Islamophobia indicators in question are closely related to other prejudicial indicators that tap xenophobia, racism and anti-Semitism. These findings raise questions over the extent to which these concepts and indicators refer to and measure different social phenomena. For example, Sniderman and Hagendoorn (2007: 56–8) found that measures for prejudice for different groups are very similar.

Even if there is a hierarchy of acceptance (see Hagendoorn 1993; 1995), those who dislike one minority group are systematically hostile to others. In his study on the US, Love (2009) argues that Islamophobia is not always about Islam and Muslims per se, but rather, often about prejudice and discrimination directed at people who look different.

Giugni and Morariu (2010) show how, in Switzerland, general intolerance values heavily affect attitudes toward Muslims. Following Schwartz's (1994) work, they imposed a high-order value dimension to differentiate between tolerance and intolerance value orientations (Giugni and Morariu 2010: 82–3). This allowed them to differentiate between intolerance and hostility toward minority groups like women, homosexuals and migrants on the one hand, versus intolerance and hostility toward those displaying perceived 'deviant' behavior – such as drug or alcohol addiction – on the other. In other words, their research speaks to the idea that there are people who are not particularly Islamophobic, but who dislike Muslims out of an impulse that makes them universally hostile toward all people who are different from them.

Working in the US context, Kerem Ozan Kalkan and Eric Uslaner make a similar point in their contribution to this volume. According to their work, it is incorrect to view Islamophobia as a mainstream Christian fear. They hold that the roots of hostility toward Muslims are much the same as those governing attitudes toward other outgroups. Accordingly, Muslims belong to what Kalkan and Uslaner call the 'band of others'. The authors also differentiate between culturally and behaviorally different groups – African-Americans and Latinos on the one hand, and illegal immigrants, welfare recipients, gays, etc. on the other hand. They argue and empirically show that Muslims are considered both ethnically and behaviorally different, as their religious practices seem strange and outside the Judeo-Christian tradition to some people. Their 'band of others' indicators prove to be by far the most powerful factors related to Islamophobic attitudes – stronger than the perceived threat of terrorism, and other typical prejudice factors.

While Giugni and Morariu (2010) and Kalkan and Uslaner in their contribution to this volume explain Islamophobia with general intolerance, other researchers prove more keenly interested in the relationship between Islamophobia and similar phenomena, such as xenophobia and anti-Semitism. The crucial question – and one that has already been asked by some researchers – is whether Islamophobia is different from xenophobia, and whether the first may be merely a particular form of the second – thus meaning nothing more than hostile attitudes toward a specific group of foreigners, that is immigrants from Muslim countries (Kühnel and Leibold 2007; Helbling 2010). Using factor analyses Stolz (2005: 559–60) as well as Kühnel and Leibold (2007) show that Islamophobia *cannot* be differentiated from xenophobia. Stolz (2005) and Strabac and Listhaug (2008) also tested the impact of a series of widely used factors on both xenophobia and Islamophobia, to see whether or not similar patterns were present. They were unable to reveal any major differences. All of these results suggest that nowadays, xenophobic people are mainly Islamophobic, since Muslims constitute a very important immigration group.

In my own work, I argue that even if the same people show hostile attitudes toward both immigrants and Muslims, it does not imply that Islamophobia is the same as xenophobia (Helbling 2010). After all, the same people might be xenophobic and Islamophobic for different reasons. For instance, if Islamophobia is indeed something new, we are obligated to show that the factors that explain it are different from those that explain hostile attitudes toward immigrants in general. To this end, I developed three arguments and tested whether people with a specific understanding of citizenship, religious persons and post-materialists have different attitudes toward Muslims and immigrants in general.

It is widely recognized that attitudes toward others are highly influenced by how we see ourselves and define our culture. Accordingly, one's understanding of citizenship and xenophobia represent two sides of the same coin. Still, favoritism directed at an in-group does not necessarily imply hostility toward outgroup members. After all, attitudes toward foreigners depend on the kind of national self-understanding that prevails in a group or a person; indeed, while some forms of national self-understanding are compatible with other cultures, others are not. Working from questions on attitudes toward naturalization criteria, I have generated three models of national self-understanding. One model includes questions concerning the Muslim headscarf, and criteria that have recently appeared in the public debate and are often related to immigrants from Muslim countries.

Second, to clarify whether immigrants from Muslim countries are seen as an ethnic or a religious group, and whether hostilities toward them result from the conviction that people with such a religious background constitute a danger for established religious groups, I have tested whether religious persons in particular are afraid of Muslims. It could also be argued, alternatively, that religious people might support Muslims out of a solidarity stemming from being confronted by similar problems, namely a secular society that leaves no space for religious matters.

The third means of revealing differences between xenophobia and Islamophobia lay in investigating the values of post-materialists. It is often argued that Muslims do not respect the principles of gender equality and oppress women. More generally, many Westerners perceive Muslims as belonging to a culture or religion where individual rights are subordinate to collective rights. It might therefore be that people who perceive the position of women in society and individualism as crucial achievements of Western societies see these attainments as endangered by immigration from Muslim countries. Thus, it might very well be that such post-modernists are Islamophobic, but have no hostile attitudes against foreigners in general.

Overall, the results of my analyses did not display different explanatory patterns for xenophobic and Islamophobic attitudes, suggesting that Islamophobia is the same as xenophobia. Since this study only focused on one country, however, adding more cases might lead to different results.

Islamic fundamentalism and the terrorist attacks of 9/11

The terrorist attacks of 9/11 and related events in Madrid and London not only brought Islam and Muslim immigrants to the front pages of national newspapers and to the top of the political agendas of national governments. These events also had a major impact on research on Islamophobia. While research on the accommodation of Islam in Western Europe has already been important since the 1980s, there were hardly any publications on attitudes toward Muslims before 9/11.

The terrorist attacks at the beginning of the new century have often been considered a major juncture in the relationship between citizens of Western countries and new arrivals from Muslim countries. It has been argued for a long time that 9/11 has had a fundamental impact on attitudes toward Muslim immigrants. Fekete (2004: 14) argues that the post-September 11, 2001 political agenda has created a culture of suspicion against Muslims. The 2004 Runnymede-backed Commission on British Muslims found that Islamophobia has increased in scope and intensity since the 1997 Runnymede report on Islamophobia. More specifically, the number of Muslims imprisoned and the number stopped by the police in Britain have increased notably.

In her study on self-reported racial and religious discrimination, Sheridan (2006) found that in the wake of September 11, 2001, levels of implicit or indirect discrimination rose by over 80 per cent, and experiences of overt discrimination by over 75 per cent (see also Echebarria-Echabe and Fernandez Guede 2006). In a US study that was conducted directly after the terrorist attacks and one year later, Person and Musher-Eizenman (2005) showed that participants both believed that they should and would be more prejudiced toward Arabs, than toward blacks. They also observed that participants reporting high levels of daily news exposure – television, radio, Internet and newspapers – were more prejudiced toward Arabs than those who reported low levels.

Working from similar concerns, the European Monitoring Centre on Racism and Xenophobia (EUMC) implemented a reporting system on potential anti-Islamic reactions in the then 15 EU member states. The report's findings show that Islamic communities became targets of increased hostility after September 11 (Allen and Nielson 2002). It also revealed how a greater sense of fear among the general population exacerbated existing prejudices and fuelled acts of aggression in many European countries. While the report gave important information on various events and trends, the fact that it was based on single case studies means that it cannot be used to yield a deeper measure of the exact impact of 9/11.

While most researchers would agree that the terrorist attacks exacerbated existing developments that had already begun in the 1980s, scholars disagree on whether or not 9/11 had a strong negative effect on attitudes toward Islam and Muslim migrants (Cesari 2005a; Fetzer and Soper 2005: 143–4; Koopmans *et al.* 2005: 243–8; Bleich 2009a). As a media study has shown, after 9/11 Muslim issues increased markedly in importance in German, Swiss and Austrian public debates (Dolezal *et al.* 2010), and there is reason to believe this happened in the other countries as well.

The question remains, however: has this development also led to a more critical discourse and attitudes, and influenced the way immigration issues are debated and perceived? Fetzer and Soper (2005: 145), for example, conclude that post-2001 Western European attitudes have been much more tolerant than the popular press suggests. Cesari (2005a: 50) argues that while 9/11 legitimized a more coercive form of government control of Islam and of Muslim migrants, it was control that had been debated earlier, even though it had not been fully accepted at that time. Koopmans *et al.* (2005: 243–8) argue that, in the past few years, tolerance toward ethnic minorities and multicultural rhetoric has declined, in part due to events related to 9/11. But in the case of the Netherlands – invoked as the paradigmatic example of multiculturalism – the authors note that similar policy changes had already been implemented as early as the 1990s. Contributions in a volume edited by Bleich (2009a) came to the conclusion that 9/11 represents but one particular event in a broader development that has led to the current securitization of Muslim issues.

One of the main questions we address in this volume is whether 9/11 had a long-lasting impact on attitudes toward Muslim migrants. The few studies that have already tackled this question uncovered rather small impacts. Using data from 1998, Sniderman and Hagendoorn (2007) were unable to study developments over time, but nonetheless showed that tensions between Muslims and Western Europeans were already evident before the terrorist attacks. Bleich (2009b) shows that, in France and Great Britain, negative attitudes toward Muslims have risen continuously over the past 20 years. Working in the US context, Panagopoulos (2006) observes sharp movements in opinion dynamics in the immediate aftermath of 9/11, but also finds that opinion levels stabilized thereafter, at around the levels they had been before 9/11. Kalkan *et al.* (2009) – also working in the US context – demonstrate that feelings toward Muslims have been shaped more influentially by general effects for outsider groups, as well as by personality and value orientations. They reveal the structure of people's evaluations of Muslim to have been very similar before and after the 9/11 attacks. Still others argue that Islamophobia is endemic in European culture, and has become more intensive at various points in time in the course of the past centuries (Allen 2004). Schildkraut (2002) found some 9/11 effects on American identity. However, she concludes that, one year after the attacks, it is too early to tell whether these effects are long lasting.

In this volume, the effects of 9/11 are investigated in three chapters, in three different ways. Kalkan and Uslaner test the extent to which their argument – concerning the validity of their 'band of others' indicator – holds before and after the terrorist attacks. First, they refer to other studies that have shown how Americans viewed Muslims as part of this 'band of others' well before the attacks on 9/11, suggesting that negative attitudes toward Muslims predated the 9/11 attacks and did not change much. In their own analyses they reveal that the changes in probabilities for the 'band of others' drops after 9/11. However, it is still by far the most powerful determinant of attitudes toward Muslims.

While most studies investigating the effects of 9/11 study the developments of attitudes, discourses or policies over time, Jolanda van der Noll is – to my knowledge – the first to use an indicator that measures the extent to which respondents feel subjectively affected by the 9/11 attacks. In her contribution to this volume she comes to the conclusion that people who felt affected by the terrorist attacks were not significantly more Islamophobic than others, and suggests that this might be due to the fact that issues related to Islam had already become prominent before the end of 2001.

Cinnirella is more generally interested in how the people's perceptions of terrorism have influenced Islamophobia. On the basis of various studies that he and his colleagues have conducted, he finds that attitudes toward Muslims prove significantly more negative under high-threat situations than in normal situations.

Furthermore, he suggests that perceptions of symbolic and cultural threat are not the only things that play a role; effects also prove to be related to xenophobia to a notable degree. Realistic threat perceptions from terrorism were also found to be very important.

Islamophobia, surveys and attitudes: providing different perspectives

The aim of this volume is to bring together scholars who work, by means of survey data, on the attitudes of ordinary citizens in Western Europe and North America toward Muslims and Islam. Such a focus has both its advantages and disadvantages. In his book on Orientalism, Said (2003[1978]: 291) bemoans the rising role the social sciences play in this field – in contrast to the dominant role that literature and philology played in earlier times – and the growing tendency 'to keep the region [of the Arab or Islamic Orient] and its people conceptually emasculated, reduced to "attitudes," "trends," statistics: in short, dehumanized'. Similar arguments have been expressed, casting doubt on research that seeks to grasp Islamophobia in Western Europe and North America by means of survey data. More generally, Said's remark speaks to a widespread controversy about the best way to analyze society.

Focusing on surveys and attitudes in this volume does not mean, of course, that such a perspective on Islamophobia is in any way superior to other perspectives. Nobody disagrees that a complex social phenomenon – such as Islam in the West, Muslim immigration, and reactions to it – can only be apprehended by approaching it on different levels, from different perspectives, using different data and applying different methods. Attitudes of ordinary citizens and population surveys are only one aspect and one method – but, I believe, crucial ones, to which rather little attention has been paid in the past.

Of course, it would have been possible to combine different methods and perspectives in this volume, and to include work based on survey research *beside* studies that followed different research traditions. In that regard, editors Katzenstein and Keohane's volume on anti-Americanism (2007) is a uniquely felicitous example. The different chapters draw on cross-national public opinion research, experiments in the field of cultural psychology, discourse analysis informed by theories of the public sphere or social frames and historical-institutional approaches.

Given that so little attention has been paid so far to the Islamophobic attitudes of ordinary citizens, and that no single book or edited volume has put survey research at the centre of its focus, I think that it is necessary to dedicate an entire volume to this particular perspective. Still, I like to emphasize that this volume includes survey data that has been used in a great variety of ways. While descriptive statistics are sometimes used to assess the extents of attitudes, inferential statistics are applied to analyze correlations and causal relationships. Two chapters present meta-analyses: analysing a large range of previous surveys in order to assess the consistency and robustness of their results. Another chapter describes the construction and testing of an Anti-Muslim Prejudice Scale, while yet another investigates Islamophobia at the aggregate level in order to circumvent some of the problems surveys pose in the context of controversial issues.

Finally, some of the chapters also look at politics, public debates, the role of the media and Islamophobic behavior (hate crimes, discrimination etc.) – not as a goal in itself, but to place the attitudes of ordinary citizens into a broader perspective. An important recurrent theme in some of these chapters concerns the influence that public debates and media coverage appear to have on individual attitudes. This brings us to the question of what social, political and cultural context might be in play.

So far, virtually all studies on Islamophobia have focused on individual countries, and specific country patterns have hardly been addressed. This stands in stark contrast to the comparative studies that investigated the integration of Muslims in Western Europe and how Western states have accommodated Islam (Haddad 2002; Haddad and Smith 2002; Hunter 2002; Cesari 2004; Pauly 2004; Fetzer and Soper 2005; Klausen 2005; Koopmans *et al.* 2005: ch. 4; Modood 2005; Abdo 2006; Joppke 2007, 2009a; Dolezal *et al.* 2010; Triandafyllidou 2010).

A laudable exception can be found in a study by Strabac and Listhaug (2008) who investigated anti-Muslim prejudice in West and East European countries. Besides the usual individual variables, the authors also investigate some important country factors, such as the percentage of Muslims and non-EU migrants, GDP per capita and unemployment rates, to explain the Islamophobic attitudes of ordinary citizens. As it turns out, however, these country level indicators have no impact.

More research on country specific patterns of Muslim immigration and Islamophobia will be necessary. Additional factors such as state-church relationships (Fetzer and Soper 2005) and integration models and multicultural politics (see Banting and Kymlicka 2006) need to be accounted for in future research. A comparative approach remains difficult, however, since there are hardly any international surveys that include relevant questions. These limitations become clear in this volume, too, insofar as it brings together studies from different countries in Western Europe and North America, yet provides few cross-country analyses, for the simple reason that such data are scarcely available.

Such studies are urgently needed, however, as factors such as national cultures and citizenship regimes may well have a crucial impact on how Muslim migrants are perceived. As it will become clearer in the various chapters, Islamophobia might constitute a different problem, or might be explained by different factors in a country such as, for example, Norway – which is characterized, at least until recently, by a comparatively low number of Muslim immigrants and the absence of high-media-profile terrorist acts – or Spain – which has traditionally had a close relationship with the Muslim country of Morocco, from where a large number of people have immigrated over the last decades.

Cross-country comparisons are also needed to investigate differences between North America and Western Europe. As Casanova (2007) notes in his work on the new religious pluralism in the US and the countries of the European Union, Muslim migrants constitute different groups in these two groups of countries. While they constitute the most important immigration group in West European countries, only about 10 per cent of all migrants in the US have a Muslim background. Moreover, a large percentage of Muslims in the US are black Africans. Thus, those people constitute an ethnic group or a race, more than a religious group, in the eyes of many Americans. Moreover, religion plays a different role in the US than it does in Western Europe (see more generally Banchoff 2007). Religion, in general, and Islam in particular, are hardly ever mentioned in debates about immigration in the US (Clark *et al.* 2010: 19). All of these factors might lead to differences in the attitudes of the native society toward Muslims.

Overview of the volume

The contributions in this volume have been grouped into four parts, each of which is dedicated to one of the main research questions discussed so far: How can we measure Islamophobia? How widespread is it? How can we explain it? And are Muslims different from other outgroups? Of course, most of the chapters address several of these questions, and also include aspects that have *not* been discussed so far.

In the *first part*, the chapter by Donald Ernst and Brian H. Bornstein on their newly developed Anti-Muslim Prejudice Scale will start off this volume. As I have mentioned above, there is an extremely pressing need for valid and reliable indicators to investigate Islamophobia. Surprisingly little effort has been invested so far in creating such indicators, however. Ernst and Bornstein's contribution allows us to take an important step forward in this domain.

In the *second part*, the scope of Islamophobia is investigated. It is often simply assumed that Islamophobia is a widespread social phenomenon – but this has scarcely been demonstrated empirically. Different strategies are used in order to put the intensity of Islamophobia into perspective: Erik Bleich and Rahsaan Maxwell, as well as Ricard Zapata-Barrero and Juan Diez-Nicolas, compare attitudes toward Muslims and toward other outgroups. Both chapters come to the conclusion that people do not always place Muslims at the bottom of the domestic minority hierarchy, and that ordinary citizens are often more concerned with other groups. Zan Strabac and Marko Valenta observe that negative attitudes toward Muslims are not more pronounced than negative attitudes toward immigrants in general. In contrast, however, there are aspects of Muslim culture that are indeed viewed more negatively.

The chapters by Zapata-Barrero/Diez-Nicolas, Strabac/Valenta, and by Pieter Bevelander and Jonas Otterbeck relate their findings on the scope of Islamophobic attitudes to the public and political spheres. They are interested in the extent to which a negative political climate has an impact on, or is reflected in, ordinary citizens' minds. For the countries of Norway, Spain and Sweden, they reach the conclusion that, although there has been much negative focus on Muslims in public debates, this atmosphere has not translated into strongly negative attitudes toward Muslim immigrants themselves.

A final strategy for assessing the intensity of Islamophobia is to let the Muslims themselves speak: to inquire about the extent to which they feel discriminated against, and the extent to which they identify with the new host society. For Britain, Bleich and Maxwell find that Muslims demonstrate remarkably high levels of positive national identification and political trust – suggesting that there is not yet a fundamental or permanent cleavage present in British society. By contrast, in their study on the experiences of young Muslims, Bevelander and Otterbeck concluded that a relatively *large* percentage of them have been exposed to some form of offensive treatment or harassment.

The chapters in the *third part* are all concerned with the question of how to explain Islamophobia. Joel S. Fetzer and J. Christopher Soper investigate the 2009 referendum vote in Switzerland that banned the construction of new minarets – seeking to explain why the Swiss voted so convincingly in favor of the ban. They argue that partisanship, ethno-religious identification and educational attainment represent key factors shaping citizen's voting behavior. In contrast to all of the other studies reassembled here, Fetzer and Soper analyze official voting *statistics*, instead of survey data. They argue that answers provided by survey respondents are not necessarily reliable, especially when concerning racially or religiously sensitive topics.

Henk Dekker and Jolanda van der Noll conducted a survey among Dutch youth. Their explanatory model includes variables from intergroup contact, socialization, social identity and integrated threat theories. Their results show that negative perceptions of Islam, perceptions of safety and value threat from Islam and Muslims, and a very positive national in-group attitude are the main Islamophobia-inducing predictors, whereas direct contact with Muslims and positive socialization about Islam and Muslims are major Islamophobia-reducing predictors.

In the third chapter in this section, Jolanda van der Noll analyzes three Dutch surveys from the first half of the 2000s, in order to discern how well Islamophobia, value orientations and the extent to which people felt concerned at the attacks of 9/11, explain tolerance toward Muslims. She comes to the conclusion that the overall attitudes toward Muslims and a multicultural value orientation are strong predictors. Concerns over the 9/11 terrorist attacks did not contribute to the explanation of tolerance toward Muslims.

Maykel Verkuyten and Edwin Poppe focus on people's political tolerance for Muslim practices. Working from an overview of empirical research conducted in the Netherlands, they show that political tolerance is relatively distinct from prejudice, that different criteria are used to determine whether particular practices are acceptable, that intergroup threat and national identity are key underlying factors, and that the historical content of the national identity – in terms of Christianity or tolerance – affects tolerance for Muslim practices among low and high identifiers respectively.

In the last chapter of the third part, Clive D. Field analyzes attitudes toward Muslims in Britain through a meta-analysis of 64 opinion polls conducted between 2007 and 2010. Using such a large range of studies allows him to provide a robust evidence base for summarizing what is known about Islamophobia in Britian. In this fashion, he avoids relying on individual surveys – which are often not conceptualized to assess Islamophobia. Overall, he comes to the conclusion that Islamophobia is multi-layered and affects one-fifth to three-quarters of adults. It is undoubtedly increasing, albeit still less pervasive than in other Western European countries, and it is by far the commonest form of religious prejudice in Britain. Muslims are thought to be slow to integrate, to have qualified patriotism and, sometimes, to be drawn to extremism. Such negativity is disproportionately concentrated among men, the elderly, the lowest social groups and Conservative voters.

The *fourth and final part* of this volume brings us back to two research questions I have already briefly addressed: Are Muslims different from other groups, and what role does terrorism play? As shown above, Kalkan/Uslaner and Cinnirella discuss the extent to which distinctions between Muslims and other outgroups can be made, and how attitudes toward Muslims are affected by perceptions of terrorism that seem to concern only Muslims and no other immigration groups.

As it appears, this volume makes some important contributions to a better understanding of Islamophobia. It is the first volume that is entirely dedicated to the study of individual attitudes toward Muslims relying on survey data. A large variety of methods and approaches are pursued in the different chapters that enable us to analyze Islamophobia from different perspectives. Thereby, the reader will hopefully gain a better understanding of how to measure and explain Islamophobia.

Obviously, at the end of this volume all will not have been said and done on Islamophobic attitudes. In this volume we make an attempt to assemble all we know on Islamophobia from population surveys so far. Some of the findings presented here contradict common ideas about Islamophobia. It seems that Muslims are not always placed at the bottom of the domestic minority hierarchy. Moreover, the terrorist attacks of 9/11 and public debates have apparently not had a major impact on attitudes toward Muslims. The evidence provided is however limited to individual countries.

Concerning other aspects the authors in this volume do not always agree. While some show that Muslims demonstrate remarkably high levels of positive national identification and political trust, others report that a relatively large percentage of them have been exposed to some form of offensive treatment or harassment. Many indicators will be discussed that explain Islamophobic attitudes. However, it will also become apparent that a clear distinction between Muslims and other outgroups is not always made. It is thus an open question whether the same factors shape Islamophobia and other phobias.

Therefore, further research is needed. More systematic country comparisons, surveys that focus more systematically on Islamophobic attitudes, combinations of methods and relating micro data to political developments are among the most important aspects that deserve further attention. However, we hope to have laid a useful starting point for further projects with this volume.

Part 1

How to measure Islamophobia

2   Prejudice against Muslims

Associations with personality traits and political attitudes

Donald Ernst and Brian H. Bornstein

Prejudice against Muslims has been extensively documented and finds expression in popular media, discriminatory governmental policies and hate crimes (Gottschalk and Greenberg 2008; Love 2009). Understanding such prejudice has become a matter of special urgency since the terrorist attacks of September 11, 2001. The Federal Bureau of Investigation (2002) reported that in the months following those attacks, hate crimes against Muslims in the United States rose 1,600 percent; subtle and overt discrimination against Muslims increased in the UK as well (Sheridan 2006). A recent review of the literature found that both implicit and explicit negative attitudes toward Muslims in the United States rose in the years following the 9/11 attacks, due in part to biased media portrayals (Cashin 2010).

Progress in understanding anti-Muslim prejudice has come on many fronts. Oswald (2005) found that prejudice and discrimination against Arabs[1] was predicted by a complex interaction of demographic, threat, self-categorization and individual difference variables – including social dominance orientation, to which we return below. In the Netherlands, where anti-Muslim sentiment is particularly strong, Velasco González *et al.* (2008) found that more than half of adolescents expressed negative feelings toward Muslims, feelings that were best predicted by a model in which intergroup contact, in-group identification, and multiculturalism fed into symbolic threat and cognitive stereotypes as mediator variables. In a very large study sampling populations throughout Europe, Strabac and Listhaug (2008) found that prejudice against Muslims was generally greater than against other immigrant groups and was negatively associated with education, white-collar occupation and female gender. Research on stereotyping has shown that although Muslims are quite heterogeneous in ethnicity, religious observance and country of origin, Americans tend to equate them with Arabs and lump together all individuals of Middle Eastern descent (Love 2009). There is also a widely held belief that most Muslims are militant fundamentalists, despite abundant evidence to the contrary (Gottschalk and Greenberg 2008).

The focus of the present volume is on Islamophobia: morphologically, the fear of Islam and Muslims. Lee *et al.* (2009) developed the Islamophobia Scale and demonstrated its validity as a measure of that construct. Our work presented here addresses broader, multifaceted prejudice against Muslims, of which Islamophobia is theorized to be a part. The Anti-Muslim Prejudice (AMP) Scale we devised surveys a wide range of negative attitudes toward Muslims and Islam, some concerning morality and social and cultural impact, which we would expect to be related to Islamophobia, and others having to do with intelligence, sophistication, and appearance and grooming. Other researchers examining general prejudice against Muslims have employed measures with more limited scope and which, though face-valid, in many cases possess unknown psychometric properties. To our knowledge, the AMP Scale is the only available measure that taps a broad range of negative attitudes toward Muslims and for which data on internal consistency, test-retest reliability, and concurrent and discriminant validity are available. We attend carefully to those data here and, in order to shed light on possible causes and consequences of prejudice against Muslims, we examine correlations of AMP with individual difference variables and political attitudes.

Perhaps no two individual difference variables relate more robustly with prejudice than do authoritarianism and social dominance orientation (Altemeyer 1996; Sidanius and Pratto 1999). Adorno *et al.* (1950) defined authoritarianism to include the traits of conventionalism, authoritarian submission, authoritarian aggression, opposition to the tender-minded, superstition, power, destructiveness and cynicism, belief in a dangerous world and exaggerated concern with sexual behavior. Unfortunately, their measure of authoritarianism, the F (Fascism) Scale, possessed numerous psychometric shortcomings (Altemeyer 1996). One was that it was unbalanced, being composed only of pro-authoritarian items, leaving open the possibility that any correlations between the F Scale and other unbalanced measures were to some extent spurious, caused by acquiescence bias (Cronbach 1946; Altemeyer 1996). Altemeyer (1981) developed an alternative measure, the Right-Wing Authoritarianism Scale (RWA), which proved to be much superior. He also refined the construct itself, presenting evidence that its core consists of only three of the nine factors originally discussed by Adorno *et al.* (1950): *authoritarian submission*, the desire to submit to those one recognizes as authorities; *authoritarian aggression*, aggression against others who do not submit to one's own accepted authorities; and *conventionalism*, adherence to societal conventions (Altemeyer 1996). Individuals high on authoritarianism are hypothesized to be prejudiced against minorities and outgroups because of their conventionalism and authoritarian aggression, especially when such prejudice is sanctioned, or at least tolerated, by authorities. Authoritarianism as measured by the RWA Scale has been found to be associated in Canada and the United States with general ethnocentrism and prejudice against gays (Altemeyer 1988), in South Africa with prejudice against blacks (Duckitt 1992), and in the Soviet Union with anti-Semitism (McFarland *et al.* 1990).

Social dominance orientation (SDO) is the preference for anti-egalitarian, hierarchical relationships among groups and the desire that one's own group dominate other groups (Sidanius 1993; Pratto *et al.* 1994; Sidanius and Pratto 1999). Sidanius (1993) argues that social dominance orientation is evolutionarily adaptive because groups that organize hierarchically have a competitive advantage over those that do not. According to social dominance theory, prejudices are 'legitimizing myths' that help to maintain group hierarchy (Sidanius and Pratto 1999: 45). This hypothesis was supported by Quist and Resendez (2002), who found that the relationship between prejudice and intergroup threat was stronger in those high on SDO. Sidanius and Pratto (1999) found SDO to correlate with prejudice against many different groups: blacks and Arabs in the United States, Asian immigrants and Native Canadians in Canada, Aborigines in Taiwan and Palestinians in Israel. Further research indicated that SDO is related to prejudice against Aborigines and Asians in Australia (Heaven and St Quintin 2003); sexism in Canada, Taiwan, China, and Israel (Pratto *et al.* 2000); and anti-gay bias (Whitley 1999).

The two empirical studies presented here examine relationships among prejudice against Muslims, authoritarianism, social dominance orientation, and other individual difference variables such as political attitudes.

Study 1

This study was cross-sectional, designed to determine the internal consistency and construct validity of the Anti-Muslim Prejudice Scale. Construct validity (Cronbach and Meehl 1955; Campbell and Fiske 1959) was tested by examining the correlations of AMP with theoretically related constructs: anti-Arab racism; posse Muslims –the degree to which one would support one's government in persecuting Muslims; modern racism (against blacks); right-wing authoritarianism; social dominance orientation; fundamentalism; nationalism; and conservatism. Two separate samples were taken, the first in February 2002 at Hillsdale College, a small, private liberal arts institution (Study 1a) and the second several weeks later at the University of Nebraska-Lincoln (Study 1b), a large, public institution.[2] Both are located in the Midwestern United States. Because Hillsdale identifies itself as politically, socially, and religiously conservative, whereas the University of Nebraska-Lincoln is considered to be more mainstream and diverse, we expected anti-Muslim prejudice and related constructs to be higher in Study 1a than in Study 1b (Altemeyer 1996).

Method

Participants

Study 1a sampled 47 students (26 female, 20 male and one unidentified) from Hillsdale College. All participants were white, and 89 percent identified themselves as Christian. Study 1b sampled 62 students (42 female and 20 male) at the University of Nebraska-Lincoln. They self-reported as 87 percent white and 89 percent Christian. All subjects participated as one means of fulfilling a course requirement.

Materials

Anti-Muslim Prejudice (AMP) Scale (Appendix A). This measure is comprised of 20 face-valid items: 10 anti-Muslim and 10 pro-Muslim (reverse scored). An example anti-Muslim item is *Muslims, as a rule, are more devious than other people.* An example pro-Muslim item is *Islam promotes kindness and love toward all people.* Because the AMP Scale is balanced in this way, scores on it should be relatively unaffected by acquiescence bias, the degree to which a respondent generally tends to agree with whatever statements are presented to him or her. The instructions and response scales for the AMP are, with minor modification, those developed by Altemeyer (1996: 12) for his Right-Wing Authoritarianism Scale, which was refined through many iterations and which has excellent psychometric properties. Response scale options ranged from −4 (very strongly disagree) to +4 (very strongly agree), with 0 being neutral.

Anti-Arab Racism Scale (Pratto *et al.* 1994). This scale consists of three negative statements, about Arabs, Iraqis and Muslims respectively, and two positive statements, about Arabs and Muslims respectively. An example item is *Most of the terrorists in the world today are Arabs.*

Posse Scale. Altemeyer (1996) designed this instrument to measure the extent to which individuals would be willing to cooperate with their government in persecuting members of a specified group. In this study, the group was named radical Muslims. The scale includes nine items. An example is *I would support the use of physical force to make radical Muslims reveal the identity of other radical Muslims.*

Modern Racism Scale.[3] Constructed by McConahay (1986), this historically has been the most widely used measure of subtle racism against blacks. An example item is *Over the past few years, blacks have gotten more economically than they deserve.*

Right-Wing Authoritarianism (RWA) Scale (Altemeyer 1996). This scale is balanced, having 15 scored pro-authoritarian items and 15 reverse-scored anti-authoritarian items, with content addressing authoritarian submission, authoritarian aggression, and conventionalism. In samples from many nations, it has been found to be reliable (alphas normally near 0.90) and construct valid.

Social Dominance Orientation (SDO) Scale. We used the 16-item, balanced version of the scale referred to by Sidanius and Pratto (1999: 67) as 'SDO$_6$'. Sidanius and Pratto (1999) report that it is internally consistent, with Cronbach's alphas ranging from 0.72 to 0.92, has good test-retest reliability, and is construct valid.

Fundamentalism Scale. Altemeyer (1996) defines fundamentalism as religious authoritarianism. The scale has 20 items, half pro-fundamentalist and half anti-fundamentalist (reverse-scored), and has good internal consistency (typical Cronbach's alpha=0.92). An example item is *God has given mankind a complete, unfailing guide to happiness and salvation, which must be totally followed.*

Nationalism Scale (Pratto *et al.* 1994). The six items on this scale address whether or not it is to the benefit of other countries to be influenced by the United States and for the United States to gain more power. An example item is *Generally, the more influence America has on other nations the better off they are.*

Demographics and general information questionnaire. This included a three-item self-report of political stance – liberal to conservative – regarding economic, social and foreign policy issues (Pratto *et al.* 1994), as well as standard demographic questions (for example, race, gender).

The demographics and general information questionnaire always appeared last. The other questionnaires were ordered by the Latin Square method, which ensures that each questionnaire appears at each ordinal position an equal number of times and that each questionnaire is immediately preceded by and immediately followed by each of the other questionnaires an equal number of times (Shaughnessy and Zechmeister 1990).

Procedure

The participants completed the questionnaires in small groups, working individually. The entire procedure took approximately 25 minutes.

Results and discussion

The internal reliabilities of each measure appear in Table 2.1, means appear in Table 2.2, and intercorrelations are shown in Table 2.3.[4]

For AMP, Cronbach's alphas of 0.93 in Study 1a and 0.92 in Study 1b provide evidence that it is internally consistent.

Compared with the participants in Study 1a, the participants in Study 1b were less conservative ($t(104)=6.6$, $p<0.001$), less religiously fundamentalist ($t(103)=4.3$, $p<0.001$), less authoritarian ($t(101)=5.0$, $p<0.001$), and lower on social dominance orientation ($t(104)=6.0$, $p<0.001$) and modern racism ($t(105)=5.2$, $p<0.001$). This confirms that the participants in the two studies differed as expected, with those in Study 1b a more mainstream young adult sample. They did not, however, differ on nationalism ($t(106)=0.71$, $p=0.48$).

In Study 1a, the mean item score on anti-Muslim AMP items was -0.63 (SD=1.7) and that on pro-Muslim AMP items was -0.57 (SD=1.5). This appears to suggest that on average, even these politically conservative participants were roughly neutral regarding Muslims. The participants in Study 1b scored lower than those in Study 1a on AMP ($t(101)=3.0$, $p=0.004$). Compared to Study 1a participants, they tended to disagree more strongly with anti-Muslim items (mean item score $=-1.2$, $t(101)=1.9$, $p=0.06$), and they agreed more strongly with pro-Muslim items (mean item score$=0.46$, $t(106)=-4.0$, $p<0.001$).

Every correlation detected in the politically conservative sample of Study 1a was replicated in the more mainstream sample of Study 1b. The strongest evidence of the concurrent validity of the AMP Scale is its high correlation with anti-Arab racism, which actually approaches unity (0.94 in Study 1a and 0.97 in Study 1b) when corrected for attenuation due to the imperfect reliabilities of the measures

Table 2.1 Scale reliabilities (Cronbach's alphas) in Study 1

Variable	Hillsdale College	University of Nebraska
Anti-Muslim prejudice	0.93	0.92
Anti-Arab racism	0.72	0.80
Posse Muslims	0.93	0.92
Modern racism	0.86	0.85
Right-wing authoritarianism	0.94	0.93
Social dominance orientation	0.80	0.93
Fundamentalism	0.92	0.93
Nationalism	0.83	0.83
Conservatism	0.86	0.82

Table 2.2 Descriptive statistics in Study 1

Variable	Hillsdale College		University of Nebraska		Range possible*
	Mean	SD	Mean	SD	
Anti-Muslim prejudice	−0.29	29.83	−16.81	26.62	−80 to 80
Anti-Arab racism	19.72	6.15	18.40	6.31	7 to 35
Posse Muslims	−13.72	17.92	−13.69	15.77	−32 to 32
Modern racism	25.98	9.44	17.40	7.48	7 to 49
Right-wing authoritarianism	4.62	42.62	−35.52	38.39	−120 to 120
Social dominance orientation	61.73	14.94	42.08	17.52	16 to 112
Fundamentalism	9.18	36.90	−19.78	31.99	−80 to 80
Nationalism	20.33	8.33	21.40	7.42	6 to 42
Conservatism	15.70	3.92	10.56	3.95	3 to 21

Note
*   This is the range of scores possible on each scale, not the measured range in our samples. High values always indicate more of the designated trait.

Table 2.3 Relationships with anti-Muslim prejudice (Pearson correlations) in Study 1

Variable	Hillsdale College	University of Nebraska
Anti-Arab racism	0.77[a]	0.83[a]
Posse Muslims	0.41[b]	0.53[a]
Modern racism	0.68[a]	0.56[a]
Social dominance orientation	0.64[a]	0.61[a]
Right-wing authoritarianism	0.49[b]	0.40[b]
Nationalism	0.45[b]	0.65[a]
Conservatism	0.46[b]	0.26[c]
Fundamentalism	0.25	0.40[b]

Note
[a] $p < 0.001$;
[b] $p < 0.01$;
[c] $p < 0.05$, two-tailed.

(Pedhazur and Pedhazur-Schmelkin, 1991). That this correlation is so high, though, suggests a possible shortcoming in AMP discriminant validity: perhaps the AMP Scale does not discriminate between prejudice against Muslims and prejudice against Arabs. We note, however, that two of the five items on the Anti-Arab Racism Scale are actually about Muslims, not Arabs. Also, for these participants in these empirical contexts, anti-Muslim prejudice and prejudice against Arabs may be highly overlapping constructs, whereas for other individuals in other contexts – for Armenians or Kurds, for example, both of whom have a long and painful history with non-Arab (Turkish) Muslims – the Muslim/Arab distinction may be more meaningful, and the AMP Scale may prove to discriminate more effectively.

Another mild source of concern about AMP discriminant validity is that AMP correlated strongly with modern racism (against blacks). Corrected for attenuation, in Study 1a this correlation is 0.76. To address this concern, we tested the difference between the correlations of AMP with anti-Arab racism and with modern racism. Using list-wise deletion to equalize N for every combination of the three variables, in Study 1a the correlation of AMP with anti-Arab racism (r (41)=0.80) was greater than that with modern racism (r(41)=0.68) by a one-tailed test (t(40)=1.75, $p<0.05$), providing evidence that the AMP Scale does discriminate between prejudice against Muslims and prejudice against blacks. This finding was replicated a fortiori in Study 1b (t(55)=3.78, $p<0.001$).

Table 2.4, showing the relationship between AMP and anti-Arab racism when other measured variables are statistically controlled, provides further evidence of discriminant validity. The relationship of AMP with anti-Arab racism does not appear to be due solely to the relationships of each of these with any other measured variable, including modern racism.

The relationship of the AMP Scale with the Posse (against Muslims) Scale provides evidence of AMP concurrent validity and suggests that prejudice against Muslims could spill over into discriminatory action at the behest of the government.

Since authoritarianism and social dominance orientation are known to be associated robustly with many forms of prejudice, their associations with AMP in our sample (Table 2.3) provide evidence of the concurrent validity of AMP, as well as further evidence in support of the authoritarian and social dominance theories of prejudice.

The relationship of AMP with nationalism provides additional evidence of the concurrent validity of AMP and suggests that, among Americans, AMP might be associated with attitudes regarding US policy toward Islamic countries, a possibility we address in Study 2.

We summed self-reported conservatism on social, economic and foreign policy matters into an overall conservatism score. The observed relationship between conservatism and AMP provides yet further evidence of the concurrent validity of AMP, echoing the findings of previous researchers (for example, Altemeyer 1996) that political conservatism is associated with prejudice.

Table 2.4 Partial correlations of anti-Muslim prejudice with anti-Arab racism in Study 1

Control Variable	Hillsdale College	University of Nebraska
Posse Muslims	0.74	0.78
Modern racism	0.60	0.76
Right-wing authoritarianism	0.75	0.80
Social dominance orientation	0.64	0.76
Fundamentalism	0.76	0.79
Nationalism	0.72	0.71
Conservatism	0.75	0.82

Note
All ps<0.001.

There was only a tendency for AMP to be associated with fundamentalism ($r(43)=0.25$, $p=0.10$) in Study 1a, but this relationship was significant in Study 1b ($r(55)=0.40$, $p<0.01$), providing additional evidence of AMP concurrent validity and suggesting that authoritarianism in religious attitudes may cause religious prejudice.

Study 2

This longitudinal study, conducted in the first week of October and the first week of November 2002, had several purposes. One was to determine the test-retest reliability of the AMP Scale. Another was to test for any relationship between AMP scores and social desirability bias, which if found would suggest that the AMP Scale over- or under-estimates anti-Muslim prejudice in the population studied. Finally, it was designed to examine the relationships of AMP with political attitudes.[5]

Method

Participants

Forty-nine students at Hillsdale College, the same conservative Midwestern American institution examined in Study 1a, participated in Study 2. Of these, 46 (31 females and 15 males) completed the questionnaires at both the test and retest sessions. Of the 49, 92 percent identified themselves as white and 86 percent as Christian.

Materials

Participants completed the AMP, RWA and SDO Scales along with a questionnaire measuring political attitudes (see Table 2.5), and they answered a number of demographic questions. They also completed a short version of the Marlowe-Crowne Social Desirability Inventory (Reynolds 1982), which is designed to measure bias toward giving socially desirable responses.

Procedure

The questionnaires were administered to small groups in sessions approximately four weeks apart. Each administration took approximately 30 minutes.

Results and discussion

Cronbach's alpha for AMP was 0.92 at time 1 and 0.94 at time 2, replicating the high internal consistency found in Study 1. The test-retest Pearson correlation for AMP was 0.92 ($p<0.001$), and AMP did not vary from time 1 (mean=-6.9, SD=27) to time 2 (AMP mean=-6.8, SD=28; $t<0.18$, $p>0.86$), indicating good test-retest reliability.

AMP correlated with SDO ($r(42)=0.45$, $p=0.002$ at time 1 and $r(42)=0.50$, $p=0.001$ at time 2) and with RWA ($r(43)=0.44$, $p=0.003$ at time 1 and $r(43)=0.49$, $p=0.001$ at time 2), replicating relationships found in Study 1.

AMP did not correlate with social desirability ($r(42)=-0.14$, $p=0.36$ at time 1 and $r(43)=-0.25$, $=0.10$ at time 2). Due to the small sample sizes, these tests were not powerful. However, the fact that the very minor tendencies of the correlations to diverge from zero were in the negative direction suggests that social desirability did not attenuate self-reported prejudice in these participants.

Political attitudes are described in Table 2.5, and the relationships between AMP and political attitudes are shown in Table 2.6. Since we calculated many correlations at each time of measurement, some would be expected to be statistically significant at the 0.05 level merely due to chance. We therefore focus on those relationships that were reliably different from zero at the 0.05 level at both times of measurement.

AMP was negatively related to favouring humanitarian aid to the Palestinians and to Iraq. Those who viewed the Muslim inhabitants of Palestine and Iraq most negatively would be expected to see them as least deserving of such aid.

Correlations between AMP and favouring the overthrow of Iraq and Iran by military or covert means were robust and moderately strong. Individuals high on AMP tended to view Muslims as devious, irrational, uncivilized, uneducated, politically unsophisticated troublemakers. It would therefore not be surprising if they saw them as incompetent and untrustworthy to determine their own governments. We also note that in all of our samples anti-Muslim prejudice was related to authoritarianism and that, in situations of conflict, authoritarians are more likely to prefer military solutions (Izzett 1971; Doty *et al.* 1997).

AMP was also associated with favouring increased immigration restrictions on people from Islamic countries. Anti-immigration attitudes might be related to Islamophobia specifically or to other aspects of anti-Muslim prejudice, such as beliefs that Muslims fall short in cleanliness, intelligence, education, or political sophistication, and therefore would make poor neighbours and fellow citizens.

AMP was reliably related to favouring extra searching and observation of people who appear to be Islamic (that is, 'racial' profiling). Of all the political attitudes we surveyed, this one is most directly related in theory to Islamophobia.

Finally, AMP was negatively associated with favouring a forum in which Islamic governments could voice their grievances. Those who viewed Muslims as irrational, devious, unintelligent, uneducated and uncivilized, thereby scoring high on AMP, would not be expected to view dialogue with Muslims as a worthwhile enterprise. They might also be relatively uninterested in listening to grievances because they tend to believe them unjustified.

We note that these associations between AMP and political attitudes can be theoretically construed with equal ease regardless of the direction of causality. It is precisely when negative views of a group might sensibly lead to a particular political attitude that such negative views can effectively legitimize the political attitude, as social dominance theory hypothesizes that prejudices do.

AMP factor structure

The AMP Scale was not designed with theoretically grounded sub-dimensions in mind, and the very high observed Cronbach's alphas of 0.92–0.94 do not compel the postulation of sub-factors. Nevertheless, we investigated AMP by way

Table 2.5 Political attitudes in Study 2

Political attitude	Mean agreement	
	Test	*Retest*
United States should supply military aid to Israel	0.90	0.83
United States should supply military aid to the Palestinians	−1.3	−1.1
United States should supply humanitarian aid to Israel, and it should do so in whatever way best promotes the interests of the Israeli people	1.5	1.4
The United States should supply humanitarian aid to the Palestinians, and it should do so in whatever way best promotes the interests of the Palestinian people	0.29	0.26
The United States should overthrow the Iraqi government of Sadaam Hussein by way of a military invasion	0.59	0.48
The United States should overthrow the Iraqi government of Sadaam Hussein by way of covert operations (e.g., using the CIA)	0.65	0.83
The United States should support the tightening of economic sanctions against Iraq that have been in place since the end of the 1991 Persian Gulf War	1.1	1.2
The United States should support the lifting of economic sanctions against Iraq that have been in place since the end of the 1991 Persian Gulf War	−0.96	−1.1
The United States should supply humanitarian aid to Iraq, and it should do so in whatever way best promotes the interests of the Iraqi people	−0.43	0.0
The United States should overthrow the Islamic government of Iran by way of a military invasion	−0.80	−0.43
The United States should overthrow the Islamic government of Iran by way of covert operations (e.g., using the CIA)	−0.53	−0.26
The United States should supply humanitarian aid to Iran, and it should do so in whatever way best promotes the interests of the Iranian people	0.18	0.22
The United States should supply humanitarian aid to Afghanistan, and it should do so in whatever way best promotes the interests of the Afghani people	0.33	0.54
The United States should support a forum in which Islamic governments could voice their grievances against the United States	−1.0	−0.41
The United States should tighten restrictions on immigration from predominantly Islamic countries because of possible threats to national security	0.20	0.43
Passengers on public transportation who appear to be Islamic should be searched and observed more carefully than are other passengers	−1.0	−0.78

Note
Standard deviations ranged from 1.6 to 2.5 and were similar at test and retest.

Table 2.6 Anti-Muslim prejudice versus political attitudes (Pearson correlations) in Study 2

Political attitude object	AMP	
	Test	Retest
Military aid to Israel	0.30[a]	0.23
Military aid to the Palestinians	0.00	−0.26
Humanitarian aid to Israel	−0.13	−0.12
Humanitarian aid to the Palestinians	−0.30[a]	−0.31[a]
Military overthrow of Iraq	0.42[b]	0.54[c]
Covert operations overthrow of Iraq	0.51[a]	0.57[c]
Tightening economic sanctions on Iraq	0.24	0.28
Lifting economic sanctions on Iraq	0.07	−0.36[a]
Humanitarian aid to Iraq	−0.37[a]	−0.55[c]
Military overthrow of Iran	0.40[b]	0.49[b]
Covert operations overthrow of Iran	0.43[b]	0.42[b]
Humanitarian aid to Iran	−0.27	−0.35[a]
Humanitarian aid to Afghanistan	−0.24	−0.25
Forum for Islamic governments to voice grievances	−0.50[b]	−0.34[a]
Restrictions on immigration from Islamic countries	0.67[c]	0.47[b]
Extra searching and observation of people on public transportation who appear to be Islamic	0.39[a]	0.51[b]

Note
[a] p<0.05,
[b] p<0.01,
[c] p<0.001, two tailed.

of exploratory factor analysis. Achieving an adequate observation:variable ratio (Russell 2002) required pooling data from Study 1a, Study 1b and Study 2 time 1. Because the mean levels of AMP were quite different in Studies 1a and 1b and the questionnaire context within which the AMP Scale was presented differed considerably between Studies 1 and 2, pooling in this way is problematic, and conclusions drawn from the analysis must be tentative. The total pooled sample size, after deletion of missing cases, was 149, yielding 7.45 observations per variable. Factors were extracted using the principal components method, and orthogonal (varimax) rotation was applied. One 'general anti-Muslim prejudice' factor had an eigenvalue of 8.59 and explained 43 percent of the total variance. Every item loaded more highly on it than on any other potential factor, with a minimum loading of 0.45. In our data there were no firm grounds for preferring a multifactor solution. We do not, however, believe AMP to be a unitary construct, and we would be surprised if future research employing larger samples did not identify AMP sub-factors, perhaps having to do with ethnic, national, religious and secular components (Konig *et al.* 2001; Glock and Stark 1966; Love 2009) or components relating to competence and beneficence (Duckitt 2003). Perceived lack of beneficence is intimately related to Islamophobia on theoretical grounds.

General discussion

The AMP Scale is a promising measure, internally consistent and stable over time. Concurrent and discriminant validity appear to be good. The construct validity of AMP is indicated by the empirical demonstration of numerous theoretically predicted relationships.

Our results should be interpreted in the light of the fact that prejudice and political attitudes and their relationships with one another change over time. For example, people high on authoritarianism are particularly supportive of governmental restrictions on rights when they are economically threatened, as many Americans were during the US economic recession of 2001, when the terrorist attacks occurred (Rickert 1998), and as they are again at the time of writing. Prejudice against Muslims has increased post-9/11 (for example, Sheridan 2006; Cashin 2010). Significantly, developments in the Middle East have continued to be prominent in the Western media since the data in the present studies were collected, with ongoing conflicts in Iraq and Afghanistan, negotiation and violence in Israel over Palestinian autonomy, and human rights abuses and nuclear developments in Iran. Continuing public attention to these issues suggests that attitudes and beliefs relevant to those measured by AMP are likely to remain salient.

Despite decades of research, the relationship between prejudice and religion has been very difficult to determine (Altemeyer 1996). We examined only religious fundamentalism, not orthodoxy, because Altemeyer (1996) argues that fundamentalism, being religious authoritarianism, is more closely related to prejudice. We note, however, that Gorsuch and Aleshire (1974) found prejudice against another religious group, Jews, to be associated with both religious orthodoxy and fundamentalism, and Konig et al. (2001) found anti-Semitism to be related to Christian worldview. Since anti-Muslim prejudice is directed specifically against a religious group, it may also be more closely related to a multitude of individual religious differences than are most other prejudices.

There are two major limitations to our work. The first is that our participants were predominantly American, white and Christian, and all were college students. It is well known that anti-Semitism varies with race, religion and education (Selznick and Steinberg 1969; Weil 1985; Konig et al. 2001; Anti-Defamation League of B'nai B'rith 2002). It would be surprising if anti-Muslim prejudice, and Islamophobia specifically, did not also vary across many such dimensions. Generalization from our research therefore requires caution. The second limitation of our data is that they are solely descriptive and correlational. We suspect that the causal relationships among the constructs we have measured are complex and often reciprocal. As discussed above, social dominance orientation and authoritarianism can drive prejudices (Pratto et al. 1994; Altemeyer 1996; Sidanius and Pratto 1999). They may also drive political attitudes, with social dominance orientation leading people to prefer policies that preserve or enhance the dominance of their own group over others, and authoritarianism affecting such political attitudes as those having to do with the power of government, the trustworthiness of officials, adherence to traditional social values and the appropriateness of harsh treatment of those who defy convention and established authority. Prejudice, in turn, may drive some political attitudes, such as those toward immigration and racial or religious profiling, rather directly, while being a moderator variable with respect to others by, for example, legitimizing or de-legitimizing them. Finally, political attitudes and especially political action may drive prejudice due to the effects of cognitive dissonance (Festinger and Carlsmith 1959) and self-perception (Bem 1972). Larger data sets than ours will be required to test such multifactorial models, and experimentation will be necessary to establish causality.

Muslims have endured centuries of conflict with other religious groups, including Christians, Jews and Hindus. Casualties in the past decade alone number in the hundreds of thousands, perhaps in the millions. Prejudice toward Muslims, as manifested in Islamophobia, both exacerbates and legitimizes inter-ethic and inter-religious conflict. The Anti-Muslim Prejudice Scale promises to be a useful measure of this malignancy in the ongoing effort to understand and alleviate it.

Notes

1   Arabs and Muslims are not identical but are overlapping groups.
2   Because anti-Muslim prejudice would be expected to vary over time, particularly in response to world events, and because the data presented here were collected several years ago, we note the dates of each of our studies.
3   Henry and Sears (2002) provide an updated measure of this construct, the Symbolic Racism 2000 Scale.
4   For all results, missing values were treated with pairwise deletion unless otherwise noted.
5   In Study 2 we also measured anti-Semitism using a newly devised Balanced Anti-Semitism (BAS) Scale. Cronbach's alphas for the BAS were 0.88 and 0.92; test-retest reliability was 0.91. For further information contact second author Brian Bornstein.

Appendix A

Anti-Muslim Prejudice Scale

This survey is part of an investigation of general public opinion concerning Islam and Muslims. You will probably find that you agree with some of the statements, and disagree with others, to varying extents. Please indicate your reaction to each statement by circling a number to the right of the statement according to the following scale:

-4 if you very strongly disagree with the statement.
-3 if you strongly disagree with the statement.
-2 if you moderately disagree with the statement.
-1 if you slightly disagree with the statement.
+1 if you slightly agree with the statement.
+2 if you moderately agree with the statement
+3 if you strongly agree with the statement.
+4 if you very strongly agree with the statement.

If you feel exactly and precisely neutral about an item, circle '0'.

You may find that you sometimes have different reactions to different parts of a statement. For example, you might very strongly disagree (-4) with one idea in a statement, but slightly agree (+1) with another idea in the same item. When this happens, please combine your reactions, and write down how you feel 'on balance'.

		Scale
1	Islam is at least as tolerant and respectful of other faiths as most major religions are	$-4\ -3\ -2\ -1\ 0\ +1\ +2\ +3\ +4$
2	Muslims, as a rule, are more devious than other people	$-4\ -3\ -2\ -1\ 0\ +1\ +2\ +3\ +4$
3	Islam, by its nature, is contrary to the American way of life	$-4\ -3\ -2\ -1\ 0\ +1\ +2\ +3\ +4$
4	Islam promotes kindness and love toward all people	$-4\ -3\ -2\ -1\ 0\ +1\ +2\ +3\ +4$
5	Muslims are controlled too much by their irrational emotions	$-4\ -3\ -2\ -1\ 0\ +1\ +2\ +3\ +4$
6	Muslims are very attentive to cleanliness and good grooming	$-4\ -3\ -2\ -1\ 0\ +1\ +2\ +3\ +4$
7	One must admit, the traditional cloth headdress worn by many Muslims looks ridiculous	$-4\ -3\ -2\ -1\ 0\ +1\ +2\ +3\ +4$
8	Muslims deserve great respect for their many cultural accomplishments	$-4\ -3\ -2\ -1\ 0\ +1\ +2\ +3\ +4$
9	Sad to say, when you get right down to it, Muslims are basically troublemakers	$-4\ -3\ -2\ -1\ 0\ +1\ +2\ +3\ +4$
10	Muslims are at least as intelligent and well educated as others are	$-4\ -3\ -2\ -1\ 0\ +1\ +2\ +3\ +4$
11	Islam has had a very positive effect on the lives of many people	$-4\ -3\ -2\ -1\ 0\ +1\ +2\ +3\ +4$
12	Muslims are often more selfish and inconsiderate than others are	$-4\ -3\ -2\ -1\ 0\ +1\ +2\ +3\ +4$
13	Overall, Muslims have made an important positive contribution to our society	$-4\ -3\ -2\ -1\ 0\ +1\ +2\ +3\ +4$
14	The basic teachings of Islam must be condemned as evil	$-4\ -3\ -2\ -1\ 0\ +1\ +2\ +3\ +4$
15	When conflicts arise, Muslims are cowards and do not fight honorably	$-4\ -3\ -2\ -1\ 0\ +1\ +2\ +3\ +4$
16	Compared with other people, Muslims are uncivilized and backward	$-4\ -3\ -2\ -1\ 0\ +1\ +2\ +3\ +4$
17	Muslims show great respect for human rights and freedoms	$-4\ -3\ -2\ -1\ 0\ +1\ +2\ +3\ +4$
18	Muslims lack the ability to think independently; they follow their leaders like sheep	$-4\ -3\ -2\ -1\ 0\ +1\ +2\ +3\ +4$
19	The understanding that Muslims have of political issues is sophisticated and advanced	$-4\ -3\ -2\ -1\ 0\ +1\ +2\ +3\ +4$
20	Muslims cherish every human life	$-4\ -3\ -2\ -1\ 0\ +1\ +2\ +3\ +4$

Part 2

The scope of Islamophobia

Public debates, attitudes and reactions

3 Assessing Islamophobia in Britain

Where do Muslims really stand?

Erik Bleich and Rahsaan Maxwell

Over the past decade and a half, the concept of Islamophobia has received an increasing amount of public attention. Islamophobia has been defined as a set of closed attitudes toward Islam as a religion or toward Muslims as adherents of the Islamic faith (Runnymede Trust 1997). Yet – much like its cognates sexism, racism, and homophobia – the word Islamophobia is often entangled in symbolic political struggles that lack analytical clarity. On the one hand, antiracist NGOs and liberal scholars use the term to mobilize sentiment against prejudice (Runnymede Trust 1997; Geisser 2003). On the other hand, skeptics of various stripes challenge the usefulness of the term and claim that anti-Muslim attitudes and actions are rare (Malik 2005; Joppke 2009b; see also Oborne and Jones 2008: 14). Unfortunately, these discussions often contain too little concrete evidence to permit an assessment of the level and nature of Islamophobia in a given society. In this chapter, we respond to this problem by examining survey evidence to address the crucial question of just how much Islamophobia exists in Great Britain and how it has evolved over time. For the purposes of this chapter, we define Islamophobia as undifferentiated negative attitudes or emotions concerning Islam or Muslims.[1]

We focus on Britain for several theoretical and practical reasons. The concept itself emerged from a British antiracist NGO report in 1997 entitled *Islamophobia: A Challenge for Us All* (Runnymede Trust 1997) and it therefore seems useful to begin by investigating its prevalence there. Admittedly, most aspects of Islamophobia are not specific to Britain. There are bodies of scholarship that trace the roots of Western Islamophobia back through centuries of history (Said 1978; Matar 2009) and that identify elements of Islamophobia in the United States and other societies (Geisser 2003; Goldberg 2006; Gottschalk and Greenberg 2008; Love 2009). Yet, since the contemporary concept grew out of an assessment of British society in the 1990s, our chapter examines the extent to which this concept is useful for understanding social and political developments where they have been deemed to be extremely significant.

Another key reason to assess Islamophobia in Britain is the growing chorus of observers who claim that Muslims are more discontented and extreme in Britain than anywhere else in Europe (Borger 2006; Pew Research Center 2006; Policy Exchange 2007; Joppke 2009b; Hansen 2011). These authors generally point to Pew surveys from the mid-2000s, which found conservative and critical attitudes among British Muslims. In addition, multiple terrorist attacks by British Muslims throughout the 2000s have heightened fears that they pose a grave security threat. These observations raise several questions about the nature of Islamophobia in Britain. Is British Muslims' extremism a response to extensive Islamophobia in mainstream society? Or is British Islamophobia a reaction to the fact that Muslims in their country are particularly radical?

Practically, Britain is an excellent site for studying Islamophobia because widespread and official concern about the term has resulted in large-n, highly systematic surveys that try to probe many of its dimensions. In this chapter, we primarily use results from the Citizenship Survey (CS).[2] The CS is a bi-annual survey that started in 2001 with the goal of providing reliable information about community cohesion in Britain. The Citizenship Survey includes an extensive set of questions on political attitudes and social behavior. In addition, each CS has a representative national sample of 9,000–10,000 people and an ethnic minority booster sample of 4,000–5,000 people. Most Muslims in Britain are ethnic minorities and do not appear in significant numbers in many national surveys, but there are between 1,400 and 2,200 Muslim respondents in each year of the CS.[3] This relatively large sample facilitates detailed analysis of attitudes of and about Muslims. While we focus on these surveys for much of our relevant evidence, we also include comparative data from other large-scale, systematic surveys of attitudes toward Muslims where appropriate.

In a first section, we provide a brief overview of the British Muslim population and discuss how this compares to other Muslim populations in Europe. The remainder of this chapter focuses on two types of survey evidence that we use to infer the presence and intensity of Islamophobia. The second section examines survey results where non-Muslims report attitudes toward Muslims; beliefs about the targets of prejudice, discrimination and disadvantage; and attitudes toward immigration from predominantly Muslim countries. If Islamophobia is rampant, we would expect to see consistent and extremely negative opinions among non-Muslims across these categories. If Islamophobia is a chimera, these sets of attitudes will not reflect significant hostility. In the third section, we turn to Muslims' attitudes toward the British state and its political institutions. As noted above, a number of studies have focused on the extent to which British Muslims are disaffected compared to Muslims in other countries (Borger 2006; Hansen 2011; Pew Research Center 2006; Policy Exchange 2007; Joppke 2009b) and have found that the British system encourages conversion of that disaffection into negative attitudes and actions (Malik 2005; Koopmans *et al.* 2005; Joppke 2009b). If these observations are correct and if Islamophobia is widespread, we would expect to see highly negative reactions by Muslims toward Britain and British institutions. However, if Muslims' attitudes are similar to those of non-Muslims, we might infer that Islamophobia is not a dramatic influence on British society. For example, moderate or positive political attitudes among British Muslims could mean that Islamophobia is not as prevalent as is often claimed or it could mean that British Muslims are not responding to Islamophobia with the severe alienation that some people predict. Because the surveys we use were not specifically tailored to address levels or intensities of Islamophobia, it is not our goal to 'prove' or to 'disprove' its presence. Rather, we use survey data to develop a nuanced analysis of Islamophobia that can more accurately assess its levels and modalities across time.

Examining all of the data suggests that Islamophobia is present in British society, and has risen gradually over the past decade by some measures, but that it is not a dominant or overwhelming vector of discrimination in Britain today. The evidence helps us flag particular ways in which Islamophobia continues to be a concern that require sustained attention. Yet it also identifies domains where British Muslims appear to be especially well integrated into their country. In sum, the data dispel the myth of runaway Islamophobia in Britain while reinforcing the notion that Islamophobia is a real phenomenon that poses specific challenges for British society.

British Muslim demographics

Although Islam has occupied a central place in recent public debates, the Muslim population in Britain is actually one of the smallest among the traditional immigration countries in Western Europe. According to a 2009 Pew Study, Muslims comprise 2.7 percent of Britain's population, compared to roughly 6 percent in France and the Netherlands, roughly 5 percent for Germany, roughly 4 percent in Austria and Switzerland, and 3 percent in Belgium (Pew Research Center 2009a). Nonetheless, according to the 2001 UK Population Census, Islam is the second-largest religion in Britain, after Christianity (which represents 71.6 percent of the population) and ahead of Hinduism (1.0 percent), Sikhism (0.6 percent) and Judaism (0.5 percent).[4]

Britain's Muslim community has developed over several centuries but the most recent large-scale migration occurred in the second half of the twentieth century. This was the period when migrants from Britain's former colonies in Africa, Asia and the Caribbean arrived to fill labor shortages in low-skill, low-wage jobs. The majority of these Muslim migrants were from India, Pakistan and Bangladesh. Since the 1980s and 1990s, there have been more Muslim political and economic refugees from Turkey, Iran, Iraq, Afghanistan, Somalia, and the Balkans (Ansari 2004). Yet, according to the 2001 Census, the majority of British Muslims are still South Asian, with roughly 43 percent of Pakistani origin, 16 percent of Bangladeshi origin and 9 percent of Indian origin.

As seen in the other chapters in this volume, the national-origin profile of Muslim immigrants varies considerably across West European countries. In addition, the strategies used to integrate Muslim migrants vary across West European countries (Laurence 2012). Therefore, it is important to acknowledge that the British dynamics examined in this chapter may not necessarily apply elsewhere in Europe. Nevertheless, our approach of empirically analyzing surveys in order objectively to assess the levels of Islamophobia can be fruitfully used in other locations.

Attitudes toward Muslims

The Citizenship Surveys were among the first major surveys to provide a set of consistent questions about attitudes toward Muslims in Britain, especially in comparison to attitudes toward other minorities. For example, since the 2003 survey, they have asked respondents which group they felt was the target of more racial prejudice today compared to five years ago (Figure 3.1).[5] Although it may seem obvious that Muslims would be at the top of the list following the events of September 11, 2001, this was not the case as of 2003, when only 16 percent of non-Muslim respondents named Muslims. As the surveys progressed, however, the responses climbed significantly, to 37 percent in 2005, and to 43 percent in 2007, at which point Muslims were judged by non-Muslims to be the primary group against whom there was more racial prejudice today compared to five years earlier, exceeding for the first time the more standard ethnic formulation of 'Asians', which then re-took the top spot in 2009. Overall, these numbers indicate there is a perception that Islamophobia has been rising over the past decade, especially compared to other forms of prejudice.

The finding that there is greater disadvantage associated with being a Muslim than in the past is echoed by 2006 and 2008 Eurobarometer surveys, which asked which types of discrimination were greater now than five years earlier. In each year, 53 percent of respondents identified religion and beliefs, which was roughly on a par with ethnic origin (54 percent in 2006 and 55 percent in 2008) and well ahead of the next most frequent answer, age (at 33 percent and 31 percent respectively).[6] These data suggest that the stigma associated with religion and beliefs – which for many respondents in 2006 and 2008 is extremely likely to reflect feelings about Muslims – is growing and has been noted by large numbers of British citizens.

Viewed in another light, however, what might be most striking about the Eurobarometer data is the fact that respondents judged discrimination based on ethnic origin to be growing as rapidly as that based on religion and beliefs.[7] After all, Britain has decades of experience dealing with ethnic differences, and many of the ethnic differences within the country do not correlate with citizenship or religious differences. It is thus important to investigate more closely attitudes toward Muslims in comparison with those toward other ethno-racial groups to understand not only trends over time, but also the relative standing of Muslims compared to other groups within the country.

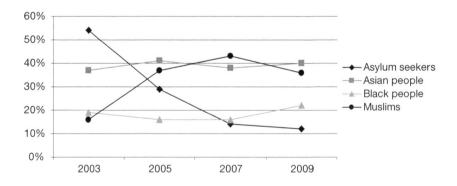

Source: Citizenship surveys

Figure 3.1 Groups there is more racial prejudice against today compared to five years ago

There is overwhelming evidence that Muslims are considered the most disliked and discriminated against group in Britain when compared to other religious groups. Viewed from the long-term perspective of religious persecution and discrimination against Catholics and dissenters in Britain, it is striking that Muslims have become the primary religious outsiders by a wide margin. It is particularly revealing that attitudes toward Muslims are significantly more negative than those toward Jews, who were very low on ethno-racial hierarchies throughout the twentieth century.

The 2005, 2007, and 2009 Citizenship Survey respondents who believed there was more religious prejudice today than five years ago overwhelmingly believed that this prejudice was directed toward Muslims. Just over 90 percent in 2005 and just under 90 percent in 2007 and 2009 identified Muslims as the targets of such prejudice, with fewer than 12 percent in each year selecting Christians, Sikhs, Hindus, or Jews as the victims of increased prejudice. Again, these surveys suggest a widespread belief in Britain that Islamophobia is a rapidly growing problem within the country.

Dislike and suspicion of Muslims has also been revealed by the Pew Surveys from 2004, 2005 and 2006. These surveys asked respondents which religious groups they had unfavorable opinions of (Figure 3.2). Significantly higher numbers had unfavorable opinions of Muslims than of Jews or Christians. In addition, just under half of all Pew respondents in 2005 thought that certain religions were prone to violence and, of those who did, over 60 percent believed Islam to be the most violent religion, with fewer than 10 percent citing Christianity, Judaism or Hinduism.[8] Moreover, in Pew Surveys from 2005 and 2006, 63 percent and 69 percent of respondents respectively believed that Muslim identity was growing; and of those that thought it was growing, 56 percent and 59 percent of Britons viewed this to be a 'bad thing' (Figure 3.3). Islam and Muslims are clearly objects of fear and aversion, when the comparison group is other religions.

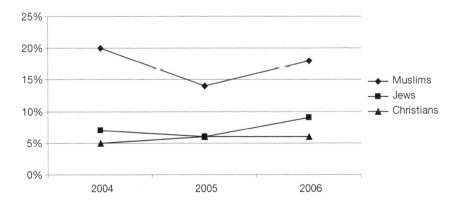

Source: Pew Global Attitudes, Release Date: June 2006

Figure 3.2 Respondents have unfavorable opinion of …

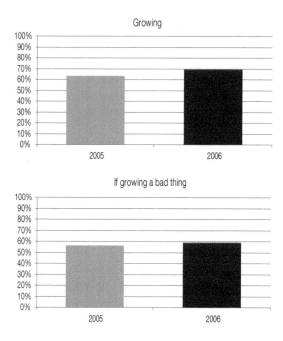

Growing

If growing a bad thing

Source: Pew Global Attitudes, release date: July, 2006

Figure 3.3 Muslim identity in our country is ...

While these surveys reveal beliefs about the presence of substantial anti-Muslim prejudice in Britain when compared to attitudes toward other religious groups – and the fact that Muslims have displaced *religious* outgroups of previous eras – they do not address Muslims' status compared to racial or ethnic groups. It may appear self-evident that Muslims have become the ultimate outsiders in Europe in the wake of 9/11, the Madrid train bombings, the assassination of Theo van Gogh and the London transportation system bombings of 2005. But are they more stigma-tized than blacks, Jews, immigrants, Roma and other ethnic minorities in Britain? Most of the polling evidence suggests that they are not, or at least not yet.

This argument may seem to contradict some evidence presented above. After all, in 2007, a thin plurality of Citizenship Survey respondents identified Muslims as the group experiencing more prejudice now.[9] However, the phrasing of this question – comparing the present day to the recent past – does not ask respondents to evaluate the relative position of these groups, but rather to assess which groups they feel are sinking most quickly on status hierarchies. These survey results support the argu-ment that there is more anti-Muslim prejudice now than in the past, but they do not provide direct information about Muslims' current status compared to other groups.

The bulk of the direct evidence suggests that Muslims are perceived as lower on status hierarchies than other important ethno-racial groups, but that they are almost never the lowest ranked group. For example, Britain's 2005 National Survey shows that 10 percent of respondents had negative feelings about black people, whereas 19 percent admitted to negative feelings about Muslims.[10] Yet 38 percent of those responding to a similar question had negative feelings about asylum seekers, placing them lower on the hierarchy than Muslims (Abrams and Houston 2006: 34). Of course, it is true that there may be some conflation between the category of 'asylum seeker' and 'Muslim', yet these results suggest that immigration status is a more significant vector of aversion or dislike than religion.

Moreover, majorities of Muslim and Asian respondents – two overlapping but not identical categories of people – said they had personally suffered discrimination based on ethnicity, whereas only minorities of those groups claimed to have suffered it based on religion (Abrams and Houston 2006: 42–3). Only further research can determine whether Muslims feel that discrimination against them was due to a perceived 'Muslim ethnicity', but it is most likely the case that victims feel they were targeted because of their Asian ethnic appearance or membership rather than on the grounds of their religious affiliation. This suggests that straightforward ethnicity was a more important vector of real-world discrimination than Islamophobia. Showing a similar low-but-not-lowest status for Muslims, close to 14 percent of British respondents to the 1999 World Values Survey identified Muslims as a group they would prefer not to have as neighbors. Yet, British respondents had a slightly greater aversion to immigrants than to Muslims, and a much stronger aversion to 'Gypsies' as neighbors compared to any other ethno-racial group.[11] As above, there is undoubtedly some overlap in attitudes toward immigrants and Muslims, but there is no perceived overlap between Muslims and 'Gypsies'.[12]

In a parallel vein, according to the 2006 Eurobarometer survey, belonging to a minority religious group is considered significantly less of a disadvantage than belonging to several other categories, most notable of which for the purposes of this essay are minority ethnic origin and Roma (Figure 3.4). Finally, it is not the case that the increasing stigma associated in the public's mind with being a Muslim has a dramatic effect on attitudes about immigration from predominantly Muslim countries. Pew research data from 2002, 2005 and 2006 demonstrate that respondents had identical and generally positive attitudes toward immigrants from the Middle East/North Africa as compared to attitudes toward migrants from Eastern Europe, who are presumably white and Christian (Figure 3.5).[13] This suggests that there is a limit to the intensity of Islamophobia in Britain, at least in certain respects according to the measures analyzed here.

Data on public attitudes toward Muslims thus reveal that there are significantly negative attitudes toward Muslims, but that these are strongest when Muslims are compared to other religious groups. When compared to other ethnic, racial or immigrant groups, attitudes toward Muslims are typically negative, but are almost never the most strongly negative. By most measures, the attitudinal aversion and concrete disadvantages of discrimination accruing to minorities remain most powerful toward people defined by some measure of race, ethnicity or immigration status, rather than by religious affiliation. Islamophobia exists, but older forms of racism are still deeply entrenched and appear to be more substantial problems for British society.

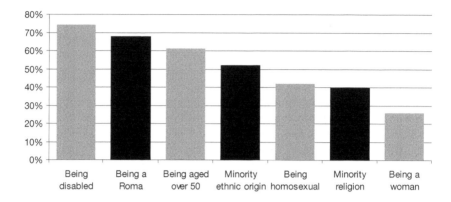

Source: Eurobarometer 65.4, 2006

Figure 3.4 Belonging to the following group is generally a disadvantage

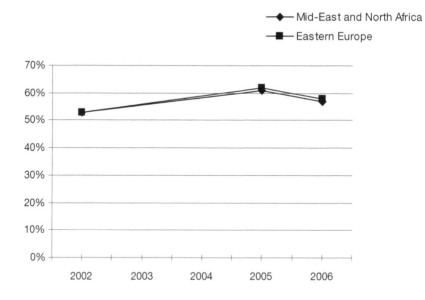

Source: Pew Global Attitudes, release date: July 2006

Figure 3.5 It is a good thing that people come to work and live in this country from …

Muslims' attitudes toward British society

Analyzing Muslims' attitudes toward British society suggests that Islamophobia and discrimination are problems in British society. However, there are also many encouraging signs of Muslims being positively attached to mainstream British political institutions and identities. This suggests a complex and nuanced role for Muslims in British society, one that involves both criticism and commitment.

One of the most sensitive issues in the public debate around Islam in Britain is the extent to which Muslims' religious views and perceptions of Islamophobia have reduced their likelihood of identifying with the mainstream national community. However, evidence from the Citizenship Surveys suggests that Muslims' levels of positive British identification are similar to – if not higher than – those of non-Muslims and the overall population. Figure 3.6 presents responses to the question: *How strongly do you belong to Britain?* from four different years of the CS.[14] The results indicate that across all four surveys Muslims are only slightly less likely than non-Muslims to respond that they 'very strongly' belong to Britain – moreover, none of the differences is statistically significant at p<.05. When the two positive categories are combined, Muslims and non-Muslims have the same levels of belonging to Britain or, at times, Muslims even have slightly higher levels of belonging, although these differences are also not statistically significant at p<.05.[15] These results run directly counter to fears about Muslim alienation from the mainstream national community in Britain.

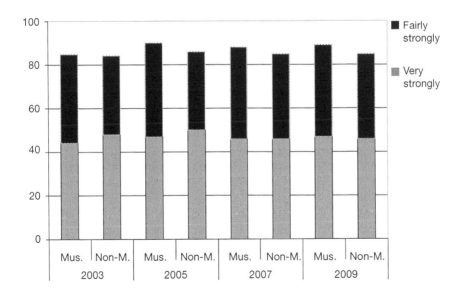

Source: Citizenship Surveys

Note: Data indicated are the percentage of responses for the two positive categories, not included in the figure are the responses 'not very strongly' and 'not at strongly'.

Figure 3.6 How strongly do you belong to Britain?

The results in Figure 3.6 may surprise some readers but they are consistent with a growing body of research arguing that most Muslims feel attached to mainstream British identities even if they recognize that there are often barriers to being recognized as fully British by others (Maxwell 2006; Hopkins and Gale 2009; Open Society Institute 2010a; Open Society Institute 2010b). Admittedly, Muslim respondents in the CS are consistently more likely than non-Muslims to claim that religion is an important – or even the most important – part of their identity.[16] This suggests that when Muslims claim a strong attachment to British identity it may not mean the exact same thing as when a non-Muslim claims that identity. However, this is to be expected and is a fairly common dynamic among minority communities that seek to shift and redefine the dominant social categories. Moreover, research suggests that the best predictor for the intensity of Muslims' identification with Britain is the intensity of their neighbors' identification, irrespective of religion (Maxwell 2010a). Therefore, even if Muslims' conception of Britishness is not exactly the same as non-Muslims' conceptions, evidence suggests that most Muslims are engaged in a broader mainstream identity and not secluded in alienated isolation.

Even if Muslims appear to identify positively with Britain, another fear is that a combination of radical religious views and Islamophobia-induced alienation has led Muslims to disregard democratic institutions and the mainstream political process. Yet, evidence from the CS suggests that Muslims' levels of trust in British political institutions are similar to or more positive than non-Muslims' levels of trust in the same institutions. Figures 3.7, 3.8, 3.9, and 3.10 present data from the CS on levels of trust in the courts, the police, Parliament, and the local council. Across each institution and each survey year, Muslims are more likely than non-Muslims to indicate the most positive response: 'A lot' of trust. When the two positive responses are combined, Muslims' levels of trust in the courts, Parliament, and the local council are still slightly higher than those of non-Muslims.

These results might not be intuitive for readers who imagine that Muslims are deeply skeptical of Western democratic institutions. Yet, the data in Figures 3.7 and 3.8 are consistent with a growing body of research on British Muslims' political trust (Maxwell 2010b; Open Society Institute 2010a; Open Society Institute 2010b). One of the key explanations for British Muslims' higher levels of political trust is that Muslims are more likely than non-Muslims to be immigrants and immigrants in general have higher levels of political trust than natives (Maxwell 2010b). This, too, may be surprising but is part of a broader and well-established dynamic in which first-generation immigrants are more likely than natives to be optimistic about the host society because they made a conscious decision to leave their home and migrate in search of a better life. First-generation migrants across a wide range of national contexts tend to be more patriotic and positive than natives, although these optimism effects decline across time and across generations (de la Garza *et al.* 1996; Kao and Tienda 1995; Michelson 2003; Wenzel 2006; Maxwell 2010c; Röder and Mühlau 2010). One of the key implications of this research is that Muslims' political attitudes to and integration in British society may be best understood as a function of their migration status and slow acculturation over time as opposed to as a distinct and permanently segregated minority.

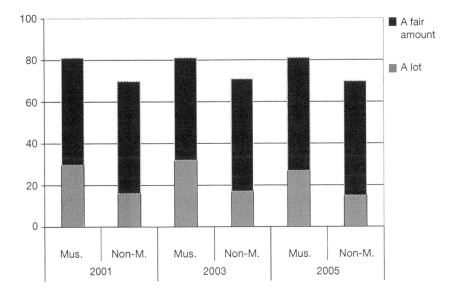

Source: Citizenship Surveys

Note: Data indicated are the percentage of responses for the two positive categories; the responses 'not very much' and 'not at all' are not included in the figure.

Figure 3.7 Do you trust the courts?

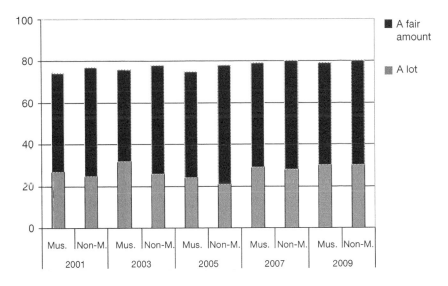

Note: Data indicated are the percentage of responses for the two positive categories; the responses 'not very much' and 'not at all' are not included in the figure.

Figure 3.8 Do you trust the police?

In addition, it is important to distinguish between attitudes toward institutions and toward fellow citizens.[17] Results from the 2007 and 2009 CS suggest that about half of Muslims think religious prejudice has recently increased in Britain and of them approximately 95 percent think Muslims have been the biggest target of that increased religious prejudice. Yet, as will be seen below in Figure 3.11, very few British Muslims – generally fewer than 5 percent – expect religious discrimination when interacting with public institutions. This suggests a distinction between the liberal British institutions that have been fairly receptive to Muslim political mobilization – especially when compared to other European countries – and the general British public that greets Muslims with suspicious looks during daily life.[18]

Despite Muslims' generally higher levels of trust in the courts, police, Parliament, and local councils, it is important to note that, when the two positive response categories are combined, non-Muslims have slightly higher levels of trust in the police. This is not surprising given the intense law enforcement scrutiny of Muslims over the past decade. And given the fact that Muslims as a group are considered prime suspects for terrorist activity, it is even more remarkable that their levels of trust in the police are so high. In each survey, there is an overwhelming majority – between 70 and 80 percent – of Muslims with positive trust in the police.

Another way of interpreting the climate of suspicion surrounding Muslims is that it could motivate Muslims to provide falsely positive responses in surveys like the CS. Some might doubt that the evidence presented here truly reflects how Muslims feel and wonder if Muslims are exaggerating their allegiance to mainstream British identities and institutions as a way of avoiding stigma as terrorist sympathizers. However, Muslims' attitudes are relatively consistent across the five surveys. Attitudes from the 2001 survey, which occurred before the September 11, 2001 attacks, are similar to attitudes from subsequent surveys. In addition, attitudes from the 2001 and 2003 surveys that occurred before the July 7, 2005 attacks are similar to attitudes from the 2007 and 2009 surveys. It is impossible to know the exact extent to which Muslim respondents felt pressured to claim more positive British identification and political trust than they truly felt. Nonetheless, when considering the results across five different surveys from 2001 to 2009, there has been no significant change in Muslim national identification and political trust in the pre and post-September 11, 2001 periods or in the pre and post-July 7, 2005 periods.

Muslims may have positive attitudes toward mainstream institutions, but it is important to remember that there are problems and Muslims remain critical about certain aspects of British society. For example, many Muslims are critical of the British government's policy toward Muslim countries elsewhere in the world. In addition, Muslims may complain about prejudice and discrimination in Britain (Abbas 2007). This raises questions about the potential effect of Islamophobia because if Muslims perceive an increasingly hostile atmosphere they may cease to hold their positive attitudes about mainstream institutions in the future.

However, survey evidence on Muslims' expectations of prejudice and discrimination provide no evidence of a widespread fear of Islamophobia. Admittedly, about half of Muslims interviewed in the recent 2008/9 CS feel that prejudice

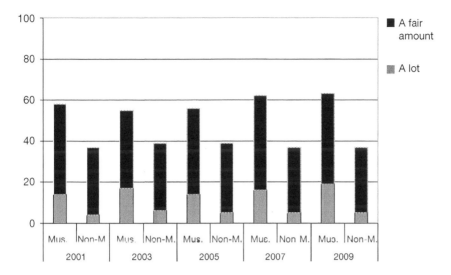

Note: Data indicated are the percentage of responses for the two positive categories; the responses 'not very much' and 'not at all' are not included in the figure.

Figure 3.9 Do you trust the Parliament?

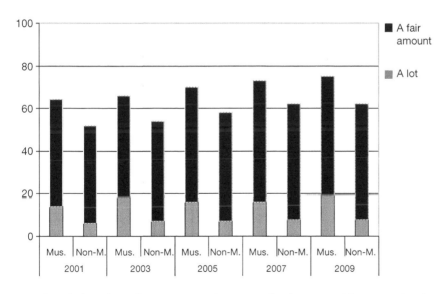

Note: Data indicated are the percentage of responses for the two positive categories; the responses 'not very much' and 'not at all' are not included in the figure.

Figure 3.10 Do you trust the local council?

against Muslims has increased in the past five years. Yet fewer than 20 percent of Muslims cite discriminatory treatment when accessing a wide range of services in mainstream society. Figure 3.11 presents data from the 2008/9 CS on Muslims' expectations of religious and racial discrimination in 12 different scenarios.[19] The results in Figure 3.11 indicate that the overwhelming majority – roughly 80–99 percent depending on the circumstance – of Muslims do not expect religious or racial discrimination when conducting their daily lives. This is especially remarkable given the fact that non-Muslim black Caribbeans – who are generally considered more assimilated than Muslims – expect much higher rates of discrimination in British society (Maxwell 2008, 2009). This suggests that even if Muslims complain of latent prejudiced attitudes in Britain, they do not necessarily believe that those attitudes are affecting their tangible access to society's services. This is reinforced by the finding from the 2008/9 CS that the overwhelming majority of Muslims – roughly 90 percent – feel that they can freely practice their religion in British society.

Another interesting finding from Figure 3.11 is that racial discrimination is much more of a concern for Muslims than religious discrimination. Aside from the question about treatment in schools, where expectations of the two types of discrimination are roughly similar, Muslims are anywhere from two to ten times more likely to expect racial as opposed to religious discrimination. These differences are quite significant, although it is not entirely clear what they mean. One potential explanation is that Britain's dominant mode of dealing with migrant issues has historically been through the frame of race relations (Bleich 2003). This may create incentives for Muslims to frame both their perceptions of discrimination and their political claims for action against discrimination in racial as opposed to religious terms (Statham 1999). However, one of the most important developments during the past two decades has been the rise of claims for greater attention to Muslims' religious needs and the inadequacy of Britain's race relations framework for dealing with their concerns (Modood 2005; Modood and Berthoud 1997). The results from the CS suggest that, despite these new claims, the racial frame remains more relevant for British Muslims' perception of discrimination. In part this may be because when Muslims face discrimination in public services it is based on how they look, which is then interpreted as a racial motivation. In comparison, religious discrimination may cover a narrow set of actions related to the practice of Islam, which the majority of British Muslims claim they are able to do without restrictions. These interpretations are speculative, but teasing out the difference between racial and religious classifications and how they apply to Muslims is likely to be a critical issue for British public discourse in the years to come.

In summary, even though Muslims in Britain are critical of stigmatization and discrimination – much of which could be considered part of Islamophobia – they also have high levels of positive British identification and trust in mainstream British institutions. This suggests that Islamophobia has not alienated British Muslims and that they are capable of being critical yet committed citizens, much like native-origin non-Muslims who can criticize society and the government without automatically being suspected of extremism.

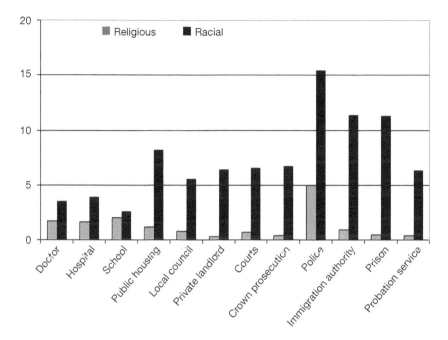

Source: 2008/9 Citizenship Survey

Figure 3.11 Percentage of Muslims who expect religious and racial discrimination

Conclusions: piecing together an accurate picture of Islamophobia

In this chapter we have argued that Islamophobia is not as severe in Britain as some critics would have us believe. This should not be interpreted as a rose-tinted view of contemporary British society and we do not ignore the many existing integration problems. Stigmatization and discrimination are problems for British Muslims on a daily basis. Conflicts over how to combine Muslims' and non-Muslims' views of society are not always easy and have led to many difficult policy struggles at the national and local levels. These tensions have led to an escalation of alienation on both sides of the divide, with some Muslims and some non-Muslims increasingly pessimistic about the possibility of ever living in harmony.

However, our focus on mass surveys draws attention to the general trends and broad tendencies around the issue of Muslim integration. As such, we find that British non-Muslims do not always place Muslims at the bottom of the minority hierarchy and may be more concerned with other groups. (This may provide little consolation for Roma and asylum seekers, but is nonetheless an important observation.) In addition, we find that despite the tense atmosphere in contemporary British society, Muslims have remarkably high levels of positive national identification and political trust.

It is worth noting that research suggests natives and immigrants tend to have different interpretations of integration dynamics. In particular, natives tend to be more skeptical of immigrants' integration progress (van Oudenhoven *et al.* 1998). This helps account for the fact that British Muslims are viewed with suspicion in the public debate despite the fact that survey results suggest an overwhelming majority of Muslims are positively attached to mainstream British identities and institutions. Even though evidence suggests that Muslims want to be a part of mainstream British society, the inevitable changes in the definition of 'mainstream British society' that accompany the integration of new immigrant groups is likely to cause further tension in the upcoming years. Nonetheless, the evidence in this chapter suggests that Islamophobia may be a real challenge and an obstacle to intergroup harmony but is not yet the most significant cleavage defining the nature of group divisions in British society.

Notes

1 For a discussion of this definition, see Bleich (2011).
2 The Citizenship Surveys were initially sponsored by the Home Office. From 2001–2005, they were thus known as the Home Office Citizenship Surveys (HOCS).
3 It is important to note that the very definition of who is a Muslim is not always straightforward. In this chapter we use a fairly broad definition that covers anyone who self-identifies as being raised as a Muslim, even if not currently practising. This has the benefit of including the wide range of people who are viewed as Muslim in the British public sphere. For the 2001 CS, this provides a sample size of 2,195 Muslims, along with 1,801 in the 2003 CS, 1,493 in the 2005 CS, 1,784 in the 2007 CS, and 2,135 in the 2009 CS.
4 Source: Census, April 2001, Office for National Statistics.
5 A first question in each survey asked respondents whether they felt there was more racial prejudice today compared to five years ago; if they answered affirmatively, a second question then asked them to identify the groups that were the target of such prejudice. The data presented here represent the answers of non-Muslim respondents.
6 Eurobarometer 65.4, 2006; Eurobarometer 69.1, 2008.
7 The difference in the response rate between the two categories is not statistically significant in either country in 2006 or in 2008.
8 Pew Global Attitudes, release date: July, 2005.
9 In the 2006 and 2008 Eurobarometer surveys, a thin plurality of British respondents tipped toward ethnic origin over religion and belief, suggesting – when combined with the Citizenship Survey results – that ethnicity and religion are perceived as essentially equal vectors of increasing prejudice and discrimination.
10 There was no direct comparison to the ethnic group 'Asians' in this question.
11 European and World Value Surveys Integrated Data File, 1999 survey. The 2008 Eurobarometer survey reinforced these findings, with 22 percent of British respondents saying they would be uncomfortable having a Roma as a neighbor, 4 percent uncomfortable with a neighbor of a different ethnic origin, and only 1 percent claiming discomfort with someone of a different religion.
12 For a useful discussion of the relationship between xenophobia and Islamophobia, see Helbling (2010).
13 Some immigrants from Eastern Europe are Muslims but most are not. Eastern European immigrants are thus extremely unlikely to be conflated with the category of Muslims.
14 The question was not asked in the 2001 CS.
15 In addition, it is worth noting that Muslim/non-Muslim group similarities also exist for responses to the additional survey questions *How strongly do you belong to England?* and *To what extent do you agree or disagree that you personally feel a part of British society.*

16 Results for these questions are not presented here in the interest of parsimony, but are available from the authors upon request.

17 The authors would like to thank Marc Helbling for suggesting this point.

18 For more on the extent to which British political institutions have been open to Muslim mobilization and what effects this may have on integration, see Joppke 2009b or Koopmans *et al.* 2005.

19 In the interest of parsimony results are presented from the most recent 2008/9 CS but the patterns are similar to those found in other editions of the CS.

4 Attitudes toward Muslims in Norway

Zan Strabac and Marko Valenta

Until a few decades ago, Norway used to be an ethnically homogenous country with fairly low levels of immigration (see, for example, Nielsson 1985). This is clearly not the case any longer. With the proportion of foreign-born resembling the level in the USA, and a diverse and fast-growing immigrant population, the country is rapidly being transformed into a genuine multi-ethnic society. The reasons for this relatively swift increase in immigration are complex and are shared by many other industrialized countries, particularly those in Western Europe. On one hand, the dual processes of European integration and the enlargement of the European Union have resulted in increased numbers of European immigrants. On the other, fairly large numbers of immigrants from developing countries are entering Norway as asylum seekers or through various family reunion schemes.

While there has been some debate about immigration from European countries, particularly since the recent eastward enlargement of the European Union,[1] there is little doubt that it is immigration from non-industrialized countries outside Europe that has sparked most controversy. This immigration has been a prominent – although not dominant – topic in political debates, and a number of political parties and organizations have opposition to immigration as a major issue on their political agendas. Some of these are fringe, far-right parties and organizations, but what is currently the second-largest party in the country, the Progress Party, has strongly focused on immigration issues for several decades. This party has been demanding more restrictive immigration policies, and has increasingly focused on cultural issues and ethnic conflicts (Hagelund 2003). In addition to political debates, there have also been debates about xenophobic attitudes and discrimination, and problems with the somewhat vaguely formulated 'integration' of immigrants into Norwegian society.

A significant proportion of immigrants in Norway come from countries with a majority Muslim population. In this way Norway has acquired a still rather small, but non-negligible and rapidly growing population that is of Muslim origin. As a part of the immigrant population, Muslim immigrants have been facing the same difficulties and prejudices as the rest of immigrants. However, in Norway, as in many other countries, there has been much negative focus on Muslims and Islam. It is therefore of interest to explore whether Muslim immigrants are particularly exposed to hostility and prejudice. In this chapter, we shall focus on negative attitudes toward Muslims that are sometimes referred to as Islamophobia. Since practically all Muslims in Norway are either immigrants or are of immigrant origin, our analyses of anti-Muslim attitudes are closely related to a broader and more established field of analyses of anti-immigrant attitudes.

We organize our presentation as following: first, we present and discuss relevant theories and empirical results that deal with negative attitudes toward immigrants and ethnic minorities in general. Thereafter, we present some relevant research results concerning Muslim immigrants in particular, followed by presentation of relevant aspects of the public debate about Muslims in Norway. We focus primarily on domestic Norwegian themes and actors, although we also present factors that can be used in an international comparison of anti-Muslim debates. Since literature concerning negative attitudes toward Muslim immigrants is still relatively scarce and not particularly well organized, we attempt to identify central themes and actors in the debate and to develop typologies that might help in conducting more systematic analyses of anti-Muslim attitudes. After these theoretical presentations, we present empirical survey data from 2009 and some simple empirical analyses of how widespread anti-Muslim attitudes in Norway are, as compared with negative attitudes toward immigrants in general.

Anti-immigrant attitudes and hostility directed toward immigrants

There is a considerable amount of empirical research and theoretical work devoted to studies of negative attitudes and hostility directed toward immigrants and ethnic minorities. Historically, an important line of research emerged in the US that focused on negative attitudes against racial minorities (for example, Schuman *et al.* 1997). In Europe, research on negative attitudes toward immigrants has been strongly developed in recent years, and a large number of high-quality studies have been produced. Some of these are single-country studies (for example, Semyonov *et al.* 2004; Sniderman *et al.* 2004), while other are focusing on cross-country analyses (for example, Scheepers *et al.* 2002a; Schneider 2008). Perhaps the most common focus in empirical studies is on determinants of anti-immigrant attitudes. Although effects of individual- and group-level determinants of negative attitudes are obviously of great practical and analytical importance, they are not the focus of our study in this chapter. In this study, we will focus on question of how widespread the negative attitudes are within the native population. Regarding this extent of anti-immigrant attitudes, findings from the large and influential study of Pettigrew (1998a) paint a rather bleak picture. The author summarizes some of his most important findings as following: '... increased prejudice, direct and indirect discrimination, political opposition, and extensive violence are major European reactions to the new minorities' (Pettigrew 1998a: 98). Concerning temporal change in anti-immigrant attitudes, Semyonov *et al.* (2006) find a considerable worsening of these attitudes in the time span between 1988 and 2000 in all 12 Western European countries included in their study. Here, we would like to point out that there is no general agreement regarding how 'exactly' to measure intensity and extent of anti-immigrant attitudes. However, there is a large degree of academic consensus that a fair amount of hostility against immigrants is present in parts of native populations, and that this hostility constitutes an important social and political problem in majority of Western European countries (see Pettigrew 1998a).

Regarding conceptual developments, a fairly large number of different theoretical concepts have been used. The one that is perhaps most commonly used, particularly in American research, is 'prejudice' (for example, Quillian 1995), although other terms, such as 'anti-foreigner sentiment' (Semyonov *et al.* 2006) or 'ethnic exclusionism' (Scheepers *et al.* 2002a) have also been used. We choose to conceptualize hostility toward a particular minority group as a negative attitude toward members of that group. We define attitudes toward a particular social group as evaluative tendencies toward members of that group that are based on their group membership, and not on their individual characteristics.

Anti-Muslim attitudes

With regard to anti-Muslim attitudes, a mention should be made about the relationship between this concept and concept of Islamophobia. There are obviously several possible definitions of Islamophobia. For example, Helbling (2010: 69) broadly defines Islamophobia as '… a rejection of Islam, Muslim groups and Muslim individuals on the basis of prejudice and stereotypes. It may have emotional, cognitive, evaluative as well as action-oriented elements (for example, discrimination, violence).' Our starting point is that anti-Muslim attitudes might be considered as one of several possible conceptualisations of Islamophobia; however, we define Islamophobia more narrowly as 'negative attitudes toward Muslims'. This simple and narrower definition is, in our view, more suitable for the empirical analyses we conduct.

A large-scale study by Strabac and Listhaug (2008) found that, in general, Muslim immigrants were more exposed to prejudice than immigrants in 13 out of 17 Western European countries that were included in the study. Authors' empirical analyses were based on high-quality data from the 1999–2000 wave of European Values study, but their measure of prejudice was very simple, consisting of a single dichotomous item. Helbling (2010), using the same simple measure as Strabac and Listhaug, finds higher levels of Islamophobia than xenophobia in Switzerland in both 1996 and 2007.

Contrary to the findings of Strabac and Listhaug (2008) and Helbling (2010), a Dutch study by Sniderman and Hagendoorn (2007) did not find notable differences in negative stereotypes of Muslim and non-Muslim immigrant groups. Their study was based on a 1998 telephone survey data and, among other things, the authors asked their Dutch respondents about their degree of agreement with a series of statements describing stereotypes of immigrant groups. The negative stereotypes of four immigrant groups were measured; two of these groups were from countries with a majority Muslim population – Turkish immigrants and Moroccan immigrants; one was from a country with majority non-Muslim population – Surinamese immigrants; and one concerned a general category of immigrants – 'refugees'. Sniderman and Hagendoorn found that around a third of the Dutch population held fairly negative views of immigrants, but they did not find that the

evaluations of the two Muslim immigrant groups were consistently more negative than the evaluations of non-Muslim Surinamese immigrants and of refugees
in general. Thus, the authors conclude that: 'The dominant pattern of evaluative
judgements [regarding the immigrant groups] is one of similarity, not dissimilarity'
(Sniderman and Hagendoorn 2007: 48).

In discussing anti-Muslim attitudes in Western European countries, one should
bear in mind that the proportion of Muslims in practically all of these countries
is still fairly low. For example, the estimates from Barrett *et al.* (2001) that were
used in Strabac and Listhaug (2008) showed that only one of the 17 Western
European countries included in the study had more than 5 percent of the population of Muslim origin; that country was France, with a Muslim population of
7.1 percent. Thus, it seems reasonable to conclude that large portions of native
populations have little or no first-hand knowledge about Muslim immigrants.
This being so, from where do the natives get the information that is necessary to
form their opinions about Muslims? Well, quite obviously, from mass media. For
this reason, portrayals of Islam and Muslims in a country's mass media are probably of great importance for the public discourse about Muslims and for formation of opinions by natives.

There is a wide variety of representations of Islam and Muslims in the media
and it is highly desirable to provide a typology of various media presentations in
order to render possible more systematic analyses of media influences. In an analysis
of depictions of Islam in the British broadsheet press, Richardson (2004) identifies four main themes that appear in the articles. These are: 1) the military threat
from Muslim countries; 2) the threat of political violence and extremism; 3) the
(internal) threat to democracy posed by authoritarian Muslim political leaders and
parties; and 4) the social threat of Muslim gender inequality. Although Richardson's
typology is based on analysis of British press, it could probably be used in analyses
of media coverage of Islam and Muslims in the majority of Western countries.
Nevertheless, we shall propose some modifications to this typology in discussions
of representations of Muslims in Norway, and this is the theme we turn to in the
next section.

Public debate about Islam and Muslims in Norway

Muslims make only a small proportion of the population in Norway. If one uses
a very broad definition of 'individuals with a Muslim origin in Norway' to mean
individuals that are either immigrants from countries with a majority Muslim
population or are Norwegian-born with both parents coming from countries
with a majority Muslim population, then Muslims constituted about 3.5 percent
of the population in 2008.[2] Using a perhaps more realistic definition of Muslims
as individuals being registered as members of various Muslim religious organisations, then Muslims make up about 1.8 percent of the total population, numbering
about 80,000 individuals.[3] Although there are relatively few Muslims in Norway,
there is a sustained focus on Islam and Muslims in the Norwegian media and in
public debate. According to a recent report from The Directorate of Integration
and Diversity (IMDi) of the Norwegian government, Islam and Muslims were

highly visible in Norwegian media. For example, in 2009, Muslims and Islam were mentioned in Norwegian media about as often as the country's Prime Minister, Jens Stoltenberg, and more often than the 'swine flu' which was the focus of heavy media attention in 2009 (IMDi 2009).

While there seems to be little doubt that Muslims are highly visible in Norwegian media, and thus in public debates in Norway, the question is whether media portrayals of Muslims are overwhelmingly negative. In particular, the question is if Muslims are portrayed in a negative manner more often than the rest of the immigrant population. To our knowledge, only one formal large-scale study of the ouput of Norwegian media has been conducted that is relevant to these questions. The study in question is by Lindstad and Fjeldstad (2005), and is based on an analysis of the content of the eight largest Norwegian newspapers over the period between 30 April and 1 June 2003. The findings show that Islam and Muslims were negatively portrayed in the Norwegian press, and much more negatively than other 'non-Western' immigrants.[4] Of 145 newspaper articles that dealt with Norwegian Muslims and Islam, only four articles – or 3 percent of the total – described Muslims in a positive manner, as ordinary citizens or as a positive resource for Norwegian society. By comparison, non-Western immigrants in Norway were portrayed as ordinary citizens or as a positive resource for Norwegian society in about a quarter of the articles that dealt with this group. The authors concluded therefore that: 'Muslims are presented more negatively in press than other immigrants' (Lindstad and Fjeldstad 2005: 67).

As mentioned before, in discussing media portrayals of Muslims it is useful to provide a typology of main themes in media presentations. Building on a typology of main themes in the British press as developed by Richardson (2004), we propose a typology of oft-mentioned and recurring themes in presentations of Muslims in the Norwegian media. In Norway, one might distinguish between three dominant themes in media depictions of Muslims: 1) family and gender relations; 2) crime, violence and social problems, and 3) 'Sharia law arguments', that is, implicit or explicit arguments that Muslims intend to replace secular liberal democracy with some form of theocracy based on traditional Islamic legal systems and values. Needless to say, in addition to these three main categories, a very large number of other themes appear in media presentation of Muslims in Norway at one time or another.

So far as family and gender relations are concerned, the focus is mainly on the position of women, arranged marriages, families' control over their children – particularly girls – and, less often, on genital mutilation of girls by some immigrant groups from predominantly Muslim countries. With regard to crime, violence and social problems, this is a theme that has already been established in media presentations of immigrants in general, and has arguably emerged in debates about Muslim immigrants simply as a result of the exceedingly strong media focus on this subset of the immigrant population. Additionally, there seems to be a sustained focus on violence and crime in media presentations of one of the largest Muslim immigrant group in the country, Pakistanis (see Chapter 4 in Lindstad and Fjeldstad 2005). Finally, with regard to 'Sharia law' arguments, it is perhaps best to illustrate the use of this kind of argument with an example. In a much-publicized and highly controversial speech given in February 2009, the chairmen of the Progress Party, Siv Jensen, warned against 'sneaking Islamization' in Norway. To illustrate what might happen, she actually used an example from neighboring Sweden, saying:

> ' … also Oslo and other larger cities in Norway can end up in a situation as the one we can see in Malmö [in Sweden], where emergency service personnel do not dare to drive into certain parts of the city because Sharia laws have taken over completely and Swedish laws are set aside.'[5]

Apart from such explicit and bombastic 'clash of civilizations type' utterances as this one, one also meets more moderate arguments criticizing giving 'special privileges' to Muslims or criticizing Muslims for not being willing enough to accept Norwegian laws. Common among all types of arguments is that Muslims are being accused of trying to form 'parallel societies' with their own jurisdiction – in a moderate version of the critique – or of trying to 'take over' and introduce Muslim laws into society at large, or at least into parts of it – in the radical version of the critique.

If we take a bit broader, international perspective, one would arguably find the three main themes in the depiction of Muslims in a majority of Western countries. Themes related to gender and family relations are explicitly or implicitly being established as important points of criticisms of Muslims pretty much everywhere in the West. Even in studies that mainly focus on the conflict of values and multiculturalism, such as in the Dutch study by Sniderman and Hagendoorn (2007), the central issue basically concerns family and gender relations.

Violence and crime is another theme that has been established in negative portrayals of different immigrant groups in many immigrant-receiving societies. To what degree this topic becomes associated with Muslim immigrants, in particular, probably depends on the degree of negative focus on Muslims, in general, and on the question of whether a particular immigrant-receiving country tends to receive one of the few national groups of Muslim immigrants that are portrayed as being particularly prone to crime and violence. Arguably, in this case 'spillover effects' are possible, leading to generalizations from that particular group to all groups of immigrants from Muslim countries.

The 'Sharia law' argument is, in its radical form, probably the most vicious portrayal of Muslim immigrants as a potential 'fifth column' that is – or will be – trying to undermine the core social values and political order in the country. This is the type of argument that possibly varies much from country to country, and its use deserves closer attention from social scientists. We shall elaborate further on its use in the Norwegian context later in the text. Arguably, also some presentations of Islamic terrorism could be included under 'Sharia law' themes. This is so particularly in instances when terrorist acts are depicted as being politically motivated, and not as a result of the personal frustrations of the terrorists.

Apart from creating a typology of main themes in the presentation of Muslims in the media and in public debate, it is useful to provide a more systematic presentation of the main *promoters* of negative descriptions of Muslims in public debate in Norway. To some degree, this is not an easy task because a wide variety of individuals can come with strongly negative utterances and sweeping generalizations about Muslims and Islam from time to time.[6] However, there are two important promoters of anti-Muslim utterances that have repeatedly and purposefully focused on Islam and Muslims. The first, and by far the most important one, is the Progress Party. It is hard to exaggerate the importance of the Progress Party as one of the key players in the anti-Muslim discourse in the country. The party has been actively promoting negative attitudes toward immigrants and immigration for decades, and has been strongly targeting the Muslim part of the immigrant population recently. The Progress Party has a reputation for being good at handling the mass media, and has generally been very successful in both local and national elections for quite awhile (see Hagelund 2003). As a result, the party is currently playing one of the leading roles in debates about Islam and Muslims.

Somewhat more controversially, we could claim that the second main promoter of anti-Muslim utterances is the Norwegian mass media itself, or at least some of the media outlets that have become important independent actors in promoting negative statements and controversies related to Islam and Muslims. This is partly a result of the general conflict orientation of Norway's mass media. Conflict sells, and once negative themes related to Muslims and Islam have been established, the media continues to keep the negative focus due to conventional news-production criteria (see Peterson 1981). However, in at least one prominent issue – the Mohammed cartoons issue – the mass media itself has playing a leading role in creating and maintaining conflictual situations. Norway has had its share of controversy and conflict related to the international crisis started by the publication of Mohamed cartoons in Denmark in 2005. But the country has also had a homegrown crisis that was a result of editorial decisions by one of the country's largest newspapers, *Dagbladet*. The *Dagbladet* is a tabloid with a greatly reduced circulation in recent years. As late as February 2010, the newspaper had an article about the highly offensive cartoon presenting Prophet Mohammed as pig. While criticizing the publication of the cartoon, the newspaper made sure that the cartoon was clearly visible on its front page. This sparked large protests by about 3,000 Muslims in Oslo, with accompanying public debate and controversies.

Attitudes toward Muslims vs. attitudes toward immigrants in general

We have seen that the relatively small group of Norwegian Muslims has been the focus of much negative attention in public debates. An interesting question is whether all this negative focus has lead to particularly negative attitudes toward Muslims among the general population of Norway. When discussing negative attitudes toward Muslims, one should keep in mind that we are talking about a subgroup of the immigrant population in the country, so the precise question to ask is: 'Are the attitudes toward Muslim immigrants more negative than the attitudes toward immigrants in general?' We shall use nationally representative survey data collected in 2009 to analyze attitudes toward Muslim immigrants, but before conducting empirical analyses, let us formulate some hypotheses about the more important aspects of anti-Muslim attitudes.

Hypothesis 1: We expect attitudes toward Muslim immigrants within the general population of Norway to be more negative than the attitudes toward immigrants in general.

Due to the reasons explained above, it seems quite probable that all the negative attention given to Muslims has resulted in particularly negative attitudes among natives toward Muslim immigrants. We therefore expect that attitudes toward Muslim immigrants are going to be more negative than attitudes toward immigrants in general.

Hypothesis 2: We expect attitudes toward Muslim immigrants among supporters of the Progress Party to be more negative than their attitudes toward immigrants in general.

The Progress Party has been one of the main proponents of negative discourses about Muslims. We shall discuss the possible reasons for the Progress Party's anti-Muslim rhetoric later, but it seems reasonable to assume that the party's supporters are particularly predisposed to accept the party's anti-Muslim rhetoric and to develop attitudes toward Muslim immigrants that are even more negative than their attitudes toward immigrants in general.

Hypothesis 3: We expect that Muslim immigrants will to a larger degree be stereotyped as being particularly prone to crime.

As we have seen, one of the dominant themes in the presentation of Muslim immigrants has been related to crime. Since we have an item in our dataset that is related to the issue of crime, we expect Muslim immigrants to be viewed particularly negatively with regard to this item.

Hypothesis 4: We expect that the culture of Muslim immigrants will be stereotyped more negatively than the culture of immigrants in general.

While 'culture' is clearly a slippery concept, it seems reasonable to believe that an average member of the public has at least some naïve ideas about 'culture' as something that is related to values and 'ways of life'. Many of the controversies regarding depictions of Muslims could be related to 'culture'; for example, the position of women, sexual mores, proper – or improper – behavior of youth in public places, etc. One of the items in our dataset is based on a question of whether or not different groups of immigrants are 'enriching the country's cultural life'. We expect Muslim immigrants to be viewed particularly negatively with regard to this item, due to the aforementioned controversies related to 'Muslim cultural traits'.

Empirical analyses

We base our empirical analyses on data from a nationally representative web survey of the adult Norwegian population – aged 18 and over – conducted in January 2009. The survey was conducted by the Norwegian branch of the international survey organization, YouGov. The sampling procedures were based on the 'Large-Panel Assembly' approach pioneered by Harris Interactive (see Berrens *et al.* 2003). In general terms, this approach tries to mimic a random probability sample of the general population by taking as a point of departure a large 'pool' (panel) of respondents who have agreed to participate in internet surveys conducted by the survey organization. From this large panel, a pseudo-probability sample is drawn by using a two-stage procedure, called *matching* by YouGov. First, a true probability sample of the target population is drawn from a large, high-quality source such as a census of the general population. (In our case, the target population is the general population of Norway.) This sample is called the *target sample*. Thereafter, for each member of the target sample, one or more matching individuals from the pool of the pre-recruited respondents are drawn. This sample is called the *matched sample*. Matching is accomplished using a set of background variables, typically involving age, sex, education, etc. Technically, the matching is conducted by an algorithm minimizing a multidimensional distance function of the attributes involved in matching and selecting the closest matching individual from the panel for each individual in the target sample. In other words, the matched sample is selected such that it resembles the target sample as closely as possible on those attributes included in the matching procedure. In the usual manner, after the surveys were conducted, weights were provided by YouGov to correct for imbalances in distribution of age, gender and education of the final sample.

One of the problems associated with studies of attitudes toward Muslims in Western countries is related to the fact that Muslims are basically a subgroup of the entire immigrant population. Since it is well-known that this immigrant population is exposed to prejudice and negative attitudes, it is challenging to separate the 'generic anti-immigrant component' from 'specific anti-Muslim component' in whichever results one might get regarding negative attitudes toward Muslims (see Strabac and Listhaug 2008). To solve this problem, we have embedded experimental manipulation in our population survey. Our total sample (n=1,000) was randomly divided into two subsamples. Most of the survey questions presented to the two subsamples were identical, but the questions that are of interest for our analyses differed slightly. The first subsample (n=477) was presented with following sett of questions:[7]

> Could you please indicate how much you agree or disagree with each of the following statements:
>
> 1   Immigrants exploit social security benefits.
> 2   Immigrants should be given the same rights as anyone else.
> 3   Immigrants make Norway's crime problems worse.
> 4   Immigrants enrich Norway's cultural life.

For all statements, five answer options were provided, coded with values from 1 to 5. The options were: 'Completely disagree' (coded 1); 'disagree' (coded 2); 'neither agree nor disagree' (coded 3); 'agree' (coded 4) and 'completely agree' (coded 5). A 'Can't say' option was also included.

The second subsample (n=523) was presented with a slightly modified version of the questions:

> Could you please indicate how much you agree or disagree with each of the following statements:
>
> 1   Immigrants of a Muslim background exploit social security benefits.
> 2   Immigrants of a Muslim background should be given the same rights as anyone else.
> 3   Immigrants of a Muslim background make Norway's crime problems worse.
> 4   Immigrants of a Muslim background enrich Norway's cultural life.

(Identical answer options as in the first subsample.)

As one can see, the only difference between the two sets of questions is insertion of the phrase 'of a Muslim background' into questions presented to the second subsample. Since the subsamples were randomly selected, we can be sure that any differences in distributions of answers are a result of differences in the questions – about Muslim immigrants compared with about immigrants in general.

To measure negative attitudes toward immigrants in general and Muslim immigrants in particular we created two additive scales. We call the first scale *Anti-immigrant*, and the scale is computed as an averaged sum of responses to the four questions presented to the first subsample. Before creating the scale, responses to questions 2 and 4 were reverse coded so that high values mean more negative views toward immigrants, that is disagreeing with the statements. In order to ease intuitive understanding of the values of the scale, the values were rescaled so to vary at the 0–100 interval, with high values meaning more negative attitudes toward immigrants.[8] The four-item scale has the reliability coefficient (Cronbach's alpha) of 0.76. The principal component analysis shows that the scale is one-dimensional. The negative attitudes toward Muslim immigrants are measured by an additive scale that we call *Anti-Muslim*. The four-item scale is coded at the basis of questions 1 to 4 that were presented to the second subsample. The coding of Anti-Muslim scale is otherwise identical to the coding of the Anti-immigrant scale. The Anti-Muslim scale has the reliability coefficient (Cronbach's alpha) of 0.81. The principal component analysis shows that the scale is one-dimensional.

To answer the empirical questions that we formulated as the four hypotheses in the previous section, we need to analyze the average values of the Anti-immigrant and the Anti-Muslim scales for the whole sample as well as for the sample of individuals who stated that they supported the Progress Party.[9] Further, we need to analyze average values of answers to question 3 (crime) and question 4 (culture) to see if our hypotheses 3 and 4 received empirical support. The relevant average values, differences between them, and p-values of the differences are presented in Table 4.1. Recall that values for question 4 (culture) have been reverse coded so that high values mean negative views toward immigrants and Muslim immigrants for all of the measures presented in the Table. In order to ease comparisons of

Table 4.1 Mean values of scales and items for questions about immigrants and about Muslim immigrants, and the difference between them

	Subsample 1 (Questioned about immigrants)	Subsample 2 (Questioned about Muslim immigrants)	Subsample 2 − Subsample 1	p-value
Scales (whole sample)	50.4	51.7	1.3	0.304
Scales (Progress Party supporters only)	62.5	65.2	2.7	0.322
Crime item (values 1 to 5)	70.8	65.9	-4.9	0.003
Culture item (values 1 to 5)	35.3	48.6	13.3	0.000

Notes
p-values are based on t-tests. Data are weighted. Total number of Progress Party supporters equals 169 (real sample size).

the average values, values of 'crime' and 'culture' items were also rescaled so to vary at the 0–100 interval, with high values meaning stronger stereotyping of the minority groups.

As one can see, the average value of the scale measuring negative attitudes toward immigrants (Anti-immigrant) is only very slightly lower than the average value of scale measuring negative attitudes toward Muslim immigrants (Anti-Muslim), and the difference is clearly not statistically significant. Therefore, we have to reject our Hypothesis 1 and conclude that attitudes toward Muslim immigrants in the general population of Norway were not more negative than the attitudes toward immigrants in general. Basically the same result is obtained when we analyzed only supporters of the Progress Party. As one might expect, supporters of the Progress Party have more negative attitudes toward both immigrants and Muslim immigrants than the population at large – recall that higher values of the scales represent more negative attitudes. However, Progress Party supporters also exhibit attitudes toward Muslim immigrants that are only very slightly more negative than their attitudes toward immigrants in general, the difference being only 2.7 points on a 0–100 scale. Additionally, the difference is clearly not statistically significant. We therefore reject our Hypothesis 2 and conclude that, among supporters of the Progress Party, the attitudes toward Muslim immigrants were also not more negative than the attitudes toward immigrants in general.

Turning to the average values of the item that measures stereotyping of minority groups as being associated with crime, a surprising result emerges. The stereotyping of Muslim immigrants is actually somewhat less pronounced than the stereotyping of immigrants in general, and the difference in levels of stereotyping is statistically significant at the conventional levels of significance. This being said, the difference is nevertheless substantively small, equalling about 5 points on a 0–100 scale (about 5 percent). We therefore conclude that our Hypothesis 3 is clearly rejected and that Muslim immigrants are actually being slightly less stereotyped as being prone to crime than immigrants in general. This result is somewhat surprising and we shall comment on it in more detail in the last section of the chapter.

Finally, with regard to the item measuring negative stereotypes of culture added by minority groups, Muslim immigrants seem to be more strongly stereotyped, with a difference equalling 13.3 points on a 0–100 scale and being highly statistically significant. Substantively, the difference is not very large but it is not negligible either. We can therefore conclude that our Hypothesis 4 has received empirical support and that the 'culture' of Muslim immigrants was viewed more negatively, or less positively, than the 'culture' of immigrants in general.

Discussion

We have seen that the results of our empirical analyses were generally not in line with the expectations that we had. Although there seems to be greater negative focus on Muslims than on immigrants in general in public debate in Norway, this did not translate in more negative attitudes toward the Muslim part of the immigrant population. In a way, this is an encouraging finding. In spite of huge amounts of negative news about Islam and Muslims, the audience does not seem to be 'buying the story', or at least not for the time being. Here, we should be quick to emphasize that we were measuring whether or not the attitudes toward Muslim immigrants were more negative than the attitudes toward immigrants in general, and not how widespread or how strong the attitudes toward immigrants, including the Muslim ones, were. Our results do not mean that there are no negative attitudes toward immigrants and Muslim immigrants in the Norwegian population but that we simply found that the attitudes toward Muslim immigrants were not *more* negative. Indeed, if we look at the distribution of values of our attitude scales we see that more than 40 percent of our respondents generally agreed with the four negative statements about immigrants and Muslim immigrants – resulting in values above 50 on both the *Anti-immigrant* and *Anti-Muslim* scales.

This is most clearly visible in analysis that only includes supporters of the Progress Party. The attitudes of this group are clearly more negative than the attitudes of the general population, with more than 60 percent generally agreeing with negative statements about immigrants, and more than 75 percent generally agreeing with negative statements about Muslim immigrants. However, Progress Party supporters also do not seem to dislike Muslim immigrants more strongly than they dislike immigrants in general. This is quite an interesting finding, since the Progress Party leadership has done its best to target Muslims in media, sometimes using really far-stretched logic and arguments, such as the 'Sharia laws in Malmö' theme. We can, of course, only speculate about reasons for the anti-Muslim utterances of Progress Party politicians, but it seems plausible that they are trying to increase the threat perceptions of the electorate. One of the ways this might be achieved is by replacing the Progress Party's usual – and successful – story about social problems and crime that are associated with immigration with depictions of a Muslim 'fifth column' that wants to change the core values and the political system in Norwegian society. For the time being, however, these attempts do not seem to have been very successful.

Turning to the stereotyping of immigrants and Muslim immigrants as being particularly associated with crime, we have seen that crime has been one of dominant themes in media depictions of immigrants in general and Muslim immigrants in particular. This shows up in our data in the form of very high average values on the 'crime' item, for both versions of the survey question. However, we actually find somewhat *less* strong stereotyping of Muslim immigrants. Although the difference in stereotyping is substantively modest, it is clearly statistically significant. This is a surprising finding. Although we believe that it is possible that there are no differences in stereotyping – that is the reason for conducting of the tests – it seems unlikely that Muslims are more positively viewed, given the current state of the public debate. We therefore wonder if a social desirability bias might be more pronounced in questions regarding Muslim immigrants. Since it is widely known that Muslims have been exposed recently to much negative media attention, including words 'of Muslim origin' in survey questions might alert the respondents that they are being tested for anti-Muslim prejudice and induce them to provide more socially desirable answers, that is, answers that are more positive toward Muslims. Nevertheless, even if we accept the argument that less negative stereotyping of Muslim immigrants is a result of stronger social desirability bias in answers to questions about immigrants 'of a Muslim background', it is still clear that Muslims are not more strongly stereotyped as being criminal. Stronger social desirability bias or not, we would argue that strongly more negative attitudes toward Muslim immigrants would show in our empirical data. Since they did not, we can be pretty sure that Muslims were not more strongly stereotyped as being criminal than the rest of the immigrants.

However, when we turn to negative stereotypes of culture of Muslim immigrants, a different picture emerges. The item we used measures the degree of disagreement with the statement: 'Immigrants – or immigrants of Muslim origin – enrich Norway's cultural life'. Although it seems that both immigrants in general and Muslim immigrants in particular are generally viewed as positive contributors to the country's cultural life, resulting in average values lower than 50, Muslim immigrants are clearly less favorably viewed in this regard. It is unfortunate that we do not have more specific measures than the one based on a general notion of 'culture', but we suspect that negative stereotypes about family- and gender-relations among Muslims are one of the major reasons for the less positive views of Muslim immigrants.

To summarize, we have seen that Muslims have been negatively portrayed in media and public debate in Norway, but that this did not translate into more negative attitudes toward Muslim immigrants. The only, but important, exception concerns the more negative views about the 'culture' of Muslim immigrants. It seems, therefore, that Muslim immigrants are not in general viewed as a particularly troublesome part of the immigrant population, but that there are aspects of Muslim culture that are viewed more negatively. Considering the geographical, cultural and socio-demographical complexity of the Muslim population in Norway, the concept of 'Muslim culture' is clearly a gross oversimplification, but it seems plausible that at least parts of the native population perceive that there is a certain degree of cultural homogeneity among Muslims. Future research should therefore investigate more thoroughly which aspects of 'Muslim culture' are more negatively viewed among natives. In addition, one should try to replicate the rather positive results regarding the lack of strongly negative attitudes toward Muslims that we obtained in our Norwegian data.

Notes

1   Norway is not a member of the European Union, but the country is closely tied to the Union through the European Economic Area (EEA) agreement. Among other things, Norway's participation in the EEA obliges the country to adopt most EU legislation, including laws regulating immigration from EU countries.

2   The percentage is calculated by authors. The absolute number of Muslims based on the broad definition is retrieved from Statistics Norway (2009), while the estimate of the total population of the country is retrieved from CIA (2009).

3   Source for total number of individuals that are registered as a member of some of Muslim religious organisations: Statistics Norway (2009) (data for 2008). Registered religious organisations in Norway receive monetary support from the Norwegian state based on number of their members, and are therefore generally open to accepting new members, without demanding active participation. Due to this reason, not all individuals registered in Muslim religious organisations are necessarily actively practicing Muslims.

4   Until recently, the distinction between 'Western' and 'non-Western' immigrants was used in Norwegian research. Western immigrants were defined as the ones coming from Western Europe, North America and Australia and New Zealand. Although somewhat oversimplified, the division was useful for many practical purposes.

5   Authors' translation of Siv Jensen's utterance as it appears in Norwegian newspaper *Verdens Gang* (VG) from 22 February 2009 (page 6).

6   Recent examples include one of country's most famous painters, Håkon Bleken and Parliamentary member Ola Borten Moe from the centre-left political party, *Senterpartiet*.

7   This is of course the English translation of questions in Norwegian

8   The rescaling is done by subtracting 1 from the original scale, and then multiplying it by 25.

9   One of the questions in the survey was about respondents' political preferences. Based on this question, we were able to extract the subsample of individuals supporting Progress Party.

5 Islamophobia in Sweden

Politics, representations, attitudes and experiences

Pieter Bevelander and Jonas Otterbeck

Introduction

In Sweden today, there is a constant stream of attention focused on Islam and Muslims. There has been a good deal of discussion of such subjects as male circumcision, female genital mutilation, the slaughter of animals in accordance with religious requirements, religious private schools, the wearing of religious dress in public places, honor violence, Sharia laws, and the granting of planning permission for mosques. In some instances the debate has been balanced and reflective, in others careless and sensationalist. In particular, Malmö, the third city of Sweden, is presented as a city soon to be completely dominated by Muslims. But the discussion of Islam and Muslim issues has roots that go back in time. Islam has long been the focus of criticism and derogatory comments, and has been perceived as representing something radically different (Gardell 2010). At the same time, policies are in place to protect minorities through legislation and make room for a plurality in Sweden. This article tries to explore the extent to which Swedish society has been affected by what has generally been called Islamophobia.

This chapter has four integrated parts. First we will discuss the political discourse on Islam and Muslims, and then we will connect that to the representation of Islam in media. We will then present statistical data on attitudes to Muslims and Islam of the general population in Sweden. Finally we will discuss Muslim experiences of stereotypes.

Instead of presuming that these four fields are permeated with Islamophobia, we will use a stipulative definition of Islamophobia to investigate different traits and nuances in Swedish discourses on Muslims and Islam.

Let us first turn to the word itself. Islamophobia is not in any way a term that should be understood through its etymological construction, that is, a phobia of Islam, much in the same way as xenophobia or homophobia cannot be attributed to psychological fears only. Rather, it has to be understood through its genealogy – in a Foucauldian (1971/1998) understanding of the concept.

Following its genealogy, it is evident that Islamophobia first was established as an activist term, implying pejorative judgments about the Islamophobe and striving to mobilize – through the acts of naming and exposure – against a wide range of discriminatory practices and values concerning Muslims, Islamic discourses, and cultural practices associated with Muslims or Islam. It was first used in 1918, in French, in this sense by Sliman ben Ibrahim in his biography of Mohammed illustrated by French painter Alphonse Etienne Diner (Otterbeck and Bevelander 2006). In 1985, Edward Said compared Islamophobia to anti-Semitism in the journal *Race & Class* claiming both to be based in the same epistemological thinking. Evidently, Said wanted to stigmatize Islamophobia through the rhetorical strength of the well-established concept of anti-Semitism, which is forceful in discussions, not least due to the accusatory power it has attained. When The Runnymede Trust introduced the concept to a wider audience in 1997, it is worthwhile noting the long commitment the Trust had had in fighting anti-Semitism.

Before attempting a scholarly definition of Islamophobia, one has to acknowledge that it gives a diverse range of practices a singular name, attaches a pejorative dimension to that term, and makes an inbuilt comparison with racism and particularly anti-Semitism. As an activist concept, Islamophobia is more useful if undefined than if it is carefully defined, allowing it to expand and retract depending on the user and the present discourse.

The discursive power of the term Islamophobia is such that it is now expected to be included – it is difficult to avoid writing about discrimination or representation of Muslims. In our use of Islamophobia, our strategy has been to consider Islamophobia an ideal type, and to avoid using the judgmental derivate 'Islamophobe' about anyone. The ideal type Islamophobia draws together a whole range of different practices and attitudes in the socio-political field, ideas about presumed Muslim culture and about Islam as a religion. At times, some acts or attitudes cover the whole spectrum – as with xenophobic populist parties targeting Islam; at other times, for example, only theological aspects are in focus – as with some churches' polemical discourses on Islam.

To create a definition covering all expressions and dimensions of Islamophobia is probably an impossible task, judging from prior definitions and the critique of them. We will, therefore, construct an ideal type consisting of four overlapping parts: identification, culturalization, subordination, and discrimination. The first part includes the important process of identifying someone as Muslim and seeing this as an important identity of the other, or claiming that a Muslim identity always is essential and central for anyone with a Muslim background. This is, in itself, not necessarily an Islamophobic act, but it is a requirement for it. The second part is to ascribe fixed religio-cultural behavior and values to Muslims, which in more vulgar discourse tends to presume that Muslim individuals are forced to act in certain ways. The third part is the subordination of these religio-cultural behaviors and values. 'Our' values are considered more humane, modern, enlightened, democratic, etc. than 'theirs'. This completes the othering process. The fourth part is the actual discriminatory practices. In line with a model presented by the Runnymede Trust in 1997, we identify four main types of discrimination: exclusion – from employment and active citizenship; discrimination – in social services and employment; prejudice – in the media and everyday contacts; and violence – verbal, physical, vandalism.[1] In the last part of the article we will return to our ideal type and compare it with our findings.

A note on the Muslim population of Sweden

The size of the Muslim population in Sweden has grown substantially over the past 60 years. The number of residents from a Muslim background increased from just a few individuals and families prior to 1950, to approximately 100,000 by the end of the 1980s, to 200,000 by around 1996, had reached approximately 350,000 by the year 2000, and probably at least 450,000 by 2010 (Anwar *et al.* 2004).[2] This is roughly 5 percent of the population. Almost 90 percent of Sweden's Muslim population have arrived in Sweden, or been born here, since in 1985. Somewhere approaching one-third of the Muslim population is of school age or younger.

The Muslims living in Sweden have their roots all over the world, not least in Turkey, the Balkans, the Eastern Mediterranean, Iraq, Iran, Afghanistan, and Somalia. Islam has undergone a transformation from being an exotic sibling to Christianity and Judaism that was practiced 'over there' to become a religion that is practiced 'at home' in Sweden. Merely the diversity of origins – national, ethnic, religious, etc. – opens up a pluralism of Islams being practiced, not to mention individual preferences, as has been made clear in several different studies (Ouis and Roald 2003; Karlsson Minganti 2007; Otterbeck 2010a).

The political discourse on Islam and Muslims

The most recent elections in Sweden were in 2010. During the years leading up to the election a populist party, the Sweden Democrats (Sverigedemokraterna), tried to win seats by profiling themselves as a party defending Swedish values against immigrants' values and behavior, primarily values said to be based on Islam or Muslim/Arab culture. The strategy and critique of Islam is similar to and often inspired by other European political contexts, and the highly profiled critique of Islam seen from some US-based think tanks and individuals (Malm 2009). The profiling proved to be politically wise. The first thing achieved was a political initiative in which few other politicians could participate, since most knew very little about Islamic history and theology or Arab societies, etc. The second was that they connected to xenophobic, neo-racist individuals through an all-legal bashing campaign. To give two examples. In October 2009, Jimmie Åkesson (2009), leader of the Sweden Democrats wrote an article for a daily in which he listed a number of phenomena which he linked with Muslim migration and called the greatest foreign threat to Sweden since World War II. In the weeks before the national elections in September 2010, the same party tried to broadcast a campaign movie pitting immigrants against pensioners. The immigrants were represented by women in Afghani-style *burkas* and Arabic-style *niqab* pushing prams. In both instances, the party attracted a lot of attention to itself and both journalists and politicians who were critical of the generalized representations of Muslims in these images and writing proved to be remarkably weak in their arguments and criticism. The Swedish democrats gained 5.7 percent of the votes and 20 seats – out of 349 – in the parliament in the 2010 national election. The party attracted even more votes in local elections in the southern part of Sweden.

In our understanding it is possible to speak about a political economy of hate (Islam 2005) when describing the populists' strategies; you attack that which it is legal to attack and make that symbolize what you cannot legally attack. In this case, by attacking Islam – which is and has to be legal in an open society – you can get to Muslim individuals. Further, in a debate climate where Muslims are the epitomized alien, you can get to all immigrants who are perceived as the other.

However, this was not the first instance of the use of Muslims as the other in Swedish politics. Leaving aside older history, such the Swedish Church's position on Muslims in the seventeenth century when Muslims – or the Turks, or Ottomans – were attacked in prayer books and in sermons on a regular basis (Gardell 2010; Otterbeck 2002), Muslims and Islam were not of domestic interest to Swedish politics until 1992. At this time some politicians in a populist party called New Democracy (Ny demokrati) picked up a fairly widespread fear in some Christian circles that the order of Swedish society was under threat from an aggressive Muslim mission and through a rapid growth in the Muslim population – through migration and birth. Typically, it was only a part of their general discourse on immigrant criminality, scams, rape, and general misbehavior. This agenda was not very successful politically, and the party disintegrated during the later part of the 1990s.

At the municipal level, at least one political party, the Scania Party (Skånepartiet), has continuously used anti-Islamic rhetoric since the 1990s. Its agenda includes the liberation of Scania – the southernmost region of the country – from Sweden and ridding Scania of Islam. In the first decade of the twenty-first century, the Sweden Democrats have become more and more focused on criticism of Islam and Muslims. In 2004, a questionnaire on attitudes showed that only 8 percent of youth in Sweden had positive attitudes toward the Sweden Democrats. Of these, 47 percent expressed intolerant views toward Muslims, and a further 42 percent were hesitant. In the same age group, as much as 56 to 86 percent of sympathizers of the established political parties expressed tolerance or high tolerance for Muslims (Otterbeck and Bevelander 2006). The high level of contempt toward Muslims expressed by the sympathizers of the Sweden Democrats also proved to be of equal size when they were asked about Jews, homosexuals or foreigners (Ring and Morgentau 2004). If one looks at really marginal political groupings, like the National Democrats (Nationaldemokraterna), the sympathizers and the activists are even more critical and full of contempt for Muslims and Islam – especially on the Internet.

Compared to the negative discourse, existing collaborative projects between political actors or organizations in civil society and Muslims are often low key. This cooperation is seldom flagged or presented as something profiling a political actor. Because of this, these collaborations remain largely unknown and marginal in political discourse even though they might form a part of civil society (Otterbeck 2010b).

Representing Muslims and Islam

Even if a political discourse – cynical or honest – of attacks on and criticism of Muslims and Islam is a fairly marginal phenomenon often shunned by established politicians and parties, the representations of Muslims and Islam in media, school textbooks, popular culture and in Christian discourse is severely criticized in several scholarly studies. Generally, conclusions are in line with the findings of well-known scholars such as Edward Said (1997) and Jack Shaheen (2001): representations have a tendency to present Muslims as a collective bereft of individualism, focus on problems and violence, present highly stereotyped, un-dynamic understandings of Islamic theology and patriarchal cultural customs, or focus on demonized male individuals who are ascribed great abilities to act, such as Osama bin Laden. It should be pointed out that the enormous output of the media also includes more realistic representations, such as those found in anti-racist journals and in the culture section in the major dailies.

Looking specifically at news media representations, one of the first studies was Håkan Hvitfelt's (1998) analysis of television news in the period 1991–95. He found that while 25 percent of news stories in general were linked to violence, 85 percent of news material related to Islam and Muslims was linked to violence. Note that Muslims were not always portrayed as the perpetrators of violence; they could also be victims. It is also important to note that the years 1991–95 were a turbulent period in several Muslim communities, with a lot of violent events that received much attention.[3]

Other studies of the news media show the same general pattern (see for example Hådell 1997). By often being associated with violence and conflicts, Muslims and Islam are associated with problems, regardless whether they are the victims or the perpetrators.

Since the Internet was introduced – especially the past ten years – the number of Islam-hostile Internet pages has grown rapidly. Journalist David Lagerlöf (2006) claims that extreme nationalist websites often see Jews as hidden conspirators, while the threat from Muslims is derived from their physical presence. Pregnant, pram-pushing Muslim women are common in pictures and propaganda films. Likewise, Muslim youth are made suspicious by simply being visible in society. The visibility of Muslims and the fact that some individual Muslims violate laws are proof of a 'low intensity war of terror' with the aim of taking over Sweden. The only cure is to extirpate all Muslims and Islam. A milder form is that Muslims will have to leave the country.

A new dimension in the representation of Muslims and Islam was introduced in the twenty-first century: the Eurabia discourse. Andreas Malm (2009) argues convincingly that this kind of discourse entered as an extremist one but has partly gained recognition by being introduced in – right wing – liberal discourse. The Eurabia discourse ascribes the power to plot and control to Muslims instead of just repeating that Islam spreads through *jihad* and pregnancies. It has also given rise to an unparalleled interest in Islam among persons critical of a Muslim presence. Nowadays it is possible to find discussions on fairly obscure Islamic concepts like *taqiyya* – the right to deny one's denomination to protect oneself against persecution – on websites dedicated to stopping the Islamization of Sweden. While the dominant representations of Muslims have been – and still are – marked by vague and general stereotypes, this new discourse, inspired by American right wing and Christian critique of Islam as a system of beliefs, is often detailed. It searches and finds problematic concepts in Islamic theology as well as in aggressive Muslim

voices or brutal acts. The critique often lacks understanding of historical processes, economic conditions, power, and of how religious discourses develop and are
articulated. So while Islam is more seldom used in general politics, it is fairly easy
to find stereotypical representations in media identifying, culturalizing and subor-
dinating Muslims and Islam. But what about the general public? Are their attitudes
similar to the political and media discourses?

Attitudes

In the numerous quantitative studies on Swedes' attitudes to Muslims and Islam
there are some noteworthy results: the rather low level of intolerance expressed
when attitudes to Muslims are measured; and the relatively higher level of
intolerance toward the Islamic religion itself. There is further an indication of
increased tolerance over time of both Muslims and Islam. Other general results
from these studies show that younger individuals who live in larger cities, have a
relatively higher educational level, are more established in the labor market, and
are women are more tolerant than those living in less densely populated areas, are
lower educated, are older, have less strong ties to the labor market and are men.
However, using advanced statistical methods – multivariate analysis – women
appear just as likely to express intolerant attitudes toward Muslims when in the
same social position as men. Moreover, negative attitudes correlate as well with
increased radical right representation in Swedish municipalities (Bevelander and
Otterbeck 2010).

The first study of adult Swedes' attitudes toward Islam and Muslims was
conducted in 1990 by Hvitfelt (1991). The result of that study showed that almost
65 percent of the Swedish population was fairly to very negative toward Islam. A
total of 88 percent was of the opinion that the Islamic religion was incompatible
with the Swedish democratic system and 62 percent had the view that the religion
led to female repression. Finally, 53 percent were of the opinion that immigration
by Muslims should be reduced. The general conclusion is that higher education,
female sex and younger age generally leads to a higher degree of positive attitudes
toward Islam, but that even the more positive were rather negative.

Later studies on the attitudes to Muslims and Islam have been commissioned
mainly by the Swedish Integration Board (Integrationsverket). The board's *Integration
Barometer* (2005 and 2006) studied the attitudes of the general public with the use
of a couple of indicators. These studies show that the ones who have a more positive attitude toward Muslims and Islam tend to be women rather than men, individuals living in large cities rather than those living in smaller cities and the country
side, and those who are better educated rather than those with lower education.
The later study also measured an age effect; the younger the respondents were,
the more positive toward Muslims and Islam. One question is similar to Hvitfelt's
study. In the *Integration Barometer* 39 percent (2005) and 37 percent (2006) of the
respondents thought that Muslim immigration should be restricted, compared to
53 percent in Hvitfelt's. Otherwise, most questions in the *Integration Barometer* are
about Muslims rather than about Islam as in Hvitfelt's. This seems to have the effect
that the attitudes are not as harsh. It is also possible that the population in Sweden

has grown more accustomed to Muslims during the 15 years that has past between the questionnaires, and that this might have had an effect.

Since 2005, the so-called *Diversity barometer* has also been conducted. The latest version (Mella and Palm 2010) shows the development over time but indicates a stable attitude toward Islam.[4] For example in response to the question *It should be forbidden to wear a headscarf in school or at work*, just less than 50 percent over this five year period answered that it should be forbidden. Moreover, the 2010 version tried to differentiate this rather crude question by asking respondents about various types of religious clothing of Muslim women. On a sliding scale it showed *burka*, *niqab*, *chador*, *hijab* and *shayla*. The results show that *burka* and *niqab* are seen as unacceptable. The acceptance for the *chador* is also less strong, whereas wearing a *hijab* or *shayla* is not seen as a problem and is accepted by the majority.

In Bevelander and Otterbeck (2010), the attitudes toward Muslims of young people in the 14–18 age group were studied by the use of logistic regression analysis. Starting at the individual level and in line with earlier studies, the study found that individual characteristics have important influence on the attitude toward others, in this case Muslims. Socio-psychological factors like aggressiveness and restlessness play an important part in the explanation of held attitudes. This was an expected result in line with the analysis in an earlier study (Ring and Morgentau 2004), theories on attitudes of right wing youth, but also socio-psychological theories like Tajfel's (Tajfel 1982a). Moreover, the article analysis shows that individuals holding stereotypical understandings of gender and a negative perception of society have more negative attitudes to Muslims. Interestingly, and in contrast to bivariate analyses, no difference between girls and boys was measured.

Robinson *et al.* (2001) suggested that attitudes were interconnected with socialisation and parental practices, but also with increasing maturity. In Bevelander and Otterbeck (2010), the socio-economic background of parents affected the attitude of youths. If the result from earlier studies of the adult population is taken into account – parents with less education and lower socio-economic status are more likely to hold negative attitudes toward Muslims – it is to be expected that these youths' attitudes are in line with their parents' and that the prejudices are likely to be part of their socialization. The opposite situation also holds. The children of parents with a higher socio-economic status and higher education generally have more positive attitudes.

An interesting and significant result is that both girls and boys born outside Sweden, and especially outside of Europe, clearly have more positive attitudes to Muslims. The likeliness of knowing a Muslim increases if you live in immigrant-dense areas. It is also possible that the joint experience of feeling excluded from the category 'Swedish' and being labelled immigrant can lead to solidarity and positive, inclusive attitudes. These interpretations are in line with the contact hypothesis stressing both general contact and common goals and experiences.

When analysing the results solely on an individual level, attitudes primarily depend on the social situation of the individual, his or her psychological well-being, and possibly age. The results of our analysis further indicate clear support for the contact hypothesis (Allport 1958), which is based on the idea that increased contact with the other induces more positive attitudes toward others. Taken together, negative attitudes would then be caused by the life situation of the individual rather than by a specific ideologically motivated Islamophobia. However, for a fuller, more complex understanding we argue for a need to take other possibilities into account.

At the group and societal level, measuring the general friend factors, Bevelander and Otterbeck (2010) found a more ambiguous result. For girls, friend factors have a significant positive effect on the attitude toward Muslims. For boys we do not find an effect of this factor. This difference between the sexes could be due to boys being more involved in so-called intolerant groups of friends. The study also found that economic, political, and demographic factors are important factors in explaining the attitude toward Muslims, especially for boys. Increased numbers of immigrants and higher unemployment levels correlate with a more negative attitude toward Muslims by boys and can be seen as threats to the status quo and increased competition for scarce economic resources in the area where one lives. This result supports the theoretical propositions of the power-threat hypothesis (Blalock 1967; McLaren 2003). We also find support for the idea that even ideas at the regional level, in this case right wing political ideas that have been incorporated into actual political parties and seats in the local government, could affect young individuals' attitudes toward Muslims. This is also in line with the power-threat hypothesis but more on a political level.

All in all, the attitudinal studies show that Islam and Muslims are categories with significance for the respondents. It is the rather socially marginal individuals that hold the most negative attitudes toward Islam and Muslims. Generally though, youth expresses a higher degree of tolerance compared to adults. However, the results of quantitative attitudinal studies need to be compared to research on how Muslims living in Sweden experience the situation.

The experience of Muslims

In the middle of the 1980s an increasing number of crimes with xenophobic and racist connotations was observed. In reaction to this, the Swedish government started to prioritize these hate crimes and has subsequently kept track of hate crime reporting, and followed up both quality and quantity of the reporting in the early 1990s (BRÅ 2010). The various types of hate crimes reported to the police are differentiated by xenophobic/racist, anti-religious and sexual disposition. It was not until 2006 that Islamophobic crimes became a separate category in the reports. For the year 2009, about 4,100 reported hate crimes (71 percent) had xenophobic/racist motives, almost 600 (11 percent) had anti-religious motives and 19 percent (1,090) had sexual disposition motives. When it comes to type of hate crimes, almost half of these crimes are unlawful threat and molesting, 21 percent are violent crimes, 13 percent are crimes of defamation, and the rest (20 percent) consist of damaging, incitement and discrimination. If we look at the results for anti-religious hate crimes, the statistics show that 42 percent of the almost 600 reported crimes were anti-Semitic, 33 percent Islamophobic, and 25 percent other religions. Islamophobic-motivated crimes in 2009 run to 194 crimes. The majority, 67 percent, of these reported crimes is in the category 'Crime against person', 12 percent is damaging/scribble and 16 percent is incitement against Muslims. From the same report, we observe that Islamophobic hate crimes were committed at a 'distance' in 44 percent of all cases. Religious places such as Mosques were the most common crime scenes. And finally, those who were exposed to crime were not familiar with the perpetrator (BRÅ 2010).

Even though there are not many reported crimes with a claimed Islamophobic content, interviews with Muslims suggest there might be a strong unwillingness to report harassment and verbal assaults, which are not seen as criminal acts by the victims but are injurious all the same. An example of this is the report 'Dialogue with Swedish Muslims' (Samtal med svenska muslimer 2003), a part of which aims to study how Muslims experienced their situation in the immediate period after September 11, 2001. The study claims that the respondents felt a more negative climate against Islam and Muslims both in the media and among non-Muslims, but also an increasing interest in the Islamic religion in general. But since we don't have earlier studies, it is difficult to say if a more negative climate really occurred, nor is it possible to say if a possible negative effect was permanent or just temporary. Further, when Åslund and Rooth (2005) analyzed the effect of September 11 on the probability of leaving unemployment by immigrants with a Muslim background, contrary to what would be expected from the result of the attitudinal studies discussed earlier, they found no increase in discrimination.

Some interesting results came out of a study by Otterbeck and Bevelander (2006) that used a questionnaire that included items on youths' own experiences of exposure to various forms of harassment and violence as a result of their religious affiliation. Almost one in four of Muslim girls and boys had been exposed to some form of offensive treatment at some point during the year prior to the survey. With the exception of exposure to physical violence, girls reported higher levels of victimization than boys.

Those living in metropolitan areas reported the lowest levels of victimization. Levels of victimization are greater among those in compulsory education than among those in secondary education, a finding which is in line with the results from previous analysis, where youths in their third year of secondary education, in particular, were found to have a more positive attitude toward Muslims.

Muslims who perceive themselves as being religious reported being exposed to offensive behavior to a greater extent than those who perceived themselves to be non-religious. Further, Muslim youth were in general subject to significantly more victimization than other youth, even more so than religious Christian youth, who were in turn exposed to higher levels of victimization than Christians who did not perceive themselves to be religious. In addition, it was found that Christian youths born outside Europe or in southern Europe reported the same level of victimization as Christian youths in general. This may indicate a greater level of intolerance toward Muslims precisely because they are looked upon as deviant, regardless of their personal religiosity. Evidence that this may be the case is found in the fact that Muslims born in southern Europe were the group who reported the highest level of victimization among Muslim youths, whereas Christians from this same part of Europe were no more victimized than others. In the same way, Muslims born outside Europe were subject to higher levels of victimization than Christians born outside Europe.

Our result can be supported and complemented by qualitative interviews made with young and adult Muslims in Malmö. Sixtensson (2009) interviewed Muslim women who wear headscarves, most of them adults, and find that almost all can relate personal experiences of verbal abuse in public places on several occasions. Further, all of the women interviewed knew about these abuses from other Muslim women's stories. The perpetrators are most often elders, both men and women. It is quite common that this abuse happens in front of the Muslim women's children. Stereotypes of Muslims were mixed with racist slurs. Experiences and narratives of experiences make the women feel uncomfortable in certain parts of the city, which they then tend to avoid. Fears of being harassed or physically attacked severely affects some of the women's mobility while others try not to bother, or try to brave it out. Regardless, this verbal abuse, and more rarely physical harassment, hinders these women from taking full part in society as active citizens. The abuses are not reported to the police.

Otterbeck (2010a) interviewed young adult Muslims who were not particularly engaged in Islam but still had a relation to Islam, being brought up with Islam as a household faith. None of the interviewees wore any visible signs of being Muslims; all were children of migrants, however. Both men and women could easily remember instances at school or downtown when they had been harassed. The patterns reported by Sixtensson are repeated in this study. At school, it is seldom teachers who are responsible for the discrimination. Rather, it is other pupils, at times themselves from migrant families, from for example Serbia. When interviewed, Ismail was 17 years old, of Arab origin and had grown up in Malmö. When asked if he had been harassed, he told of some instances:

As can be seen, his reaction varied in different instances. Ismail wanted to protect his mother when insulted by the old man. He further mentioned how hurt he was for his mother's sake and probably by his own impotence in getting back at him. The other occasion is defused by the shared experience with the father; they experienced the woman as crazy and laughed about it instead of being hurt. But it, too, was remembered. As in the study of Sixtensson mentioned above, different individuals make sense of similar experiences in their own ways and according to the situation. What everyone shares, however, is that the insult serves to remind the respondent what it may mean to be categorized as Muslim and different from the majority, and it forces the respondent to develop strategies in relation to this. These strategies may affect where you feel safe, self-confidence when in contact with public institutions, or when applying for work, or looking for housing, just to mention a few situations.

Concluding this section, the only study using a representative, sample study is Bevelander and Otterbeck (2006). It shows a higher negative experience for individuals with a Muslim background compared to other youth in the same sample. This may indicate that, in general, a low negative attitude toward Islam and Muslims may go hand in hand with Muslims' negative experiences in certain specific places and situations. Since Swedish statistics do not keep record of individuals' religion, surveys are not useful when trying to map to what extent individuals are excluded and discriminated against due to religion in access to employment or in society at large. The few quantitative studies that have been done taking religious identity into account show little tendency toward a general exclusion because of religious belonging. However, qualitative data show that, in particular, verbal assaults are fairly common, and indicate in which situations these negative experiences occur.

Final words

This chapter has focused on the politics, representation, attitudes toward and experiences of Muslims and Islam in Sweden over the past decades. In order to do this we have looked into the political discourse on Islam and representations in the media. We have further looked into the results from a number of questionnaires on attitudes toward Muslims and Islam and statistical reports from public authorities on Islamophobic hate crimes committed during the most recent past. Finally, we have focused on Muslim experience of stereotypes and discrimination.

Recapitulating the stipulated definition of Islamophobia and its interlinked dimensions – identification, culturalization, subordination and discrimination – we can conclude that the first step of identification figures prominently in our material. People of a Muslim family background are often perceived as Muslims regardless of their individual self-identification. As pointed out earlier, this identification is not Islamophobic in itself. It is through the processes of culturalization and subordination that Islamophobia becomes an issue. Populist parties promote a discourse that uses fixed stereotypes and denigrating value judgments about Islam and, at times, Muslims. The analysis of the media becomes more problematic. The identity label Muslim is used a lot in news media, which tends to focus on negative happenings – as always – and seldom puts Islam or Muslims in connection with promoted values like peace, humanism, and human rights. Further, the brief, short format of news seldom allows in-depth descriptions or analysis. Statements are seldom denigrating. It is rather the aggregate amount of statements that produce the otherness of Muslims and Islam, not the individual statement as such. The constant lack of positive images signals a negative understanding of Muslims and Islam. However, on the Internet you can easily find websites hostile to Muslims and Islam that culturalize and subordinate and call for a discriminatory politics toward Muslims and Islam. Some of these websites are run by politicians from the Sweden Democrats.

In contrast, we found that negative stereotypes and harsh views of Muslims were fairly rare in different attitude studies, especially in the data from 2004 researching youth. Still, when Muslim youth answered the questionnaire from 2004, the self-evaluation of discrimination was higher than that of other comparable groups. Examples of verbal abuse and racist slurs were also given from qualitative research. Results indicate clearly a difference between young and old people in Sweden. Older individuals have in general more negative attitudes toward Muslims than younger people. This is also signaled in interviews with Muslims who give accounts for being verbally attacked, mainly by elderly persons, not because of their own actions or words, but just for being there.

A possible explanation – at least in part – for the low level of intolerance among youth might be the fact that many of the well-to-do middle class youth are skilled in filling in questionnaires in a way that portrays them as 'good' holding the correct, human rights–based values, much in the same way as others might take the opportunity to break taboos and be perceived as 'bad'. The design of the study makes it impossible to see if the large group of tolerant youth would have spontaneously identified Muslims as a first step in an othering process. For example, philosopher Étienne Balibar (1991) claims that a neo-racist agenda among the educated classes starts with the use of identity categories like immigrant, Muslim, Arab, implying a subtle othering process seldom expressed in blunt words. The possible value of Balibar's critique should be tested in future questionnaires.

The process of identification is dominant. Muslim is a common category held to be meaningful in society, much more so than labeling someone as Christian. Certain sections of politics and the media culturalize Muslims and Islam, reducing historical dynamics and processes to more stable categories – contrary to academic knowledge. This is also seen in parts of the statistical material presented. Subordination is most visible in certain political parties' discourse, the Sweden Democrats being the best example. Subordination is, however, much more difficult to find in the other material, apart from in some right wing discourse calling for discrimination. Thus, it is obvious that the experiences of Muslims will have to be examined more systematically to be able to paint an accurate picture of Islamophobia today.

With a growing Muslim population and increased visibility of Islam as a religion in everyday life in Sweden over the past two decades – just like in other European countries – the issue of how to understand negative attitudes and discrimination has become critical. In the general debate, Islamophobia is at times used as a pejorative trying to stigmatize opponents and critiques. As an activist concept, it is obviously useful. As an academic concept it becomes problematic. In our research, we treat Islamophobia as an ideal type to enable us to see discursive and social phenomena rather than to label someone, a group, or an act as Islamophobic. By using different types of scholarly work a larger picture is discernable. It is obvious that different research design and methods produce contrasting results that are hard to reconcile. We see this as an incentive to draw from differing results and sharpen the tools of research and pose questions in surveys that take theories on racism into account as well as further advancing qualitative interviewing. It is in this that we see the future of the research on Islamophobia.

Notes

1 We acknowledge the relevance of the criticism posed toward certain parts of the definition of Islamophobia proposed by the Runnymede Trust (see for example Allen 2010), however, the Trust's model for discrimination is well balanced.
2 Sweden has no official records of the citizens' denomination. The last figure is built on estimations of the percentage of recent immigrants that is likely, nominally, to be Muslims.
3 During 1991–95, for example, the following occurred: the Gulf War and its prelude (1990 onwards), the Algerian crisis (1992 onwards), the Bosnian crisis (1992 onwards), the many wars in Afghanistan (not least the Taliban entered the media in early 1995), and the on-going Israel–Palestine conflict.
4 The questions were focused on Islam or on Muslims practicing Islam in public.

6 Islamophobia in Spain?

Political rhetoric rather than a social fact

Ricard Zapata-Barrero and Juan Díez-Nicolás

Introduction[1]

In this chapter we challenge conventional views that the tensions and difficulties surrounding the integration of Muslims derive primarily from Islamophobia. As the Spanish case study shows, the reluctance to give visibility to Islam in the public space is much more a political issue than a social reality. In Spain, the political construction of the 'other' is not skin-color- and race-based, but rather religion-based. The purpose of this chapter is to argue that current policies limiting Muslims' public visibility may be based in tradition and have a structural basis of legitimacy in Spain (Zapata-Barrero 2010b: 383), but they are also directly part of the anti-Muslim rhetoric; even if socially, as we will see in section three, there is no way to justify these policies. We want to show that there is a contrast between the foundation of certain policies aimed at limiting the public expression of Muslims, and public opinion and attitudes.[2] Xenophobia is then considered as a political and media construction, rather than a social fact. Anti-immigrant policies respond much more to the rhetoric of electoral strategy than as a channel answering real needs and demands of citizens, as the recent *burka* debate promoted by several Spanish municipalities shows – see Spanish newspapers during June and July 2010 – as we will see later.

Here Spain is following some European trends. The recent Swiss referendum decision to ban minarets on Muslim worship centres, the current French online debate on national identity, and the French and Spanish discussion on whether *burka* should be banned in the public sphere have raised the unfinished question of the growing phobia against Islam in Europe. But is it a phobia against Islam or, as we want to discuss, a general stigmatization of foreigners and immigrants? (Bader 2008; Triandafyllidou 2010; Vertovec and Wessendorf 2010). It might even be argued that this phobia is not directed to Muslims in general, but to Islamic fundamentalist terrorism. The point is not that prejudice against Muslims does not exist – it certainly does. However, generalized fears and prejudices are always articulated within specific local contexts and inflected in the process. While Muslims might be a particularly vulnerable group, especially following September 11, 2001 (New York) and March 11, 2004 (Madrid), negative reactions to their presence are not uniform across the country. In fact, a national survey conducted immediately after the 11-M train bombings in Spain and Madrid showed no significant increase of negative attitudes toward Muslims immigrants. Rather, such reactions must be understood within the broader assemblage of relations present in any given setting (Rasinski *et al.* 2005).

The approach we follow is a contextual conflict-driven approach, using empirical data and existing surveys. The chapter is divided into four main sections: in the *first* we present an overview, within the European framework, of the main characteristics distinguishing Spain both from a historical – the tradition against Moors – and social point of view – mapping the main social conflicts related to Muslims immigrants. We will then look, at the citizenship and political reactions to manage these conflicts. We will argue that these are at the core of the Islamophobia rhetoric, nourishing, instead of separating the perception that stigmatizes between visible and invisible immigrants, which in Spain is religious-based. In the third section, we will compare the attitudes of Spaniards toward Muslim immigrants with similar attitudes in other EU countries. Finally, we will compare the attitudes of Spaniards toward Muslim immigrants with similar attitudes toward other groups of immigrants and other socially excluded groups – Gypsies, people with AIDS, heavy drinkers, etc. A last concluding section will allow us to summarize our main findings and arguments: the fact that Islamophobia in Spain is much more a matter of political and media rhetoric than a social phenomenon.

Overview: Spanishness and Islam, tradition and society

In terms of the religious history of Europe, what sets Spain apart from northern European countries – such as France, Germany and England – is that is did not witness the clash of Protestant and Catholic, or even the massacre of Jews. Rather, in Spain, the conflict was between Catholicism and Islam, because much of Spain was occupied by an Islamic population during most of the Middle Ages up to the coming of modernity. However, a large number of history books have provided evidence that peaceful and often very fruitful coexistence of Christians, Muslims and Jews, in both the Christian- and Muslim-ruled territories in Spain was not the exception, but rather the rule during that long period of almost eight centuries. This is not to ignore the fact that there were violent conflicts and battles between Christians and Muslims, and also between Christian kingdoms, as well as between Muslim kingdoms. Every European country has its 'dark historical side' in religious political management and, in this sense, Spain also belongs to this European trend.

Religion (Catholicism) has often been presented by politicians and the media as one of the main pillars of Spanish identity or *Hispanidad* (*Spanishness*), but Spaniards do not mention this trait as one of the important ones to be a real Spaniard.[3] This discourse of identity has created a strong narrative of similarity and difference: similarity regarding those who profess Christianity or simply have been born within this context; and difference regarding those who profess other religions, particularly those who today are most visible in number and in practices, such as Muslims. (There were very few Muslims in Spain, nationals or immigrants, until the recent immigration flows since 1990). This discourse of belonging to *Spanishness* has not only shaped the narratives of nationhood, but also determined the bases for access to membership. Let us go back to the roots of this tradition.

It is meaningful that Spanish identity was initially codified in the late fifteenth century – though many historians argue that the concept had existed since the Roman conquest, when the country was named Hispania, and that a sense of Spanishness persisted during the long period of Islamic presence in most of the peninsula – and particularly in the symbolic year of 1492, when Sephardic Jews, Muslims and Gypsies were expelled from the peninsula, and Spain officially started the conquest of America and what could be labeled as the global expansion of Spanish Catholicism and the practice of messianism. The politics of the so-called 'Catholic Monarchs' – a religious Catholic alliance between two kingdoms, Castilla and Aragon, that for the first time politically unified the whole territory of the Iberian peninsula – had many elements of what today we would refer to as *ethnic cleansing* (Zapata-Barrero 2006: 146). Since then Islam has historically been excluded from the formation of the Spanish identity in which a Christian 'us' has been particularly opposed to an Islamic 'other'.

The term *Hispanidad* was developed at the beginning of the twentieth century to counterweigh the loss of the last colonies (Cuba, Puerto Rico and the Philippines) by emphasizing cultural proximity and historical ties. In the mid-twentieth century it was re-used during the Franco dictatorship 'precisely to comprise the whole Spanish area of influence, designating a linguistic (Spanish) and religious (Catholic) community, and creating a sense of belonging, excluding non-Spanish speakers, atheists and Muslims' (Zapata-Barrero 2006: 148) as well as Protestants, Jews and practitioners of other religions. The political Francoist argument *'habla cristiano'* (*'speak christian'*) is a clear example of how the regime promoted the confusion between Spanish (language) and Christianity (religion) so as to build a culturally homogeneous society and exclude any sort of diversity (Zapata-Barrero 2010b: 387). The Spanish Constitution (1978), which resulted from the Transition period (1975–78) left aspects linked to religion unresolved. For instance, the Catholic Church still has certain control over the cultural hegemony in the educational system.

The construction of differences in interactions between Spanish majorities and Muslim minorities should then be understood within the context of the historical presence of Islam in the Iberian Peninsula for almost eight centuries. These interactions have not been free of contradictions, as shown by the fact that under Franco's dictatorship the official foreign policy had three main axes: the Arab states in North Africa and the Middle East – though foreign Muslims were a very small minority and not socially visible in the public space – Latino America, and the Vatican. Interaction with Europe became a priority much later and more officially after the death of Franco in 1975 when democracy was restored. As we have seen, the religious component in the self-identification of Spanish majorities is reproduced today in the context of interactions with Muslim minorities in general – including Spanish Muslims – and Moroccan Muslims in particular – who mix foreignness and religion. Although the demands for mosque establishment and responses of local authorities have also been influenced by other structural factors, especially – the lack of – citizenship and the existing legal framework of religious freedom and equality, there is a large gap between legal and de facto recognition of religious rights of Muslims. While Hispanic identity over time has become more cultural than religious – in addition to the importance of Spanish language – it has been built up against the category of the Moor, traditionally referring to Berbers from North Africa. The binary logic of Hispanic versus Moor is reproduced today in the context of an increasing presence and visibility of Moroccan migrants.

Let us now discuss current policies, and how they can have this tradition as a legitimating basis, but also how these policies can also be part of the anti-Muslims rhetoric, even if socially, as we well see in section three, there is no way to justify these policies. The main issues concerning Muslim communities are structural. They are related to religious infrastructures and education. The greatest problem has not only been the limited implementation of the 1992 Agreement,[4] but also the difficulty the State has had in finding representatives to negotiate with.

In this respect, the process of incorporation of Islam into the system of cooperation between State and Church makes us question the capacity of the Islamic Commission and the federations of associations to represent the growing Muslim community – national, nationalized and foreign – and to fulfil the relative functions for implementing the 1992 Agreement, as well as the capacity and willingness of local administrations to develop it. Alvarez-Miranda (2009: 185) points out that comparisons with Britain, Germany and France show that although all states guarantee freedom of worship and permit plural religious teaching, the institutional adjustments and the levels of support given to the collective practice and teaching of Islam varies. The Spanish design appears to resemble the German one more closely, which is more liberal than the other two.

In addition, Spain cannot escape from the governance problems posed by the link between security, Islam and terrorism on a global level (see Zapata-Barrero and Qasem, 2008: 81), nor from the need to reposition its relations with the Catholic Church in order to ensure a secular state, which is considered to be one of the likely responses to Muslim demands.[5] Therefore, the issue of the space and support that should be given to Islamic worship and teaching poses wider questions in relation to the effects religious recognition may have on the integration of immigrants (Díez -Nicolás 2005: 293). Spain has yet to resolve the dilemmas generated by the demands of people of Islamic faith. In this regard, Spanish policies of governance need to take steps in the practical field rather than in the theoretical field of the 1992 agreement, which has hardly been implemented.

There are still many questions to be resolved around the accommodation of the Muslim community. If wide recognition of religious difference is achieved, will there be a tendency toward an intercultural coexistence, isolating communities and prolonging inequalities in time? If this recognition is denied, will there be a reaction of dissatisfaction and badly channeled demands around the issues of Muslim identity? Which of these two cases promotes coexistence between religious communities and the numerous Europeans and immigrants from Muslim countries who do not practice any religion? Such questions still remain in the political and social arena today. The politics of governance is then a key point in the current debate (Zapata-Barrero 2009). The argument we will put forward is that these policies are really at the core of the anti-Muslim rhetoric, and these 'virtual fears' coming from tradition and still present in the current institutional structure, rather than from the existence of a social xenophobic attitude.[6]

Conflicts and policies related to Muslims

One should start by saying that, despite having a particular history related to Islam, there are no specifically Spanish conflicts that are different from those in other European countries. Maybe the distinction arises from the foundation of these conflicts and, in some case, as we will show, from specific policy answers. The most distinctive example is perhaps related to tradition and festivals.

Conflicts around Islam should first be understood in the context of the Spanish identity construction which is based, as explained above, on a traditional negative perception of the Muslim and more particularly the Moroccan, considered in pejorative terms as 'the Moor' (*el moro*) (Zapata-Barrero 2006: 143). These conflicts should also be explained in the context of a double and apparently contradictory process: the secularisation of the state but while the Catholic Church still maintains a predominant position – as in England, where Anglican Church is really dominant, in Central and Northern Europe, where Lutheran Protestantism is dominant, and in Morocco, where Islam is absolutely dominant. While the shift to a secular state has tended to relegate religious practices to the private sphere, the asymmetrical relation with the Catholic Church has implied in practice non-compliance with some of the agreements signed with minority religions. Finally, like in many other European countries, some cultural practices of Muslim communities have increasingly been perceived by public authorities, rather than by society, as we will show in section three, as opposed to liberal values such as human dignity, freedom or equality. Let us review the main Muslim-related conflicts in Spain.

Muslim places of worship

The conflicts around mosques, oratories and cemeteries consist of different elements:

- *Some opposition against the building of mosques* and/or opening of religious centres or oratories from both citizens and government. This shows that society experiences certain difficulties in the social recognition of Muslims in some public spaces.
- *Discussion about the access of women* to mosques and oratories, particularly the fact that women either have been prohibited from entering the mosques or have been forced to use separate rooms. This is often perceived as unacceptable in terms of principles of sex equality and religious freedom.
- *Opposition against foreign-funding of mosques.* The main concern is that poorly resourced mosques depend on funding from foreign sources, including extremist-oriented groups.
- *Critique on radical imams leading mosques.* As these religious leaders are either educated abroad or not educated at all, there are fears that they will advocate interpretations of Islam that are in conflict with the legal and social norms of Spanish society. In an attempt to prevent imams from spreading hateful and violent ideas, the government proposed the monitoring and censoring of mosque sermons in May 2004. Protests by Muslim and civil liberty groups made them retract the proposal. As an alternative, the main Moroccan

immigrant workers organisation (ATIME) proposed a system of self-control of mosques – including supervision of mosques and appointment of imams – led by local and national Muslim councils.

Religious education

Conflicts around religious education have been articulated around three main topics

* *Discussion on the predominance of Catholic education.* It is compulsory for public schools to offer Catholic education, although students may choose to opt out. While in primary schools no alternative needs to be provided, in secondary schools an alternative course – history of religions – must be offered, but students are free to choose neither of these options. There have also been debates about the presence of Catholic symbols in schools. Interestingly, when a few parents criticized the presence of crucifixes in the classroom, the council of education of the Autonomous Community of Castilla y León asked them to be 'tolerant', arguing the need for toleration in a sphere of *convivencia* (peaceful coexistence).
* *Discussion on the right of religious education in both public and private schools.* Although the agreements between the Spanish state and the Jewish, Evangelical and Muslim communities guarantee the right of religious education, in practice most schools do not provide this possibility. (In most cases this is because of lack of demand. Demand for such courses only becomes important in big cities.)
* *Discussion on the new compulsory course* – offered in the final year in primary schools and all years in secondary school – called 'Education for Citizenship and Human Rights' (*Educación para la ciudadanía y derechos humanos*). Following recommendations from both the Council of Europe and the European Union, in 2006, this new course was introduced with the aim of teaching individual and social ethics and democratic values, including topics such as climate change, human rights, immigration, multiculturalism, etc. Arguments *for* were the need to create democratic citizens and prevent inequalities between sexes, minorities, etc. Arguments *against* come from the Catholic Church and related parties who argue that it might lead to value indoctrination by the state and goes against the freedom of ideology and religion.

Conflicts around some festivities

The climate generated after the Cartoon Affair provoked a debate on the traditional Festivals of Moors and Christians (*Moros y Cristianos*) celebrated in almost 400 localities in Spain. The Festivals celebrate the Spanish *Reconquest* (Christian victory over Islam) of the peninsula after eight centuries of Muslim presence, by the re-enactment of local victories over invading Moorish armies. The celebration basically consists of a symbolic battle for the local territory, a dramatization of the struggle of Moorish and Christian military units, resulting in the victory of Christians. 'In the Festivals, the Moors are defeated in combat and then converted to Christianity, or, in the case of some villages [...], they are "symbolically" thrown into the sea' (Flesler and Pérez Melgosa 2003: 153). Harris (2006: 45) highlights that the *fiestas* combine religious processions and secular parades. Dramatized battles between Muslims and Christians became occasional after the Conquest of Granada in 1492.[7] Tourism has also increased the popularity of the festivals over time, as well as the showiness of the festivals (Flesler and Pérez Melgosa 2003: 151). Through time, however, the 'battle' part of these festivals has lost presence in favor of the 'parade' part, to the point that in most cities there is a great competition among Spaniards to be members of the parading Muslim army, and local citizens spend a lot of money to compete in providing luxurious costumes for members of both armies.

In contrast to making the places of worship of contemporary 'Moors' – Muslim immigrants – invisible, during the festivals the 'imagined Moor of the past' is made extremely visible, as both an exotic and a barbaric figure – however this picture is being reconsidered in recent years (Zapata-Barrero and de Witte 2010: 185). The self-censorship debate arising just after the Danish cartoon affair demonstrates the problematic interaction between representations of present and past Moors, as changing the representation of the 'past Moors' is justified by the presence – and fear – of the 'real Moor'. In contrast to the time of the *reconquista*, the freedom of religion within the context of Spanish liberal democracy makes the idea of 'Christians' being the *only* legitimate heirs of the territory problematic. Interactions between Muslim minorities and the majority in Spain today, therefore, present not only a challenge of accommodating religious diversity, but also of reconstructing national identity. The question is therefore not *if*, but rather *when* Spanish society will be ready to accept their cultural and religious 'Other' as part of the 'Self' (Lindkilde *et al.* 2009).

Conflicts around dress code

Conflicts have arisen around the use of headscarves in schools, and *burkas* and *niqabs* in public spaces. The terms of the debates have been the following:

*   *Headscarves in schools.* Until very recently the use of the Muslim headscarf in public schools has not been as controversial as in other European countries. Opinions, however, have been divided between those who defend religious symbols as part of religious liberty and those who would like to see the prohibition of religious signs in the public sphere in the name of liberal-republican values. When schools prohibited girls wearing the Islamic veil (*hijab*) based on their own internal rules that prohibit all elements of discrimination, the responses have also been diverse. For instance, Madrid's right-wing government, in 2002, and the Catalan government, in 2007, intervened to reverse the school prohibition by arguing that the right to education had priority over the regulation of – religious – symbols (press releases in 2002 and in 2007). In spring 2010, Madrid's right-wing regional government supported a school prohibition, while the Socialist national government opposed it arguing that the right to education came first. This latter case has generated a huge national debate that continued with the discussions around the draft of the

new Organic Law for the Freedom of Conscience and Religion. Nevertheless, it could be argued that the cleavage in Spain is not so much between leftist and rightist, but between dogmatic-intolerants, and pluralist-tolerant.

• *Burkas and niqabs in public spaces.* In May/June 2010 some municipalities – first in Catalonia and then in Andalusia, see main newspapers during this period –started to ban the wearing of the *burka* and *niqab* in public buildings. In June the Senate also approved – though only by a slight majority – a proposition made by the right-wing *Partido Popular* (People Party) to ban the wearing of the *burka* and *niqab* in *all* public spaces. Those who defend these measures argue that these practices violate women's dignity and the principle of equality, and that they pose a threat to public security, making a person invisible and posing an obvious problem of identification. Those against the ban argue that these measures have the effect of shutting women in their houses and polarizing positions around Islam. We can interpret this issue as a debate not only on the limits of diversity in our societies, but also on the use of legal means, rather than social and political means, to solve the fact that women wear a *burka* and thus pose an obvious problem of visibility and identification. It is not a quantitative problem, since it is estimated that not more than 20 people in Catalonia wear a *burka*, but an electoral strategy addressing public opinion and some new anti-immigrant political formations, such as *Plataforma per Catalunya* (Platform for Catalonia), which pressurizes most cities governed by socialist and centre-left political parties on the need to make a visible reaction against Islam. Here we have a clear example of how Islamophobia is not a social fact, but a product of these political measures, addressed to people that can have difficulties in differentiating common Muslims, especially from Morocco and Pakistan, from the *burka*, which is a real exception in the Muslim communities, and an extremist reading of Islam.

Attitudes of Spaniards toward Muslims

In order to evaluate the degree of 'Islamophobia' in Spanish society it seems necessary to compare it with other countries and, furthermore, to compare it with the degree of 'racism', 'xenophobia' or 'social exclusion' of other social groups.

In this particular case, the Values Surveys [European Values Study (EVS) and World Values Survey (WVS)][8] provide a huge volume of comparable data for almost 100 countries in five waves covering a period of more than 25 years. The analysis presented below is based on 355,298 face-to-face personal interviews in 97 countries collected by both projects around 1981, 1990, 1995, 2000 and 2005. The questionnaire in the five waves included a multiple-answer question that asked respondents to mention those social groups that they 'would not like to have as neighbors'. Respondents were presented a list of social groups that were likely to be socially excluded or rejected in greater or lesser degree in most countries. The social groups selected for this analysis were those most commonly found in all countries and waves: drug addicts, heavy drinkers, homosexuals, people with AIDS, Gypsies, people of different religion, Jews, Muslims, immigrants and foreign workers, and people of a different race.

The main findings from the total sample are as follows. The percent of respondents mentioning they would not like each of the mentioned social groups as neighbors varies from 72 percent who mention drug addicts, to heavy drinkers (61 percent), homosexuals (48 percent), people with AIDS (42 percent), Gypsies (41 percent), people of different religion, and Jews (20 percent), Muslims and immigrants and foreign workers (19 percent), and people of a different race (16 percent). Variation of these percentages from 1981 to 2005 is in general very small, and the relative ranking of each of these groups is maintained with very few alterations which are not really meaningful. The only large variation is that Jews were excluded by only 15 percent in 1990 but by as much as 72 percent in 2005. Part of this change may be due to the growing number of Muslim countries included in the 2005 wave compared to previous waves. Probably that also explains why Muslims were rejected by 26 percent in 1990 and only by 16 percent in 2005. The limitations of this paper make it impossible to present a detailed analysis of the exclusion of each one of the 10 social groups over five waves and 97 countries.

The group 'Muslims', which is the third-least rejected social group by the total sample, has been analyzed in more detail because they are the main object of this paper. Their rejection as neighbors is higher in countries such as Turkey, Moldova, South Korea, Romania, Albania, India and Slovenia (54–30 percent) and is lowest in Chile, Canada, Switzerland, Argentina and Guatemala (less than 10 percent). Table 6.1 shows the proportion rejecting Muslims as neighbors for EU member countries – with the exception of Cyprus, for which there is no available data. Sweden and Spain are the two EU member countries that show the lowest rejection of Muslims as neighbors (less than 13 percent), while Romania, Lithuania and Slovenia show the highest rejection (more than 30 percent). Results are very similar when only the data for the 2000 wave are taken into account – the 2005 wave excluded the question on Muslims in almost all countries. Between 57 and 30 percent reject Muslims in South Korea, Moldova, Romania and Albania. And, considering only the EU, while rejection was around 30 percent in Lithuania and Malta, it was lower than 14 percent in Spain, Netherlands, Germany, Sweden and Portugal.

To summarize, worldwide Muslims are less rejected as neighbors than many other social groups. And, secondly, they are excluded more in some countries where they are either a majority or a large minority (Turkey, Albania), while they receive a very low rejection in countries with high Muslim minorities resulting from immigration (United States, Sweden, Spain, Netherlands, Germany or Switzerland). A regression model to explain the reference to Muslims as not-liked neighbors shows that, other things being equal, older and conservative – ideologically in the right – persons tend to mention Muslims as not-liked neighbors in greater proportions than younger and progressive persons, and that those who are oriented toward post-materialist – self-expression – values tend to mention them in lower proportions than those with a more materialist value orientation (Inglehart 1977, 1990, 1997; Díez-Nicolás 2007a).

Spain presents a very unique example of a country where two different research teams have conducted the values surveys. Thus, while one team[9] conducted the EVS surveys in 1981, 1990 and 1999, another team[10] conducted the WVS surveys in 1990, 1995, 2000 and 2005. Results in both groups of surveys are very consistent

Table 6.1 Percentage of people who would not like to have Muslims as neighbors, EU member countries, average 1981–2005

	No Muslim neighbors %		No Muslim neighbors %
Austria	14.7	Italy	15.8
Belgium	23.9	Latvia	19.9
Bulgaria	27.5	Lithuania	32.3
Czech Republic	24.3	Luxembourg	15.4
Denmark	15.9	Malta	23.5
Estonia	21.3	Netherlands	13.1
Finland	24.6	Poland	22.2
France	16.6	Portugal	13.9
Germany	19.9	Romania	32.9
Great Britain	15.5	Slovakia	29.4
Greece	20.9	Slovenia	30.5
Hungary	18.3	Spain	12.2
Ireland	13.9	Sweden	11.9

Source: Produced by J. Díez-Nicolás from Values Surveys (www.jdsurvey.net)

in time, as well as when EVS and WVS are compared for the same wave (1990 and 1999–2000). Heavy drinkers, people with AIDS, drug addicts, homosexuals, Gypsies, and Jews (only in WVS-2000) show consistently higher percentages of rejection as neighbors in the seven WVS and EVS surveys than Muslims. Actually, Muslims are rejected in Spain only between 10 percent (EVS-1990) and 16 percent (WVS-2000), and they are among the least rejected social groups – together with people of a different race, immigrants and foreign workers, and people of a different religion. The only inconsistent result is the one referring to Jews in WVS-2000, when they were mentioned as non-desirable neighbors by 34 percent of respondents, while in EVS-1999 their rejection was only 9 percent, and 8 percent and 13 percent in EVS and WVS 1990 respectively. A reliable explanation is still being searched for this rather surprising change. A very tentative hypothesis that cannot be pursued in this paper is that Spaniards tend to favour Palestine over Israel in their historical confrontation in the Middle East.[11] One should also underline the sharp decline in rejection of people with AIDS and homosexuals, from 30 percent and 31 percent respectively in 1990, to 16 percent and 7 percent also respectively in 2005.

Different regression models calculated for the WVS-EVS Spanish surveys, whether aggregated or separated by wave and/or study, show consistently that age and income have a significant and positive relationship with mentioning Muslims as not-liked neighbors, while education and post-materialist values show a significant and negative relationship with it. In fact, the same variables explain the higher or lower degree of racism or xenophobia among Spaniards (Díez-Nicolás 2007b: 124; 2009a: 247; 2009b: 21) based on ASEP's monthly surveys 1991–2009. Therefore, it seems appropriate to conclude that, other things being equal, the older and richer a person is, the greater the chances that he/she will mention Muslims as non-desirable neighbors. And, on the contrary, the more educated and the more oriented to new post-materialist values a person is, the greater the chances that he/she will not mention Muslims as non-desirable neighbors. And these relationships seem to be valid not only for all countries but also for the seven Spanish surveys within the values studies, regardless of whether EVS or WVS.

In any case, the evidence seems to reject the hypothesis that Muslims – and in a similar manner, Jews or other national groups – are particularly exposed to being socially excluded by Spaniards, at least when compared with several other minority groups. Gypsies, however, are three times more exposed to being socially rejected than Muslims or Jews. And these findings seem to hold over time and when comparing results from two different research teams. If there is 'Islamophobia' in the Spanish population, it seems to be very much hidden, though it must be asserted that even little social exclusion of any group must be considered as excessive.

A second set of data used for this analysis of presumed 'Islamophobia' in Spain is a series of 19 annual national surveys conducted by ASEP between 1991 and 2009 on attitudes of Spaniards toward immigrants.[12] The question used in these surveys was similar to the one used by the Values Surveys, and refers to the social groups that would not be liked as neighbors. However, while in the Values Surveys respondents only had to mention or not mention the groups they wouldn't like as neighbors, in the ASEP-Spanish surveys a rating scale was used to evaluate each group from zero ('I would not care at all having them as neighbors') to 10 ('I would be very much upset to have them as neighbors'). A total of 13 social groups were included in the question – although three of them began to be included between 1993 and 1995. Consistently, drug addicts, Gypsies, ex-convicts, prostitutes, and people with mental

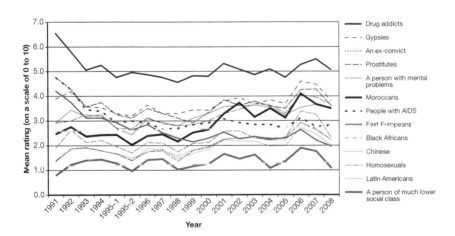

Source: Produced by J. Díez-Nicolás from ASEP's The Public Opinion of Spaniards (www.jdsurvey.net)

Figure 6.1 Mean rating (on a scale 0 to 10) of social groups that would not be liked as neighbours, Spain, 1991–2009

problems – except in 2006 and 2007 – were rejected as neighbors in higher degree than Moroccans.

Homosexuals were more rejected than Moroccans until 1998, and people with AIDS were more rejected than Moroccans until 2000. The change for those two groups was not due to an increase in the rejection of Moroccans but, on the contrary, to a steady and sharp decline in the social rejection of homosexuals and people with AIDS. It is true, however, that the rejection of Moroccans also increased a little since 2000, a fact that seems consistent with changes already mentioned both in the Spanish and the world data. It must be noticed that all immigrant groups – Moroccans, East Europeans, Black Africans, Chinese, Latin Americans – are less rejected than other social minorities – drug addicts, ex-convicts, prostitutes, people with mental problems – and, until not many years ago, also homosexuals and people with AIDS. The least rejected group, however, has always been 'people of a much lower social class'.

A regression model to explain the rating of Moroccans as not-liked neighbors – based on the same explanatory variables as the model used for the total sample of countries in the values studies – shows that older, higher income and higher socio-economic status and more conservative persons are more likely to dislike Moroccans as neighbors, while persons with higher education and oriented toward more post-materialist and self-expression values are less likely to dislike Moroccans as neighbors.

To summarize, the relevant findings derived from the regression models are: 1) there seems to be no difference between Spain and the rest of the world with respect to the variables that explain rejection of Muslims as neighbors – age, right ideology and cultural values seem to be the most powerful predictors, even though in both cases the models explain a very small percentage of the variance; and 2) more important than that is that religiosity – regardless of a person's religion – does not contribute to explaining rejection of Muslims as neighbors when some other variables such as those mentioned are present in the model. Besides, one should always remember that both in Spain and in the world rejection of Muslims, Arabs, Moroccans or the like is lower than rejection of other social minority groups, and this is particularly true of Anglo Saxon and West European countries, among them, Spain.

A final question frequently used to measure social exclusion of social groups refers to a person's reaction toward a daughter falling in love with a person belonging to particular social groups. In the Spanish set of 19 surveys that question was included, asking for the reaction of respondents if a daughter were fall in love with a Gypsy, a North African, a Black African, or a Latin American. The majority of respondents in all surveys answered that they would let their daughter do whatever she wanted to do, and only between 25 percent and 30 percent would give one of the two more negative (exclusionist) answers: 'would advise her to break the relationship' or 'would forbid her to continue with it'. Differences among the social groups mentioned were usually fewer than 10 percentage points, and certainly the lowest opposition was regarding Latin Americans, and the highest referred to Gypsies, with North and Black Africans being more or less equally rejected.

Concluding remarks

Empirical evidence from the Values Surveys (EVS and WVS) suggests that social exclusion of minority social groups – drug addicts, heavy drinkers, people with AIDS and homosexuals – is greater, in general, than social exclusion of national or ethnic minorities – people of a different race or religion, immigrants and foreign workers, Muslims, Jews. The only exception is Gypsies. Comparing regions and countries it has also been found that social exclusion in general, toward Muslims in particular, is more common in less developed countries than in more developed ones as those in the EU and Anglo Saxon countries, confirming previous analyses (Díez-Nicolás 2005: 347). Additionally, it has been found that older, more conservative persons, in the total sample of countries, and in the Spanish sub-sample within the Values Surveys, are more likely to mention Muslims as not-liked neighbors, while persons with more formal education and oriented toward post-materialist (self-expression) values are less likely to mention them in that respect.

On the basis of a question asked in 19 annual surveys conducted only in Spain by ASEP since 1991 till 2009 on the rejection of different social groups as neighbors, using questions similar to those used in the Values Surveys, it seems that Spaniards do not differ from other world citizens. Ethnic, racial or national groups – Moroccans, East Europeans, Black Africans, Chinese, and Latin Americans – have been less socially rejected as neighbors than other social groups – drug addicts, ex-convicts, prostitutes, people with mental problems, people with AIDS, and homosexuals – for most of the period 1991–2009. The only exception has always been Gypsies, the second least liked social group of all, only a little less rejected than drug addicts. Nevertheless, it must be underlined that social exclusion of any group, at least as measured by this question, does not seem to be very high, because the intensity of rejection as neighbors has been below five points – on a scale zero to 10 – for all social groups and across 19 surveys, with the exception of drug addicts, who have always been rated around or above five points. Moroccans, however, have always been mentioned as not-liked neighbors more than any of the other four national or ethnic groups – but less than Gypsies – but usually with ratings below 3.5 points. Statistical analysis has confirmed the same findings as the values surveys, in the sense that older, more conservative, less educated and more materialist persons tend to reject Moroccans as neighbors more than younger, more progressive, more educated and more post-materialist persons.

Many other findings that cannot be reported here seem to demonstrate two very important assertions. First, Spaniards are not more racist, xenophobic or social exclusionist than other West Europeans or Western citizens in general and, if anything, it can be argued that Spaniards are less exclusionist than most other nationals, very similar to the Swedish and the Swiss. Second, even when attitudes toward Moroccans, Muslims, Arabs or the like, are taken into consideration, Spaniards do not show any signs of 'Islamophobia', at least not more, but generally less, than most other Europeans, and certainly much less than the rest of world citizens. Those statements imply that social exclusion of Moroccans or other groups in Spain is relatively lower than in most other European countries, and in absolute terms they are limited to generally older, low educated, extreme rightist, and more traditionally value oriented very small minorities.

Given these main findings, we can ask why there is such a media and political interplay between Muslims and social conflict, and wonder why there is such a contrast between the foundation of certain policies aimed at limiting the public expression of Muslims, and public opinion and attitudes that show that Spanish people are not so Islamophobic as it is thought. Maybe one additional finding when we contrast attitudes with the political management of Muslims affairs is that xenophobia has to be considered as a political construction, rather than a social fact, policy-independent. Anti-immigrant policies respond much more to rhetoric, an electoral strategy, rather as a channel answering the demands of society and real needs of citizens. The real question is then not why citizens are or are not Islamophobic, but rather why certain powers and political hegemonic groups have real difficulties in sharing their power or even accepting that they may lose their power within the political realm. The question to be answered is whether the alleged Islamophobia is a rhetorical construction of politicians and the media to distract from other problems that really concern society.

Notes

1 This introduction, the following two sections and the concluding remarks are related to R. Zapata-Barrero's findings in the Accept Pluralism research project which is co-funded by the European Commission (7th Framework Programme, Socio-Economic Sciences and Humanities). The project is coordinated by the Robert Schuman Centre for Advanced Studies, European University Institute, Florence, Italy, Prof. Anna Triandafyllidou. For more information: http://www.accept-pluralism.eu

2 On the link between policies and public opinion toward immigrants in Spain, see R. Zapata-Barrero (2008: 1101)

3 Together with language, see for instance, Zapata-Barrero (2006: 143, 2010a: 181, 2010b: 383). On the interface between national identity and attitudes toward immigrants, see the seminal work of Díez-Medrano (2005).

4 Spain has one of the most advanced agreements with the most important religions in Spain – Jews, Protestants and, of course, Islam (Jefatura del Estado, 1992). With the Islamic Commission Agreement it officially guaranteed the right of Islamic education to Muslim students in both public and private schools. But the main problem is the lack of application of this most liberal agreement in Europe (Moreras 2003: 52).

5 On the governance of Islam in Europe, see the overview of Maussen (2007).

6 Research has demonstrated that most negative attitudes toward social groups are a product of the 'fear of the unknown'. Thus, Spaniards who have not had any personal direct contact with police stations and courts have a worse image of police and judges than those who have had such contacts. Similarly, Spaniards that have interacted with immigrants or Gypsies have a better image of those groups than those who have never interacted with them in any way (Díez-Nicolás 2005: 283).

7 The beginning and incorporation of the Festivals of *Moros y Cristianos* into the annual festive calendar is probably a combination of the *soldadescas* – the formation of local militias that guarded the coasts against the Turkish navy and Berber pirates in the late sixteenth century, who sometimes dressed as Moors or Turks – and the much older *fiesta del patron* – the annual procession of the town's patron saint (Harris 1994: 46).

8 www.europeanvaluesstudy.eu ; www.worldvaluessurveys.org ; www.jdsurvey.net

9 DATA and Deusto University, Bilbao.

10 ASEP and Complutense University, Madrid.

11 Results of different questions from the monthly national surveys conducted by ASEP since 1986 till the present seem to confirm this assertion (ASEP, 'La Opinión Pública de los Españoles', in www.jdsurvey.net). Thus, in the November 1991 survey, when asking for the reason of the conflict between Israel and Arab countries, 34 percent of Spaniards answered that Israel did not accept the territories given to them by the UN and recurred to the occupation of other Arab territories, while 25 percent answered that Arabs have never accepted the state of Israel. In April 2002, 8 percent justified Palestinian terrorist attacks in Israel and 74 percent did not justify them, but in October 2003 only 2 percent justified Israel's attacks on Syria and 79 percent did not justify them. In this same survey, when asked about which actions were worst and less justified, 13 percent mentioned Israel's attacks on Palestinian cities against 8 percent who mentioned Palestinian attacks on Israel (64 percent mentioned both and 7 percent none). Many other questions in ASEP's monthly surveys during the past 23 years suggest Spaniards show more sympathy toward Palestinians and Arabs than toward Israel.

12 Data files can be accessed in www.jdsurvey.net, Immigrants Collection. And there are many other questions about foreigners and immigrants in particular in the ASEP collection – 242 monthly surveys between 1986 and 2009 – on the same web site.

Part 3

How to explain Islamophobia

7 An ecological analysis of the 2009 Swiss referendum on the building of minarets

Joel S. Fetzer and J. Christopher Soper

The Islamic percentage of the European population has grown dramatically over the past several decades. In response, many states initially adopted policies that sought to accommodate the religious practices of their Muslim population (Fetzer and Soper 2005). In turn, European far-right activists helped engineer a populist backlash against Muslims, and the results have been felt in mainstream public policy and electoral politics throughout the region. France has banned the wearing of the *hijab* in public schools and the French legislature voted to outlaw the wearing of the *burka* in public places, the lower house of parliament in Belgium passed a similar *burka* ban, and the Netherlands and Britain have proposed doing the same. The latest of these actions was the 2009 referendum vote in Switzerland that banned the construction of new minarets. A clear majority of Swiss voters (57.5 percent) affirmed the proposal, making Switzerland the only country in Europe with an outright prohibition on the construction of these religious structures (Antonsich and Jones 2010). That the Swiss referendum is consistent with what other states have done to restrict the rights of European Muslims does not, however, explain why the Swiss voted so convincingly in favor of the ban. We suggest that the ideal way to interpret the meaning of the vote is to analyze official voting data from the referendum itself. Based on our analysis of these votes, we argue that partisanship, ethno-religious identification, and educational attainment were the key factors shaping citizens' behavior.

Background

The referendum vote came as a surprise to many observers. Prior to the election, the Swiss Federation of Businesses, the Bundesrat – the seven-member executive body – and leaders of both the Catholic and Protestant communities in the country came out in opposition to the referendum (Mathwig 2009; Hirter and Vatter 2010: 18). By a vote of 132 to 51 with 11 abstentions, the Federal Assembly similarly recommended that the Swiss people reject the referendum (Swiss Parliamentary Commission 2009). Moreover, a pre-election poll found that 53 percent of respondents *opposed* the ban, and only 37 percent supported it (Wälti 2009). Given elite opposition to the minaret ban and the fact that pre-election polls seemed to indicate that the referendum would fail, the results of the vote caused widespread surprise and concern. France's Foreign Minister Bernard Kouchner expressed shock at the outcome, and the Vatican called it 'a blow to religious freedom' (West 2009). In its 2009 Human Rights Report on Switzerland, the United States Department of State (2010) suggested that the referendum vote 'contradicted basic values in the country's constitution' and potentially 'violated its international obligations'.

The vote, however, is less surprising given the long history of anti-immigrant referenda in the country, the political success of far-right parties in national elections, and the politics surrounding Switzerland's naturalization process. Between 1968 and 2000, Swiss voters opined on eight popular initiatives on issues related to immigration, seven of which called for stricter limits on the foreign population. While none of those initiatives passed, they nonetheless suggested broad dissatisfaction with Swiss immigration policy and the political potential for xenophobic parties (Gross 2006: Annex 1; Marquis and Bergman 2009).

One party that has taken full advantage of this electoral opportunity has been the Swiss People's Party (SVP). While the SVP and its predecessor parties have existed since the early twentieth century as a nationalist, socially conservative movement, the organization began to take a more militant anti-immigrant stand in the 1990s (Norris 2005: 62–3; Mazzoleni 2008). In 1991, the party received just fewer than 12 percent of the popular vote in Swiss parliamentary elections. Eleven years later, the party's support more than doubled to 28 percent, and the party's leader, Christoph Blocher, obtained a cabinet position (McGann and Kitschelt 2005). In the most recent parliamentary elections, in 2007, the SVP won 29 percent of the popular vote, and the party secured the largest number of seats in the Federal Assembly (Cumming-Bruce 2007). Finally, the SVP was the driving force behind the 2009 referendum vote, collecting over 100,000 signatures and submitting them to the Federal Chancellery for approval (Müller 2009; Tanner 2009).

In many respects, the referendum reflected Switzerland's bifurcated immigration history (Ireland 1994). On the one hand, the country has promoted immigration to meet its chronic labor shortages. In 2000, as an example, 19.3 percent of the Swiss population was foreign born (Gross 2006: 6). While this statistic was relatively high by historical standards, over the past century the average percentage of the Swiss population that has been foreign-born is 13.3 percent. Switzerland, in short, has always had one of the highest proportions of foreign-born residents in Europe. On the other hand, the presence of immigrants has coincided with the rise of such xenophobic groups as the SVP. The SVP's targeting of minarets was politically novel, but it reflected an important change in Swiss immigration patterns: the country of origin of migrants. For decades, the majority of the inflow into Switzerland was from Western and Southern Europe. In more recent years, however, immigrants have come increasingly from Eastern Europe, particularly Yugoslavia, and many of those immigrants and their families are Muslim (Iseni 2009; Schneuwly Purdie 2009). By 2000, 400,000 Muslims were living in Switzerland, representing just under 5 percent of the country's total population (GRIS and Institut Religioscope 2009). As they settled in the country, tensions between the religious needs of Muslims and Swiss church-state policy intensified (Aldeeb 2009). Eventually, Muslims built an estimated 160 mosques, four of which had a minaret (Hirter and Vatter 2010: 18). At least for the immediate future, the referendum has put a stop to the building of any mosques with a minaret, but the law might be vulnerable to a legal challenge at both the national and international level (Müller 2009; Tanner 2009).

The Swiss naturalization process has proved to be a final impediment to the political power of immigrant groups and a final reason why the referendum result was not perhaps quite so shocking. While Switzerland has one of the largest foreign-born populations in Europe, its naturalization process is one of the most cumbersome in the world. While close to half a million Muslims live in the country, no more than 20 percent are Swiss citizens. Under federal law, applicants for naturalization must have lived in Switzerland for at least 12 years, established proof of social integration, and demonstrated a knowledge of the Swiss way of life (Gross 2006: 36–7). However, the decision to grant citizenship is made not at the national level, but in both the canton – equivalent to a US state – and 'commune' – equivalent to a subdivision of a US county, perhaps as small as a village (Helbling 2008: 12-13). An informed review of relevant empirical studies (Wanner and Piguet 2002; Helbling and Kriesi 2004) leads one to conclude that many communes and cantons are basing their decisions on such supposedly extraneous factors as cultural, religious, and political considerations. In larger communes where the SVP is particularly strong, the rejection rate is correspondingly higher (Helbling and Kriesi 2004). Not surprisingly, the difficulty of gaining citizenship thus curtails the political power of immigrant groups who might have opposed the referendum.

What became the national campaign against minarets originated in a local dispute over a Turkish association's 2005 effort to build a 'symbolic minaret' in Wangen (Mayer 2009; Müller and Tanner 2009; Antonsich and Jones 2010: 57). The publicity surrounding this campaign led eventually to the effort to ban minarets via the initiative process. Like the debate on the *hijab* and *burka* in other European countries, the minaret became a symbol of the permanence of the Islamic presence in Switzerland (Behloul 2009; Hawthorne 2009). Proponents of the ban were quick to point out that restricting the construction of minarets would not limit Muslims' right to practice their faith but, if that claim were true, it only reinforced the vote's symbolic significance. Led by the SVP, the pro-referendum campaign said that it was opposing the 'creeping Islamization of Switzerland' (Wille 2009). What was left unsaid by the SVP was that only a small percentage of the Swiss Muslim population practices their religion, only four minarets exist in the entire country, two of which date from 1963 and 1978, and no evidence suggests that Islamization, whatever that might be, is more likely to come from Muslims who worship at mosques with a minaret. The SVP presented Islamic values as inherently incompatible with Europe's democratic and religious traditions. One of its more colorful posters during the campaign depicted a fully veiled woman standing next to a sea of minarets made to look like missiles emerging from the Swiss flag. The word 'STOPP' is written underneath in bold letters (minarette.ch 2010). The SVP claimed that the referendum was not a covert attack on immigrants per se, but rather an effort to defend women's rights and democracy (Müller 2009; Tanner 2009; Frauen gegen eine Islamisierung der Schweiz 2009) from an illiberal, intolerant ideology. In doing so, they were making arguments that were similar to those of critics in French- and German-speaking Europe who did not come out of an extreme right-wing background, but nonetheless felt it was a duty to be 'intolerant' of intolerant Islam (for example, Tribalat and Kaltenbach 2002; Broder 2008).

If the results of the referendum were not as shocking as originally thought, what was surprising was that the pre-election poll was so far off from the actual results. Although 37 percent of respondents in the pre-election survey conducted a month before the election indicated that they would vote for the referendum, in actuality, almost 58 percent of voters approved it. We argue in this chapter that such divergent results often occur when citizens are asked about sensitive, racially charged questions (see Jackman 1973; Berinsky 2002). Because many respondents do not want to appear prejudiced, they lie to interviewers about such matters but do allow racial considerations to influence their behavior in the privacy of the voting booth. We therefore contend that the Swiss opinion and exit polls on the minaret initiative are inherently unreliable and cannot be used – at least by themselves – to isolate the definitive causes of the vote. We therefore offer an 'ecological' analysis of official votes on the initiative – see methodological discussion below – which should not suffer from such bias. Using this technique, we propose to test four theoretical approaches to explain support for the 2009 referendum: post-materialism, status politics, rational choice theory, and partisanship. We test these political theories for two reasons. First, the demographic variables that are measured in the different theories – education, religion and ethnicity, social class, and party identification – are generally understood to shape an individual's political behavior, and those variables have historically been important in Swiss politics. What remains to be seen is if those factors also explained vote choice in this referendum. Second, the four theories are some of the most commonly tested in the literature on attitudes toward immigration. While not all Swiss Muslims are migrants, the rhetoric of the referendum campaign presented the issue as part of a larger conversation about immigration. Consequently, theories about popular attitudes toward immigration seem ideal for explaining the referendum vote.

Theories to be tested

Post-materialism theory was developed in the 1970s by Ronald Inglehart (1977). Inglehart theorized that a country's political culture is directly linked to its economic development. Based on extensive survey research, Inglehart suggested that Western societies were undergoing a change from materialist to post-materialist values. Materialist concerns focus on economic and physical security; they predominate in times of economic insecurity and result in class-based political conflict. However, as countries experience economic growth and material security can more easily be taken for granted, citizens turn their focus to such post-materialist values as personal autonomy, self-expression, and quality-of-life issues. In many countries, today's educational system tends to reinforce those post-materialist values. Inglehart includes under the penumbra of these values gender equality, environmental protection, tolerance for outgroups, and diversity. Since Muslims constitute the ultimate outsider group within Swiss culture, public attitudes toward them fit easily within this post-materialist framework.

If we apply this perspective to attitudes toward Muslims, the theory would predict that younger respondents and those with more education would be more post-materialist and therefore less likely to support the anti-minaret initiative.

Empirical studies of popular attitudes toward immigration have found that education increases support for immigrant minorities (Bogardus 1928: 98–102; Westin 1984: 255–9, 296–301; Hoskin 1991: 108–110; Chandler and Tsai 2001; but see Fetzer 2000: 113). Moreover, studies also find that, in general, older respondents exhibit less sympathy for the foreign-born (Hoskin 1991: 110–12; Heath and Tilley 2005).

A status politics model suggests that politics are shaped by membership in key ethnic or religious groups (Gusfield 1963). Those groups socialize members in social values, shape partisan attachments, and become the mechanism for political competition. Collective action by the group is designed to raise or maintain the prestige of the group. Particularly when they feel that their values are being threatened by newcomers or social change, members of the majority try to shape politics to reflect their particular cultural values, while members of ethnic or religious minorities oppose those efforts. At stake is which group will receive the government's cultural imprimatur.

In the Swiss context, a status politics model would highlight language and religious affiliation as the most historically significant points of political cleavage. Historically, German speakers have constituted the ethnic or linguistic majority. They have promoted policies that reflect this position of cultural dominance while the minority French, Italian, and Romansh have opposed them. Status theory would interpret the referendum as the attempt by the culturally dominant Germans to get the government to endorse their cultural values, 'the Swiss way of life'. The perceived threat from Muslim immigrants would explain the timing of the referendum. Status theory would predict that ethnic Germans would be the most likely to support the ban, while ethnically French and Italian Swiss would be less enthusiastic. There is some evidence from the immigration literature that belonging to a disfavored, disadvantaged, or 'marginal' cultural group sometimes increases sympathy for such other non-mainstream individuals as immigrants (Fetzer 2000; Hayes and Dowds 2006).

Religion is frequently a variable that is a part of status politics models, and certainly religious identity has been important in Swiss history. At present, however, Catholics (41 percent of Swiss citizens) and Protestants (43 percent) are close to equally represented, making behavioral differences between the two groups less likely according to status theory. Religious minorities and those with no religion (16 percent) are a significant portion of the electorate, but they are likely to feel disadvantaged by a dominant-Christian religious power structure. Consequently, status theorists would expect them to disproportionally oppose the initiative.

A partisanship model argues that the most important variable shaping electoral choices is party identification. The theory proposes that parties shape political values and socialize voters to adopt the policy positions of the party with which they identify (Campbell *et al.* 1960). Traditionally, left-of-center parties have supported working class interests, sometimes even including the rights of immigrant workers. Voters who identify with those parties might consequently be expected to be more supportive of the political rights of immigrants. Conservative parties, by contrast, have traditionally appealed to business interests and socially conservative voters, and party members would be less likely to support immigrants. In the broader immigration literature, there is a good deal of evidence that identification with a right-of-center party usually correlates positively with opposition to immigration (Girard 1971; Holzer and Münz 1995; Lange 1995; Ilias *et al.* 2008).

The situation in Europe has become increasingly complex, however, with the rise of extreme-right populist parties (Norris 2005). These parties combine economic liberalism with a very strong opposition to immigration (Kitschelt 1995). As we noted above, the Swiss People's Party has been electorally effective at mobilizing voters, and the party led the successful referendum campaign. Not surprisingly, a party theory would predict that voters who identify with the SVP would be more likely to support the referendum. Conversely, the Social Democratic Party opposed the referendum and we would anticipate that members of that party would have been more likely to oppose the referendum. What is less clear is what to expect from partisans of the right-of-center Christian Democratic Party. On the one hand, the party came out against the minaret ban as did the leaders of the Catholic Church, which is historically the party's base of support. What remains to be seen, however, is whether these culturally conservative voters followed the wishes of party and church leaders on the referendum. We would expect that support for the minaret ban from members of the Christian Democratic Party would fall midway between support from members of the SVP and the Social Democratic Party.

Finally, a rational choice model posits that political values are shaped by economic self-interest. People vote on the basis of how they think a particular party, candidate, or issue will affect them economically (Downs 1957). For the referendum vote, this theory would predict that those voters who saw immigrants as an economic threat would have been most likely to support the minaret ban. Rightly or wrongly, members of the working class would more likely perceive the largely blue collar Muslim population as economic competitors than would members of the upper classes. To test this theory, we will look at a composite figure for social class that includes income, education, and occupation.[1]

The empirical immigration literature has generally found that belonging to the working class or being employed in a less-skilled job often increases xenophobia (Jones and Lambert 1965; Kassim 1987; Hoskin 1991: 104–8; Fetzer 2000: 97, 102; Kunovich 2002), presumably because such employees feel more threatened economically by the generally working-class immigrants (Mayda 2006). However, previous studies of immigration attitudes find that neither being unemployed oneself (Hoskin 1991: 82–84; Citrin and Green 1997; Fetzer 2000: 144, 148) nor living in a region with a high unemployment rate (Schissel *et al.* 1989) influences attitudes toward immigration.

Data and methods

As we mentioned above, the difficulty in analyzing polls on the referendum is that the answers provided by survey respondents, even in exit polls, are not necessarily reliable, especially on racially or religiously sensitive topics like this one. For example, the most methodologically rigorous exit poll, that by Hirter and Vatter (2010), arrived at results that were nine percentage points below the actual yes vote on the initiative. This discrepancy suggests that many Swiss voters were embarrassed to admit to interviewers that they supported the minaret ban. Official voting statistics would not suffer from this bias, but one may not simply infer individual behavior from such aggregated data (Robinson 1950). This 'ecological fallacy' problem hindered statistical analysis of aggregated voting data for decades, but Gary King's (1997) development of a maximum-likelihood approach to this issue made possible the kind of analysis that we employ in this chapter. In a nutshell, this method relies only on actual, official, voting and census data, which are not subject to response bias from surveys. Instead, the model estimates what the underlying individual-level relationship would have to be given the observed relationship between the two aggregated variables, such as the vote on the minaret initiative and the religious background of the individual voter.[2] King (1997: 197–245) has demonstrated its accuracy, by comparing the results of his ecological analysis of aggregated data with the actual population statistics from all individuals. While the method is ideal for a controversial issue such as the minaret vote, where one might not trust self-reported behavior, King's technique also has some potential limitations. As an example, multivariate analysis is cumbersome, and variables – percent Roman Catholic, college educated, women – whose averages are close to 100 or 0 percent often do not allow precise estimations – that is, large standard errors and/ or a failure of the maximum-likelihood routine to converge to a plausible result.

Voting data on the 2009 minaret initiative and data from the 2000 census came from the Swiss Federal Statistics Office. Because the boundaries of some electoral districts had changed between 2000 and 2009, we recalculated the relevant statistics for these newly created voting districts by hand.

Results

The data confirm several of the theories tested (see Table 7.1). As post-materialism would predict, educational attainment was strongly correlated with vote choice. According to our results, fewer than 10 percent of voters with a tertiary education supported the minaret ban. The education data might also illustrate the chasm between elite opposition to the ban and popular support for it. As we noted earlier in the chapter, the Swiss political, social, and religious elite were nearly uniform in their hostility to the referendum. It was precisely this elite group, however, that is most likely to have a university education and to have been exposed to a set of political values – tolerance for diversity, the rights of minorities, social equality – that would explain their opposition to the ban. This interpretation is consistent with the broader literature on immigration attitudes which finds that education produces tolerance for immigrants via the learning of multicultural norms rather than the acquisition of skills that remove one from direct competition with immigrants (Hainmueller and Hiscox 2007; Hainmueller and Hiscox 2010; but see Helbling 2011).

The data also partially confirm the partisanship and status theories. As expected, members of the SVP were much more likely to vote 'yes' on the initiative than were Christian Democrats and, especially Social Democrats. The ethnic German majority does seem more likely to have supported the ban, possibly as a way of affirming its status position, while the minority French were less supportive. The

Table 7.1 Ecological analysis of 2009 Swiss minaret initiative

Variables	% Yes	Standard error (%)
Official results	57.5	n/a
Economic/rational choice		
Upper classes#	53.2★	9.8
Post-materialism		
College educated#	8.3★	0.2
Ethno-linguistic		
German	64.6★	7.0
French	51.6★	6.8
Italian	68.9★	5.4
Political		
Swiss People's Party	86.1★	6.2
Christian Democrats	63.9★	7.8
Social Democrats	6.5	37.5
Religious		
Catholic	62.8★	7.4
Protestant	64.1★	8.6
Other/None	26.3	n/a

Note
Estimates obtained with EI2 (see King 1997). Confidence intervals computed at 95 percent certainty.
★ p<.05. # = unit of analysis equals canton, not district/Bezirk. n/a = not applicable.

even smaller minority of Italians, on the other hand, appear to have been slightly more supportive than even the Germans, which is not what status theory would predict. The religious data similarly confirm the status theory. Most of the majority Catholics and Protestants voted yes, while nearly three out of four religious minorities and non-religious citizens opposed it.[3] Finally, some evidence supports an economic, rational choice theory. Based on our composite data for social class, Swiss voters who belonged to the upper class of class structure were less likely to vote for the initiative than were their counterparts below the class average.

It was hardly surprising that supporters of the anti-immigrant SVP voted disproportionately for the arguably anti-Muslim initiative. This result begs the question of who is most likely to identify with the SVP in the first place. In Table 7.2, therefore, we have conducted an ecological analysis of the 2007 Federal Assembly election. In that contest, 28.9 percent of all voters cast their ballots for the SVP. Support for the party was particularly robust among Germans (33.9 percent) and Protestants (44.6 percent), while college educated (17.0 percent), French (18.0 percent), Italians (5.7 percent), and non-religious or religious minority voters (3.1 percent) were much less likely to vote for the SVP ticket. Overall, these results for the SVP vote parallel those for the minaret initiative. The Italians are the one notable exception, with a very low SVP support, but a very high 'yes' vote on the minaret initiative (68.9

Table 7.2 Ecological analysis of 2007 Swiss Federal Assembly election

Variables	% SVP	Standard error (%)
Official results	28.9	n/a
Economic/rational choice		
Upper classes	30.0*	10.1
Post-materialism		
College educated	17.0*	0.5
Ethno-linguistic		
German	33.9*	6.9
French	18.0*	4.1
Italian	5.7*	0.2
Religious		
Catholic	24.0	14.4
Protestant	44.6*	0.6
Other/None	3.1*	0.3

Note
Estimates obtained with EI2 (see King 1997). Confidence intervals computed at 95 percent certainty. Unit of analysis is canton. * $p < .05$. N/A = not applicable

percent). Swiss Italians are concentrated in the single canton of Ticino, a Christian Democratic stronghold. We would therefore hypothesize that local party politics, rather than pro-Muslim sentiment explains this paradoxical outcome.

Our findings broadly confirm the weighted, survey-based results of Hirter and Vatter (2010). As we do, they found strong partisan, ethno-linguistic, and religious effects in the vote. According to their survey, 54 percent of the Christian Democrats and 93 percent of Swiss People's Party affiliates voted 'yes', while our equivalent estimates were 64 and 86 percent respectively. Their estimate for the percentage of Social Democrats who voted 'yes' is 26 percent, about 20 percentage points higher than our estimate, but for that variable the King method did not allow for a precise estimate. Similarly, their ethnic results – 60 percent 'yes' for Germans, 49 percent for French, and around 68 percent for Italians – mirror our own for the three major Swiss linguistic communities. Finally, our data approximate those of Hirter and Vatter for the two largest religious communities: Roman Catholic and Protestant. Our ecological analysis thus supports their use of weighting to achieve the same overall percentages as the recorded vote.

Discussion

Ethno-linguistic and religious identities have long formed the core of Swiss domestic politics. While it appears they are also determining Swiss citizens' views of religious outsiders, these factors are doing so in ways not fully consonant with their historical role. Catholics and Protestants who have traditionally found themselves on opposite sides of any number of issues differ little in their opposition to minarets. Religious minorities and the non-religious, however, are much more supportive of the rights of Muslims. Religion remains a key factor in Swiss politics, in short, but it is no longer a conflict between Protestants and Catholics, but is instead a divide between the historically dominant Christian churches and the non-Christian and non-religious. Similarly, the ethno-linguistic factor looms large on this issue. As expected, the majority Germans overwhelmingly supported the initiative, arguably as a way to defend their status as the dominant ethnic group in the country. The French minority, by contrast, was more likely to sympathize with the Muslim minority. The even smaller Italian community, on the other hand, was more supportive of the initiative than even the Germans, possibly as a way to confirm their status as 'real' Swiss.

Partisanship similarly played a key role in the electoral outcome. Members of the far-right SVP, the party that was responsible for putting the initiative on the ballot, unsurprisingly supported the minaret ban by a factor of nearly nine-to-one. That nearly two out of three affiliates of the centrist Christian Democratic People's Party also supported the initiative is somewhat more surprising given the opposition of CVP party leaders and church officials. This result suggests an elite–mass divergence on this issue that is potentially problematic for both party and church leaders. For the party, it indicates a potential market for the SVP to exploit, while for the church, it may accelerate the alienation between pew and pulpit.

This chasm can also be seen in the data on education. Those Swiss with a tertiary education voted quite differently than those with lower levels of education, but they were not a large enough proportion of the electorate to defeat the referendum. As members of the cultural and political elite, highly educated Swiss urged opposition to the minaret ban from the pulpit, the printing press, and the party apparatus, but most Swiss voters simply ignored their advice.

This result also suggests that the minaret initiative fits within the larger history of anti-immigrant initiatives in Swiss politics. The SVP tried to reach out to women and the highly educated by claiming that the ban was necessary to preserve liberal democracy, but the vote was yet another example of Swiss xenophobia. This was the latest in a series of attempts by the party to present itself as a 'mainstream', non-racist political movement, but highly educated voters were most likely to oppose the measure and reject the SVP assertion that it was necessary to be 'intolerant' of those who were 'intolerant'. Moreover, our analysis of the 2007 SVP vote in Table 7.2 confirms that the party's base of support was nearly identical to that for the 'yes' vote on the minaret initiative. In this case, Islamophobia is not a new plant, but an offshoot of the same xenophobic tree (Helbling 2010). Talking about 'Islamic extremism' or a defense of traditional Swiss values has therefore arguably become a form of symbolic racism or Islamophobia in the same way that the discourse around crime in the United States has become a way for politicians to activate voters' prejudice against African Americans (Kinder and Sears 1981; Sears 1988).

Our empirical results and those of Hirter and Vatter suggest that this vote was primarily about Swiss identity. In this regard, Switzerland is like much of Western Europe in wrestling with issues surrounding the rights of Muslim citizens and migrants. We can only hope that this initiative is not the final word on what it means to be Swiss, on what religious practices are protected, and on how the country will come to terms with its multi-religious population.

Notes

1   The composite is based on six indicators that measure educational attainment, occupation, and income. The data are from the Swiss Federal Statistics Office and are available at http://www.bfs.admin.ch/bfs/portal/en/index.html

2   As King details in his book-length explanation of the technique (1997: 28–140), the maximum likelihood routine estimates two major parameters. The first, labeled βb, could be the proportion of some subset of all citizens – for example, African-Americans – who turn out to vote in a particular election. The second, labeled β^w, is the proportion of all remaining citizens – not members of that subset – who turned out to vote. EI also provides standard errors for both of these estimates, which allow researchers to calculate the precision of EI's estimates of βb and β^w. MLE triangulates in on the most plausible values for these two parameters by searching across a two-dimensional plane that represents all possible combinations of βb and β^w and plots all observed pairs of the independent and dependent variables by district – for example, the proportion African-American in a given county versus the proportion of citizens who turned out to vote in that same county. EI represents this plane as a MRI-like tomography plot that highlights the most likely combination of these two statistics in the underlying population of individuals.

3   We computed the results for other/no religion based on the number of such voters who would have had to vote 'yes' to achieve the total number of 'yes' voters for the initiative. We assumed that the turnout rate was constant across religious groups and that our ecological-inference-based estimates for Catholics and Protestants were accurate.

8 Islamophobia and its explanation

Henk Dekker and Jolanda van der Noll

Introduction

How can we explain Islamophobia? That is the intriguing question we want to answer in this chapter. Islamophobia is on the rise in several countries in Europe and is also clearly present in the USA and various countries in Latin America and Asia (Pew Research Center 2007, 2008). It is important to study Islamophobia because it is one of the main explanatory factors of negative behavior toward Islam and Muslims. Increasing negative attitudes toward Islam and Muslims among non-Muslims may result in increased social exclusion and discrimination against Muslims by non-Muslims, which then may result in radicalization among Muslims, which in turn may contribute to a further increase in negative attitudes among non-Muslims, and so forth. Attitude research provides an indication as to whether there is fertile ground for more negative behavior and how to stop the negative spiral. The academic inspiration to carry out this study came when we discovered in 2005 that there was no generally accepted instrument for measuring Islamophobia, and we could not find an explanation for this attitude in the existing literature. In this chapter we present our new Islamophobia measure, a predictive model, the survey findings, and our conclusions about the origins of Islamophobia.[1]

Islamophobia

In our study Islamophobia is viewed as an attitude. The major characteristic of an attitude is its affective nature. An attitude is 'the amount of affect for or against some object' (Fishbein and Ajzen 1975: 11). In line with Ajzen and Fishbein (1980), we have opted for the one-dimensional interpretation of the attitude concept, instead of the multi-dimensional interpretation that also includes cognitions and behavior. In our opinion, cognitions – knowledge and perceptions, including clichés and stereotypes – and behavior are not dimensions of an attitude, but rather variables that may explain variance in an attitude or an effect of an attitude, respectively. Although the concept of Islamophobia primarily refers to Islam, we decided to include both the religion and its adherents in the definition and measurement of Islamophobia: we define Islamophobia as 'having a negative attitude toward Islam and Muslims'. It should be clear that 'phobia' does not signify a kind of mental illness here; a negative attitude toward Islam and Muslims may be 'normal' and based on rational considerations.

Predictive model

Our predictive model is based on the theories that have been successful in explaining attitudes toward foreigners, immigrants, and ethnic or national minorities in general. The intergroup contact theory explains a reduction of negative outgroup attitudes. The social identity and integrated threat theories explain an increase in negative outgroup attitudes. The socialization theory can explain both reduction and increase, depending on the socialization contents.

Intergroup contact theory states that direct contact with an outgroup prevents or reduces negative outgroup attitudes (Allport 1954). Positive intergroup contact may result in affection for one or more outgroup members that can spill over to include the majority of the outgroup (Pettigrew 1998b). A meta-analysis reviewing more than 500 studies showed that the frequency of intergroup contact has a reducing effect on negative attitudes, and that this is stronger than the reverse effect of attitudes on the intensity of intergroup contact (Pettigrew and Tropp 2006). Besides quantity, the quality of contact, evaluated positively or negatively, can also have an important effect on attitudes toward outgroups (Tausch *et al.* 2007). Positive intergroup contact diminishes perceptions of threat (Ward and Masgoret 2006). In line with the intergroup contact theory we hypothesize that more contacts, and more positively evaluated contacts, with Muslims reduce negative attitudes toward Islam and Muslims (H1a-b).

Socialization theory holds that people are not born with negative attitudes toward ethnic outgroups – or negative outgroup 'genes' – but rather that these attitudes are the result of processing the emotional and informative messages that individuals receive from relevant others (Lasswell 1977; Jennings 2007). Family, school, church, mass media, peer group, and political leaders form the main socialization agencies (Jennings *et al.* 2009; Boomgaarden and Vliegenthart 2007). Messages about Islam and Muslims in the mass media are more negative than positive (Nacos and Torres-Reyna 2006, Poole and Richardson 2006; Shadid 2007). Violent incidents involving Islam throughout the world have dominated the headlines for several years, and have probably contributed to the association of Islam and Muslims with terrorism and to a perception of Islam and the Middle East as being a civilization in direct opposition to that of the West (Cashin 2010), and are likely to have fuelled safety and value threat perceptions (Riek *et al.* 2006). The Internet also offers various sites containing strong anti-Islamic and anti-Muslim messages (Larsson 2007). In popular culture, messages are also more negative than positive (Shaheen 1997). In several countries political leaders, driven by their own attitudes or by political goals, publicly express negative feelings about Islam and Muslims and may act as 'sewers' of Islamophobia (Allen and Nielsen 2004). In line with the socialization theory we hypothesize that negative messages about Islam and Muslims from relevant others and mass media induce negative attitudes toward Islam and Muslims (H2a-b).

Social identity theory argues that people have a fundamental need for a positive self-identity, and that to a large extent this is derived from social group membership

(Tajfel and Turner 1986; Abrams and Hogg 1990). To maintain or enhance their self-esteem, people compare the group they belong to with other groups and evaluate their own group positively, whereas they evaluate other groups less positively or even negatively. The national group is one of the main groups to identify with (Bloom 1990). Two national attitudes have been empirically distinguished, patriotism and nationalism (Dekker *et al.* 2003). Nationalism has more impact on negative outgroup attitudes than does patriotism (Gijsberts *et al.* 2004). In line with the social identity theory we hypothesize that low self-esteem and a very positive national in-group attitude – nationalism - induce negative attitudes toward Islam and Muslims (H3a-b).

Integrated threat theory states that negative outgroup attitudes are caused by threat perceptions, negative stereotypes, and intergroup anxiety (Stephan and Stephan 2000). Perceived 'realistic' threats refer to a conflict of interests over scarce resources. Perceived 'symbolic' threats refer to a conflict of values, norms, and behavior. Several studies have shown that threat perceptions are related to negative outgroup attitudes (Scheepers *et al.* 2002a; McLaren 2003). Stereotypes are characteristics that an individual ascribes to a group. Intergroup anxiety refers to the fear of being treated negatively in interactions with the outgroup (Stephan *et al.* 2005). Several studies have shown that negative emotions such as anxiety have an important effect on attitudes toward ethnic minorities (Mackie and Smith 2003; Brader *et al.* 2008). In line with the integrated threat theory we hypothesize that perceptions of threat posed by Islam and Muslims, negative clichés regarding Islam, negative stereotypes of Muslims, and intergroup anxiety induce negative attitudes toward Islam and Muslims (H4a-d). Recent studies suggest that the integrated threat theory variables work as mediators for the effect of intergroup contact (Stephan *et al.* 2005). The same might apply to the effect of socialization and national attitude. Therefore, we hypothesize that perceptions of threat, negative clichés and stereotypes, and anxiety mediate the effects of direct contact, socialization, and national attitude (H5a-c).

Besides these theories and their main explanatory variables we included knowledge about Islam and Muslims as an independent variable in our analysis. Various educational publications expect a positive effect of knowledge on attitudes. Several studies have shown correlations between knowledge and attitude (Dekker *et al.* 1998). Therefore, we hypothesize that more knowledge of Islam and Muslims reduces negative attitudes toward this religion and its adherents (H6).

Background variables are age, gender, education level, social class, and religiosity. A fairly common finding is that older respondents have more negative attitudes toward ethnic outgroups than the younger ones (Chandler and Tsai 2001), males have more negative outgroup attitudes than females, and that more education leads to less negative attitudes toward ethnic outgroups in general (Hello *et al.* 2004) and Muslims (Fetzer and Soper 2003). Lower socio-economic status usually translates to more negative attitudes toward ethnic outgroups. Research findings show that there are no or only weak relations between religiosity and negative outgroup attitudes (Hunsberger and Jackson 2005; Scheepers *et al.* 2002b, respectively). However, highly religious people and religious traditionalists from other religions have shown more negative views of Islam (Kalkan *et al.* 2009; Nisbet *et al.* 2009).

Focus group and survey

In order to test the hypotheses we conducted a survey among Dutch adolescents. We focused on the Netherlands because the percentage of Muslims in the Netherlands is one of the highest in Europe, and much higher than in the USA (Pew Research Center 2009a). The Netherlands is also one of the countries with the most ambitious multiculturalism policy (Sniderman and Hagendoorn 2007). We focused on young people as the research population because there is growing empirical evidence that fundamental political attitudes are developed at an early age, and that these attitudes, once developed, tend to be long lasting (Sears 2003). Moreover, adolescents and young adults can become very politically active and have a greater-than-average preference for protest.

In order to prepare the questionnaire we held open group discussions with non-Islamic adolescents from the lowest level of secondary education, because we wanted to find out how these youngsters talk about Islam and Muslims. The most important finding was that Muslims are almost always connected to a nationality or ethnicity; all conversations were about Turks or Moroccans. This is not surprising, because more than 90 percent of the people with a Turkish or Moroccan background declare themselves to be Muslim (SCP 2005: 119), and more than 60 percent of the Muslims in the Netherlands are of Turkish or Moroccan background, while the other 40 percent are dispersed over many small groups (CBS 2004). The participants in the discussions did not distinguish between the various Muslim religious groups such as Sunnites and Shiites. (A more extensive report of the focus group meetings is available from the authors on request.)

We used secondary schools to gain access to the respondents and to obtain a sample for our survey that was stratified along divisions of educational level, gender, and opportunity for contact. The fieldwork in 33 third-year groups of 11 secondary schools in the Netherlands was conducted between 14 March and 26 April 2006. In this period no major national or international events took place that could have influenced answers. The questionnaire, containing 104 mainly closed-ended single- and multi-item questions, was completed during regular school hours. Various measures were taken to prevent socially desirable and politically correct answers, including questionnaire self-administration and anonymity.

Since we knew from the focus group sessions that Dutch youngsters strongly associate Muslims with Turks and Moroccans, we decided to ask questions about these two minorities instead of about 'Muslims'. To avoid an excessive focus on or any priming toward Islam and Muslims, the study was presented to the respondents in general words as a study of 'how youngsters think about particular groups in Dutch society', and questions referred not only to Turks and Moroccans, but also to Jews and Dutch. Likewise, questions referred not only to Islam but also to Judaism and Christianity. We developed sets of questions for almost all variables rather than just one per variable. Reliability was checked using Cronbach's alpha. The six respondents who had missing values on the questions used to construct the dependent variable were dropped from the sample. The following analyses are based on data from 580 non-Islamic youngsters aged 14–16. Girls and higher-level general education students are slightly over-represented in the sample.

Measures

Islamophobia was measured by seven questions, asking about the respondents' general attitude toward Islam, general attitude toward Turks and Moroccans, the level of trust in Turks and Moroccans, and any positive or negative feelings they felt they would experience should they be having new neighbours with a Turkish or Moroccan background. The correlations between attitudes toward Islam and Turks or Moroccans were strong (r = .54 and .57 respectively, *ps* < .01), and between attitudes toward Turks and Moroccans very strong (r > .78, *ps* < .01). Confirmatory factor analyses using AMOS 18 show that the answers to all seven questions form one factor ($\chi 2$ (9, $N = 580$) = 20.86, $p = .01$, CFI = .996, TLI = .992, SRMR = .018). The three components – general attitude toward Islam, general and specific attitudes toward Turks and Moroccans, any feelings about new neighbours with a Turkish or Moroccan background – contributed equally to the Islamophobia factor. We averaged the scores of the single questions into a scale ranging from 1 to 5; the higher the score, the more negative the attitude toward Islam and Muslims.

For intergroup contact two variables were constructed, one related to frequency and one to the evaluation of the contact. Intergroup *contact frequency* was measured by asking about the frequency of contact in class, at school, in the neighbourhood, and 'elsewhere'. The answers related to Turks and Moroccans were used to construct an index of direct contact. The value of this direct contact index was the mean score of the answers on these eight subquestions – contacts with Turks and Moroccans, in four possible situations – and varies from 'no contact' (1) to 'much contact' (4). *Contact evaluation* was measured by asking respondents' overall evaluation of the contacts with each of the groups – 'How do you in general evaluate the contact with the people from these groups?'. The five-point scale ranges from 'very negative' (-2) to 'very positive' (+2). The mean score of the evaluation of contacts with Turks and Moroccans was included in the analysis.

Two socialization variables were constructed: one related to socialization through persons; and one regarding socialization through mass media. We measured socialization as perceived by the respondents, because we know that parents' and adolescents' reports of socialization are only moderately correlated and that adolescents' reports are the most important in predicting adolescents' attitudes (Hughes *et al.* 2009). *Socialization by persons* was measured by asking the respondents about the attitudes of their grandfather, grandmother, (foster) father, (foster) mother, favourite teacher, and best friend toward three religions – Islam, Judaism, and Christianity – and four groups – Turks, Moroccans, Jews, and Dutch. The mean scores of the answers to the questions concerning the perceived attitude toward Islam, Turks, and Moroccans for all six socializers were averaged into one scale, varying from very negative (-2) to very positive (+2). *Socialization by media* was measured by the perceived content of the information provided by newspapers, television news, other news programmes on TV, and the Internet. The Internet was left out in subsequent analyses because there appeared to be hardly any variation regarding the use of this medium. The mean scores for the answers to the questions about the content of newspapers, TV news and other news programmes on TV with respect to Islam, Turks and Moroccans were averaged into one scale, varying from very negative (-2) to very positive (+2).

Self-esteem was measured by means of 10 statements, which were translations and adaptations of items from Rosenberg's (1965) 'self-esteem scale' – for example, 'On the whole, I am satisfied with myself' and 'At times I think I am no good at all'. The answer categories ranged from 'totally disagree' (1) to 'totally agree' (5), and all statements were coded in such a way that a higher score represented higher self-esteem. The reactions to the statements form a reliable scale (alpha = .91) and the mean score of the statements was included as the scale value.

National attitude was measured by statements reflecting differences in positive feelings toward people's own national group and country (Dekker *et al.* 2003). All statements were measured on a five-point scale ranging from 'totally disagree' (1) to 'totally agree' (5). Factor analysis revealed two distinct factors, representing *patriotism* (factor loadings > .77; alpha = .89) and *nationalism* (factor loadings > .63; alpha = .91). Both scales consist of the mean scores of the statements; higher values reflect stronger patriotism or stronger nationalism, respectively.

Perceived threat was measured by statements reflecting economic, safety, and value threats. One of these statements refers to Islam – 'Islam and democracy are hard to combine'; two to Muslims –'Muslims and the Dutch generally hold the same opinions', 'Muslims who maintain their own culture threaten the Dutch culture'; and four to Turks and Moroccans – 'Turks [Moroccans] take the jobs of the Dutch', and 'I feel unsafe when I meet a group of Turks [Moroccans] on the street'. All statements were coded in such a way that a higher score indicated a higher perceived threat. Three subscales of perceived threat were constructed; one concerning *perceived economic threat* (two items, alpha = .98), one concerning *perceived safety threat* (two items; alpha = .94) and finally, one referring to *perceived value threat* (three items; alpha = .68).

Negative clichés and stereotypes were measured using questions asking whether or not the respondent thought that certain characteristics apply to the religions – 'old-fashioned', 'violent', 'dominant', and 'unfriendly toward women' – and the ethnic groups – 'rude', 'selfish', 'aggressive', 'arrogant', 'clumsy', 'dominant'. To prevent bias we included an equal number of negative and positive clichés and stereotypes in the questions, and asked the questions for all three religions and four groups. Respondents received one point for every negative cliché or stereotype assigned. Two scales were constructed: one reflecting *negative clichés* of Islam and one reflecting *negative stereotypes* of Muslims – that is, Turks and Moroccans.

Intergroup anxiety was measured by asking respondents whether they had experienced emotions of 'fear' and 'uneasiness' with respect to the religions and the groups. Respondents received one point for the emotions experienced. Fear and uneasiness with respect to Islam, Turks, and Moroccans were averaged into one reliable scale of intergroup anxiety (alpha = .82).

Knowledge was measured by the self-assessed level of knowledge about the three religions and four groups. The answers to the questions about Islam, Turks, and Moroccans were averaged to construct one scale for *knowledge about Islam and Muslims*, with values ranging from 'no knowledge' (1) to 'much knowledge' (5).

Age, gender and *education* level were measured by the usual single items. *Social class* was measured subjectively by the estimated relative income of the parents.

Religiosity was measured by asking respondents to indicate how often they attend religious services, on a five-point scale ranging from at least once a week (1) to never (5).

Results

More than half of the respondents had negative to very negative *attitudes toward Islam and Muslims* (54 percent), while four out of ten respondents had positive to very positive attitudes toward Islam and Muslims (40 percent). This finding is similar to the findings from the Pew Research Centre 2005 poll, in which 51 percent of the Dutch respondents reported unfavourable opinions about Muslims. Attitudes toward Islam were significantly more negative than the attitudes toward Turks (t (579) = -7.42, p <.01) and Moroccans (t (579) = -2.61, p <.01); attitudes toward Moroccans were on average more negative than the attitude toward Turks, regardless of whether this was in terms of general attitude (t (579) = 7,76, p < .01), trust (t (579) = 7,5, p < .01), or the 'new neighbours' preference (t (579) = 5.85, p <.01).

Regression analyses show that after controlling for the demographic variables all theories contribute to the explanation of Islamophobia. The *intergroup contact theory* variables explain 50 percent of the variance in attitude (Table 8.1, model 1) and it is especially the evaluation of contact that is strongly associated with respondents' attitude (β = -.58, p < .001). Regression analysis including the *socialization theory* variables (model 2) explains 45 percent of the variance, and the perceived attitude of personal socializers is a strong predictor of attitude (β = -.58, p < .001). Model 3 includes the *social identity theory* variables. Regression analysis shows that self-esteem is a weak (β = -.14, p < .001) and nationalism is a strong predictor of attitude (β = .55, p < .001), whereas patriotism, as expected, has no significant effect. This model explains 38 percent of the variance of attitudes toward Islam and Muslims. *Integrated threat theory* variables (model 4) explain 51 percent of the variance, mainly because of the strong effects of perceptions of value and safety threats (β = .32 and β = .26, ps < .001, respectively). The perception of economic threat and negative stereotypes are weak predictors (β = .09, p < .01 and β = .09, p < .05, respectively), whereas negative clichés and intergroup anxiety are not significantly associated with attitude. The *knowledge model* (model 5) explains a mere 13 percent of the variance in attitude; knowledge of Islam and Muslims has a very weak negative association with negative attitudes toward Islam and Muslims (β = -.13, p < .01).

To test how the individual theories perform when they are analyzed in combination, we conducted a regression analysis including the predictors from all theoretical models. This model explains 68 percent of the variance in attitudes toward Islam and Muslims (model 6). The intergroup contact theory (contact evaluation, β = -.30, p < .001) and socialization theory (perceived attitude of relevant others, β = -.23, p < .001) contribute most to the explanation of attitudes toward Islam and Muslims. Positive contact with Muslims and positive messages from relevant others reduce the level of Islamophobia. Other predictors are perceived safety threat (β = .15, p < .001), perceived value threat (β = .13, p < .001), negative clichés about Islam (β = .07, p < .05), and nationalism (β = .14, p < .001).

We also hypothesized that integrated threat theory variables would mediate the effects of direct contact, socialization, and national attitude. To test these hypotheses we removed the variables belonging to the integrated threat theory from the model, and examined how the other variables were affected by this removal – not shown in the table. The changes are marginal: the explained variance slightly decreases to 62 percent – from 68 percent. The effect of nationalism on attitude toward Islam and Muslims is most strongly influenced by the removal of the integrated threat theory variables ($\beta = .26$, was $\beta = .14$, $ps < .001$). Nationalism is associated with heightened levels of perceived safety and value threats, which in turn increases Islamophobia, but the indirect effects are very weak ($\beta = .03$ and $\beta = .04$, $ps < .001$, respectively). The changes in other variables are negligible. The results do not support our hypotheses that integrated threat variables mediate the effects of intergroup contact and socialization on Islamophobia.

Conclusion and discussion

Our analyses show that the main predictors of Islamophobia are contact evaluation and socialization by personal socializers, that is, variables from intergroup contact and socialization theory. Both have a reducing effect on negative attitudes toward Islam and Muslims. Perceptions of safety and value threats from Islam and Muslims, negative clichés of Islam, and a very positive attitude toward one's national in-group – nationalism, all variables from integrated threat and social identity theory, have an important positive effect on Islamophobia. The data do not justify a rejection of our explanatory hypotheses relating to direct contact evaluation, perceived attitudes of personal socializers, perceived safety and value threat, negative clichés of Islam, and national attitude. However, we found no support for our hypotheses relating to perceived mass media content, negative stereotypes, negative emotions, knowledge level, and self-esteem level.

Ours was the first empirical study to explain attitudes toward Islam and Muslims in the Netherlands. Another study carried out among the same research population in 2006–7 supports our findings of a high percentage of respondents with negative attitudes (47 percent), positive relationships with negative stereotypes and perceived symbolic threat, and a negative relationship with intergroup contact (Velasco González *et al.* 2008).

Future studies would benefit from improved measures for some of the variables. When we developed the questionnaire we decided to ask a question about subjective knowledge, that is, self-assessed knowledge about Islam and Muslims, instead of objective knowledge because we were afraid of the possible negative effects on the respondents' motivation to answer the subsequent questions after they discovered their own lack of knowledge. Subjective knowledge was found not to be a predictor of attitude in the overall analysis (model 6). The question remains whether objective knowledge of Islam and Muslims has a positive effect on attitude toward Islam and Muslims. There are indications that this is the case (Pew Research Center 2009b). Socialization via schools could be further studied by including socializers other than the favourite teacher, such as lessons and textbooks about Islam and Muslims. Furthermore, we would then include questions through

Table 8.1 Regression analyses on Islamophobia

	Model 1			Model 2			Model 3		
	B	(SE)	β	B	(SE)	β	B	(SE)	β
(Constant)	01.51	(00.60)		01.80	(00.63)		00.42	(00.68)	
Gender (male)	00.21	(00.05)	00.12***	00.29	(00.06)	00.17***	00.37	(00.06)	00.22***
Age	00.13	(00.04)	00.10**	00.07	(00.04)	00.05	00.15	(00.04)	00.12***
Educational level	−00.06	(00.02)	−00.08*	00.00	(00.02)	00.00	00.02	(00.03)	00.02
Social class	−00.00	(00.01)	−00.02	−00.00	(00.01)	−00.02	−00.00	(00.01)	−00.02
Religiosity	−00.20	(00.02)	−00.03	−00.01	(00.02)	−00.01	−00.03	(00.02)	−00.05
Direct contact frequency	−00.11	(00.04)	−00.11**						
Direct contact evaluation	−00.52	(00.03)	−00.58***						
Socialization by persons				−00.66	(00.04)	−00.58***			
Socialization by mass media				−00.10	(00.05)	−00.07			
Self-esteem							−00.16	(00.04)	−00.14***
Patriotism							−00.05	(00.04)	−00.06
Nationalism							00.43	(00.03)	00.55***
Perception of economic threat									
Perception of safety threat									
Perception of value threat									
Clichés about Islam (negative)									
Stereotypes Muslims (negative)									
Anxiety									
Knowledge of Islam/Muslims									
R^2		00.50			00.45			00.38	

	Model 4			Model 5			Model 6		
	B	(SE)	β	B	(SE)	β	B	(SE)	β
(Constant)	0.10	(0.60)		01.36	(0.79)		0.96	(0.52)	
Gender (male)	0.35	(0.05)	0.20***	0.50	(0.07)	0.29***	0.17	(0.05)	0.10***
Age	0.08	(0.04)	0.06	0.15	(0.05)	0.11**	0.07	(0.03)	0.05*
Educational level	-0.02	(0.02)	-0.03	-0.04	(0.03)	-0.05	-0.00	(0.02)	-0.01
Social class	-0.00	(0.01)	-0.01	-0.01	(0.01)	-0.05	0.00	(0.01)	0.00
Religiosity	-0.02	(0.02)	-0.03	-0.03	(0.03)	-0.05	-0.01	(0.02)	-0.01
Direct contact frequency							0.03	(0.04)	0.02
Direct contact evaluation							-0.27	(0.03)	-0.30***
Socialization by persons							-0.27	(0.04)	-0.23***
Socialization by mass media							-0.08	(0.04)	-0.05
Self-esteem							-0.04	(0.03)	-0.03
Patriotism							-0.02	(0.03)	-0.02
Nationalism							0.11	(0.03)	0.14***
Perception of economic threat	0.07	(0.03)	0.09**				0.02	(0.02)	0.03
Perception of safety threat	0.19	(0.03)	0.26***				0.11	(0.02)	0.15***
Perception of value threat	0.26	(0.03)	0.32***				0.10	(0.03)	0.13***
Clichés about Islam (negative)	0.13	(0.09)	0.05				0.19	(0.08)	0.07*
Stereotypes Muslims (negative)	0.25	(0.11)	0.09*				0.03	(0.09)	0.01
Anxiety	0.17	(0.09)	0.07				0.06	(0.08)	0.03
Knowledge of Islam/Muslims				-0.16	(0.05)	-0.13**	-0.02	(0.03)	-0.02
R^2			0.51			0.13			0.68

Note
* $p < 00.05$;
** $p < 00.01$;
*** $p < 00.001$

which to study the socializing effect of politicians. Some politicians currently active in the Netherlands and in other countries voice a very negative attitude toward Islam and Muslims. Other possible explanatory variables are people's basic values and value hierarchy (Inglehart and Welzel 2005; Entzinger 2007). Furthermore, in future research we hope to involve various age groups, conduct the study in different countries – although Strabac and Listhaug found at most weak effects in their 2008 multilevel analyses of 'anti-Islam prejudice' – and add indirect or implicit measures for the variables (Park *et al.* 2007).

In the study described here data were collected simultaneously, which makes it impossible to establish a temporal sequence for the variables in question. The likely causal order of the variables has been reconstructed within a correlational design. Although this reconstruction was based on findings from previous studies and seems fairly plausible, we cannot be certain that the proposed relations are correct in terms of causality. In a future study involving a panel design and/or experiments we would like to check the causal relationships hypothesized here.

An interesting question is whether Islamophobia is a unique phenomenon or merely a new expression of xenophobia. Social identity theory provides reasons to expect members of the majority or dominant group to tend toward denigrating outgroups generally. To answer the question whether or not Islamophobia is a special case, we have to measure attitudes toward Islam and Muslims and attitudes toward other comparable religious-political-ideological outgroups – for example, Jews, Hindus, Buddhists and their religions – or outgroups in general – for example, 'foreigners', 'immigrants', or 'refugees' – compute the correlations between these attitudes, and analyze the similarities or differences in the explanatory models. A few studies have started to explore the field (Stolz 2005; Maher *et al.* 2008; Helbling 2010), and findings suggest that there are different levels of negative attitudes toward different outgroups, that there is a fairly high level of consensus within countries regarding the ranking of different groups in an 'ethnic hierarchy' (Hagendoorn 1995), and that predictors for negative attitudes toward different groups have different explanatory power.

Another important question is about the attitudes of Muslims toward non-Muslims. Sniderman and Hagendoorn studied mutual 'global evaluations' among both non-Muslims and Turkish and Moroccan Muslims in the Netherlands. Their conclusion was that Muslims in the Netherlands 'are as likely to dislike the Dutch as the Dutch are likely to dislike them' (Sniderman and Hagendoorn 2007: 26; see also Pew Research Center 2006). It is academically and socially relevant to find out whether Muslim attitudes toward non-Muslims can be explained by the same variables used to explain Islamophobia among non-Muslims.

Insights from our study and research by others may help political leaders and policy makers to design policies that will prevent further increases in unfounded negativity about Muslims among non-Muslims. Since direct contact has proven to be an important variable, these policies need to promote positive direct contact. Heterogeneous neighbourhoods and mixed schools facilitate contacts between Muslims and non-Muslims, and joint activities can contribute to more positively evaluated contacts. Recommendations for schools and teachers may be to motivate students to test the empirical evidence of the various clichés and threat perceptions, help students to reflect on their own Islam and Muslim socialization, and stimulate positive contacts between non-Muslim and Muslim students. More positive direct contacts together with a more balanced socialization at home, at school, and in the mass media, and a critical analysis of perceptions of safety and value threats from Islam and Muslims and negative clichés of Islam, are the main ingredients for a programme aiming at reducing Islamophobia.

Acknowledgements

The authors would like to thank the anonymous reviewers for their constructive comments and Ineke Smit for her proofreading.

Note

1   The data set, including the questionnaire, is available for secondary analyses and replication at the Data Archiving and Networked Services from the Royal Netherlands Academy of Arts and Sciences and the Netherlands Organisation for Scientific Research: http://easy.dans.knaw.nl/ui/datasets/id/easy-dataset:40201 under ID p1725.

9 The aftermath of 9/11

Tolerance toward Muslims, Islamophobia and value orientations

Jolanda van der Noll

Introduction

In recent decades, relations between Muslims and non-Muslims have been the subject of increased debate. Especially since the terrorist attacks of September 11, 2001 on the World Trade Center and the Pentagon in the United States, more attention has been paid to the negative attitudes toward Muslims held by non-Muslims. Several opinion polls conducted after the attacks showed that negative attitudes toward Muslims were widespread, especially in the Netherlands where a majority of the population (51 percent) indicated having a negative attitude toward Muslims, compared to 34 percent in France, 22 percent in the USA and only 14 percent in Great Britain (Pew Research Center 2005). In addition, a substantial part of the population believed that the culture and lifestyle of Muslims was incompatible with the Western way of life (Pew Research Center 2006; Sniderman and Hagendoorn 2007). Because the attacks of 9/11 were carried out by Muslims who had also been living in Western societies – the USA and Germany – it further was questioned to what extent Muslims should have the freedom to follow their own practices within Western societies.

The development of relations between Muslims and non-Muslims within Western societies will have a determining impact on the political and social cohesion of these societies. Muslims are the largest minority group in many Western societies (EUMC 2003), and to hamper Muslims' freedom to perform their own activities and follow their own way of life may cause major societal problems such as increased discrimination, marginalization, social isolation and radicalization of Muslims. Furthermore, despite the negative attitudes and beliefs one may have toward other groups, a well-functioning democratic society requires that the right to follow an own way of life and the accompanying practices be recognized and respected, as long as this does not encroach upon the limits of the democratic order (Sullivan and Transue 1999). It is therefore important to know what drives people to be willing to limit the – democratic – freedom of Muslims to follow their own practices.

In this chapter, I focus on explaining variation in the opinion on whether Muslims should have the freedom to follow their own practices in the Netherlands. Explanations are sought in a negative overall attitude toward Islam and Muslims (Islamophobia), value orientations and the impact of the 9/11 attacks.

Islamophobia

In public discourse, the term 'Islamophobia' is increasingly used to refer to the collection of negative attitudes and behaviors directed at Muslims and Islam. Some studies, following the initial conceptualization by the Runnymede Trust (1997), define Islamophobia as a hatred of Islam, as well as the practical consequences of this hatred, such as discrimination and exclusion of Muslim groups or individuals (EUMC 2003). This definition refers to a behavioral dimension of Islamophobia, which can be observed and measured relatively easily. It is more challenging, however, to measure Islamophobia as an attitude. Some scholars argue that Islamophobia entails a prejudice against Islam and Muslims (Stolz 2005; Zick *et al.* 2008; Van der Noll and Dekker 2010), but others use Islamophobia as an equivalent of a negative attitude toward Muslims (Halliday 1999; Brown 2000; Yalonios *et al.* 2005). Finally, some studies also include support for Muslims' rights and liberties, such as the building of mosques or the ability to follow their own religious rules (Cattacin *et al.* 2006; Bevelander and Otterbeck 2010).

I would like to argue that tolerance for Muslims is a related, yet different concept from Islamophobia. In my opinion, Islamophobia refers to the negative attitude toward Islam and Muslims, which can result in negative behavior or intolerance with respect to Islam and Muslims. For the concept of attitudes, I follow the one-dimensional interpretation of an attitude as 'a person's general feeling of favorableness or unfavorableness' (Ajzen and Fishbein 1980: 54). In tolerance research, the assumption is often made that supporting the rights and liberties of others only has relevance for those who have a negative attitude toward these others (Vogt 1997; Marcus *et al.* 1995). In line with this assumption, I expect that people who have a negative attitude toward Muslims will be more inclined to limit Muslims' freedom to perform their own activities than those who have a positive attitude toward Muslims.

However, in contrast to this assumption, several studies have shown that although people have indicated having a positive attitude toward an outgroup, they are still reluctant to grant this outgroup the same rights and liberties as the majority population (Sniderman and Hagendoorn 2007; Van der Noll *et al.* 2010). Studies have found moderate associations between the two concepts at best and show that between 10 and 20 percent of the people with a positive attitude do not support the rights and liberties of these others (McIntosh *et al.* 1995; Saroglou *et al.* 2009; Van der Noll *et al.* 2010). This relationship is therefore not unambiguous. Following these studies, I expect that there will be a substantial amount of people with a positive attitude toward Muslims who are opposed to Muslims' freedom to follow their own practices.

Value orientations

The issue of tolerating dissenting beliefs and practices is not only related to intergroup attitudes, but also to ideas about what society should look like. Value orientations are more abstract than attitudes; value orientations focus on ideals, whereas attitudes refer to more concrete objects. Values can be defined as 'enduring beliefs that a specific mode of conduct is personally or socially preferable to an opposite or converse mode of conduct or end state of existence' (Rokeach 1973: 5). Values can give meaning to actions and are used as a standard against which behavior, from others or oneself, can be judged (Hitlin and Piliavin 2004). As such, value orientations can play an important role in explaining attitudes and tolerance toward outgroups.

One set of value orientations that is clearly linked toward intergroup attitudes is multiculturalism; the more abstract belief that a culturally diverse society is desirable and that all cultural groups should be treated with respect and as equals. Multiculturalism encourages maintenance of minority identities and cultures (Fowers and Richardson 1996;Verkuyten 2005; Berry 2006). Several studies have indicated that people who adhere more to multiculturalism are less negative and more tolerant toward outgroups (Verkuyten 2005;Ward and Masgoret 2006;Velasco González *et al.* 2008; Van der Noll *et al.* 2010). In line with previous studies, it is expected that multiculturalism is positively associated with attitudes toward Muslims and support for Muslims' freedom to perform their own activities.

It is, however, not only value orientations related to cultural diversity that can be expected to influence attitudes toward and support for outgroups. Theories of symbolic racism argue that aversion toward outgroups does not, as with traditional racism, stem from a belief in the − biological − superiority of the own group, but rather finds its origins in a perceived clash between the society's traditional values and those of outgroups (Kleinpenning and Hagendoorn 1993; Sears and Henry 2003). People who adhere more to conservative values are found to be less positive and less likely to respect and support equal rights for outgroups (Biernat *et al.* 1996; Stolz 2005; Saroglou *et al.* 2009). Opposite to these conservative values of traditionalism and conformity are self-expression or emancipative values, which emphasize individual choice rather than the subjection of individual autonomy to community discipline (Welzel *et al.* 2003: 342). A stronger orientation toward emancipative values entails an emphasis on individual liberty and freedoms. People who emphasize their own liberty are more likely to respect and support the liberty of others and are more likely to be tolerant of diversity (Welzel *et al.* 2003; Helbling 2010). It is therefore expected that there is a positive relation between the strength of emancipative values and the support for the freedom of Muslims to perform their activities.

Based on the assumption in tolerance research that granting rights and liberties to others is only an issue among those with a negative attitude toward these others (Marcus *et al.* 1995;Vogt 1997), I expect that the impact of value orientations on support depends on the overall attitude toward Muslims, and that the endorsement of multiculturalism or emancipative values will have a stronger effect on the level of support among those with a negative attitude toward Muslims. For those with a positive attitude toward the outgroup, tolerating and granting equal rights and liberties is the natural predisposition, whereas people with a negative attitude need additional justifications for granting these rights and will therefore rely more on their value orientations.

Value orientations play an important role in explaining tolerance judgements (Sullivan and Transue 1999; Saroglou *et al.* 2009;Van der Noll *et al.* 2010) as well as in explaining overall intergroup attitudes (Stolz 2005;Velasco González *et al.* 2008).

Since both concepts are often studied independently, it is unknown to what extent value orientations have an independent influence on tolerance, or whether it is mainly an indirect effect mediated by the overall attitude toward the outgroup. It is expected that, next to direct effects, stronger multiculturalism and emphasized emancipative values improve attitudes toward Muslims, which in turn leads to more support for Muslims' freedom to perform their own practices.

The effect of 9/11

The debate about relations between Muslims and non-Muslims, and about the attitudes and beliefs these groups have toward one another intensified after the attacks on the World Trade Center and the Pentagon by Islamic extremists. Studies have shown that, after the attacks, Muslims and Islam in European societies have increasingly been the targets of verbal harassments, physical attacks and negative media coverage (Larsson 2005; EUMC 2006). It is more problematic to determine how attitudes toward Muslims and Islam have been affected by the terrorist attacks. A 2002 opinion poll in the Netherlands revealed that more than half of the respondents had changed their opinion about Muslims since the attacks. Furthermore, 95 percent of these respondents indicated that their opinion had become worse (Nieuwenhuizen and Visser 2005). However, this was based on self-reports, and little empirical information on how the attitude is affected by 9/11 is available. Furthermore, despite the common notion that the attacks of 9/11 had a decisive impact on the deterioration of attitudes and beliefs toward Islam and Muslims, several studies showed that, even before 9/11, Muslims were generally evaluated more negatively than immigrants in general (Stolz 2005; Sniderman and Hagendoorn 2007; Strabac and Listhaug 2008), and that mass media reports about Muslims and Islam were predominantly characterized by negative content (Larsson 2005; Vercauteren 2005). An impact of 9/11 on attitudes and tolerance toward Muslims has been found on the aggregate level. Fetzer and Soper (2003), for instance, found a decline in public support for the accommodation of Muslims' religious needs in several Western countries. However, other studies showed that 9/11 caused a short disruption, after which the mean level of attitudes toward Muslims returned to their pre-9/11 level (Kalkan *et al.* 2009). It is expected that we will find the same pattern in the present study; attitudes toward Muslims and support for the freedom of Muslims to perform their own activities will have deteriorated between 2000 and 2002, but are expected to have recovered for the most part by 2004. There are no *a priori* expectations that the relations between support, the overall attitude and value orientations differ across the years.

At the individual level, there are no studies that empirically examine the impact of 9/11 on attitudes and tolerance toward Muslims. To test the impact of the attacks, studies generally compare cross-sectional survey waves conducted before and after the attacks. This is problematic because differences cannot solely be attributed to the attacks. To overcome this deficit, in addition to a comparison of survey waves, this study includes an individual measure of whether people feel concerned about the attacks. I expect that people who felt more concerned about the attacks of 9/11 will have a more negative attitude toward Muslims and a lower level of support for Muslims' freedom to follow their own practices.

Methods

Sample

The data have been collected by the Netherlands Institute for Social Research (SCP) as part of the cross-sectional *Culturele Veranderingen in Nederland* (Cultural Changes in the Netherlands) surveys that aim at measuring the changing opinions of the Dutch population. The survey program started in 1975 and is conducted biannually. The present study involves the analysis of data from 2000, 2002 and 2004.[1] During the fieldwork in 2000 and 2002, there were no major incidents that could have influenced the responses of the survey. In 2004, however, the Dutch film director Theo van Gogh was murdered by an Islamic extremist during the period of fieldwork. Inspection of the interview dates revealed that only three interviews were conducted after the murder (November 2) and were subsequently omitted from the analyses. In addition, respondents who considered themselves Muslim were omitted from the analyses. This resulted in sample sizes of 1,548 (2000), 1,891 (2002) and 2,193 (2004) respondents.

Measures

The dependent variable, *support for the freedom of Muslims to perform their own activities*, was introduced as follows: 'There are various religious streams in our society. For each of these streams, I would like to know from you to what extent, in your opinion, they should have the freedom to perform their own activities.' The answers were on a four-point scale ranging from 'completely free' (1) to 'not free at all' (4). The religious streams not only included Muslims, but also Catholics, Protestants, Jehovah's Witnesses and 'various other streams'. The items were recoded and a higher score indicates more support.

Islamophobia was measured by means of a single question concerning the overall attitude toward immigrant groups. The question reads 'What is your overall attitude toward immigrant groups in our society, such as Turks, Moroccans and Surinamese? Positive, negative, or neither positive nor negative?' Despite the fact that this question does not specifically ask for the attitude toward Muslims, I presume that most people had Muslims on their mind while answering this question. Opinion polls have shown that the concepts of immigrants and Muslims are increasingly used interchangeably (Nieuwenhuizen and Visser 2005). This is not surprising, because Turks and Moroccans are by far the largest immigrant groups in the Netherlands and large majorities of the Turks (87 percent) and Moroccans (92 percent) identify themselves as Muslim. Surinamese constitute the third largest immigrant group and although only 10 percent of Surinamese are Muslim, they represent the third largest Muslim minority group in the Netherlands (Forum 2010: 7). The single question is a rather limited operationalization of the concept of Islamophobia, but it is the only possibility with these surveys to achieve an identical operationalization across different years. The item was recoded to a three point scale of having a negative attitude (0), a neutral attitude (0.5) or a positive attitude (1).

To construct a composite measure for the value orientation of *multiculturalism*, three items were selected that touch upon cultural diversity and were asked in all years. The first item reads 'What do you think of the number of people with different nationalities that live in our country? Are there too many, many but not too many, or not many at all?' The answers were recoded into a dummy variable with 0 indicating too many with a different nationality, and 1 indicating that there are not too many or not many at all. The other items are 'The settlement of immigrants in the Netherlands is not only a problem, but also an enrichment of the society' and 'Foreigners should not hold strongly to their own culture and habits'. Both statements were rated on a five-point scale ranging from 'strongly agree' to 'strongly disagree'. The items have been recoded with 0 indicating the weakest and 1 the strongest support for cultural diversity. The three items are internally consistent ($\alpha > .61$) and are averaged into one scale with a higher score indicating a stronger endorsement of multiculturalism.

Screening the questionnaires for items that represent *emancipative* values identified two groups of items that emphasize freedom of expression or equality of opportunity. The first set of items addressed the equal opportunities and read as follows: 'If you have to choose between different families or persons, who, in times of housing shortage, should receive a newly available house?'; 'Assume that there are two employees, who differ on one point but are equal on all other aspects. When one of them has to get fired because it is not going well with the company, who should that be?' and '[....] When only one of them can be offered a promotion, who should that be?' In all three items the respondents had the choice between a foreigner and a native Dutchman. Dummy variables were created with 1 indicating that there should be no difference. Because the items address a choice between a foreigner and a native Dutchman, there is the risk that they are closely related to the dependent variable. However, correlations with attitude toward Muslims and support for the freedom of Muslims to perform their own activities were weak ($< .36$). Therefore, I suspect no problems with including these items as an aspect of emancipative values.

In addition, three items referred to equal opportunities in terms of gender, but were only part of the surveys in 2002 and 2004. These items read 'Women are more qualified to raise little children than men'; 'Men and women should equally divide household tasks'; and 'Men and women should equally divide paid labor'. All items had to be answered using a five-point scale ranging from 'strongly agree' to 'strongly disagree'. The items were recoded to a scale where a higher score indicates a stronger focus on equality. The items formed a reliable scale ($\alpha = .82$, for the three items in 2000 and $\alpha > .60$ for the six items in 2002 and 2004).

The second group of items emphasized the freedom of expression. Respondents were asked to give their first and second priority for what should be done in the Netherlands choosing between 'maintaining order'; 'giving people more say in government decisions'; 'fighting inflation'; and 'protecting freedom of speech'. Prioritising 'giving people more say in government decisions' and 'protecting freedom of speech' are indicators of the freedom of expression component of emancipative values. A four-point scale was constructed by assigning 1 point (maximum score) for both items on the first and second rank, 0.67 points for one of these items on the first rank, 0.33 points for one of these items on the second rank and 0 for none of these items as either the first or second priority. In addition, respondents were asked about local government: 'The extent to which people have a say in local government should be (much) bigger or (much) smaller.' The answers from the five-point scale were recoded to a scale ranging from 0 to 1, with 1 representing a stronger focus on expression. The scores on the subscales of equality and expression were averaged in an overall index of emancipative values, ranging from 0 for the strongest rejection to 1 for the strongest support of emancipative values.

To measure the *concern about 9/11*, respondents in 2002 were asked to indicate their concern about a number of incidents that had happened over the past years. The question was introduced as follows: 'To what extent do you feel personally concerned about a number of shocking incidents that have happened in the last couple of years. Can you indicate that for the following incidents?' and continued with 'September 11, 2001 (the attacks on the Twin Towers in New York and the Pentagon)' and other major national incidents. Respondents could indicate whether they felt 'very concerned'; 'concerned'; 'not concerned'; 'not concerned at all'; or 'has in the end made no impression on me'. The answers were recoded into a scale with a higher score indicating stronger concerns about 9/11.

Background variables include gender, age, years of education, income and religiosity.

Analyses

Analysis of variance with Scheffé's post-hoc comparison was used to identify differences across the years in the level of support for Muslims' freedom to perform their own activities and other variables. Analysis of variance is preferred because general mean comparisons between the years would inflate the risk of falsely rejecting the null hypotheses (Type I error). Scheffé's post-hoc comparison is one of the more conservative methods and was used to locate the significant differences between the years. Bivariate correlations (Pearson's r) were calculated to examine the associations between support for Muslims' freedom and the selected predictor variables.

Regression analyses were conducted to examine to what extent Islamophobia, value orientations and 9/11 explain variation in support for Muslims' freedom. The confidence intervals of the obtained coefficients were compared to see if there were differences in the strength of the effects between the years. Missing values among the predictor variables did not exceed 2 percent of the sample size and were excluded via list-wise deletion. To control whether there were problems of multi-collinearity between the independent variables, the variance inflation factors (VIF) were checked. These did not exceed the value of 2, indicating that multicollinearity was not a problematic issue among these variables.

Results

Descriptives

A majority of the respondents in 2000 (58 percent) and 2004 (51 percent) fully agreed that *Muslims should have the freedom to perform their own activities* (Table 9.1). As expected, the support was considerably lower in 2002, with only 31 percent of the respondents giving this response. The rejection of Muslims' freedom to perform their activities doubled from 7 percent in 2000 to 15 percent in 2002. In 2004, 12 percent of the respondents rejected Muslims' freedom. Analysis of variance with Scheffé's post-hoc comparisons showed that the mean level of support significantly differed between all years (2000: $M = .76$, $SD = .32$; 2002: $M = .60$, $SD = .35$; 2004: $M = .70$, $SD = .36$, and F $(2, 5632) = 99.78$, $p < .001$, $\eta^2 = .03$), but the substantial differences were rather small. Muslims' freedom received significantly less support than Catholics' and Protestants' freedom (over all years: $t (5603) = -48.53$, $p <.001$, $r =.30$).

In 2000, 16 percent of the respondents indicated having a negative attitude toward Muslims, a majority (61 percent) was neither positive, nor negative, and almost one-fourth had a positive overall attitude toward Muslims. In line with the expectations, the attitude toward Muslims deteriorated in 2002. In 2004, the percentage of people with a negative attitude stabilized at around one-fifth of the respondents. There was a slight increase, though, in the number of people with a positive attitude toward Muslims (20 percent). Despite statistically significant differences, the differences over time in the attitude toward Muslims were small (F $(2, 5586) = 15.94$, $p < .001$, $\eta^2 = .006$).

Table 9.1 Descriptive information support for Muslims' freedom to perform their own activities, overall attitude toward Muslims and concern about the 9/11 attacks (percentages)

		2000	*2002*	*2004*
Muslims should have the freedom to perform their own activities	Not at all	7.2	14.6	11.7
	Slightly	14.9	22.2	17.0
	Considerable	20.3	32.1	20.7
	Completely	57.6	31.1	50.7
	Total (N)	100 (1548)	100 (1891)	100 (2193)
Attitude toward Muslims	Negative	15.9	21.7	20.9
	Neutral	60.9	61.4	58.2
	Positive	23.3	16.9	20.9
	Total (N)	100 (1548)	100 (1891)	100 (2147)
Concerned about 9/11 attacks	Made no impression		0.6	
	Not concerned at all		2.5	
	Not concerned		15.7	
	Concerned		57.1	
	Very concerned		24.0	
	Total (N)		100 (1884)	

Supporting the rights and liberties of others is often considered only an issue for those who have a negative attitude toward these others. However, the results show that a substantial proportion of people with a neutral or positive attitude toward Muslims were also reluctant to give full or considerable support to the statement that Muslims should have the freedom to perform their activities (Table 9.2). In 2000, 12 percent of the respondents with a positive attitude toward Muslims and one-fifth of those with a neutral attitude, did not support, or only slightly supported this statement. In 2002 this percentage almost doubled (21 percent) for those with a positive attitude. The correlations between support for Muslims' freedom and the attitude toward Muslims were weak (r < .32, p <.001). These results support the expectation that tolerance toward Muslims is distinct from the overall attitude toward Muslims.

On average, the majority of the respondents in all years seemed to be slightly opposed to a cultural diverse society and this has been stable during the years (2000: M = .44, SD = .28; 2002: M = .45, SD = .27; 2004: M = .47, SD = .27, and F (2, 5627) = 5.57, p = .004, η^2 = .002). In line with previous research, it was found that people who were stronger supporters of multiculturalism were more likely to have a positive attitude toward Muslims (r < .52, p < .001) and to support the freedom of Muslims to perform their own activities (r < .40, p < .001).

The endorsement of emancipative values has also been stable during the years (2000: M = .56, SD = .21; 2002: M = .53, SD = .15; 2004: M = .52, SD = .16, and F (2, 5632) = 17.4, p < .001, η^2 = .006). A stronger endorsement of emancipative values was positively associated with the attitude toward Muslims (r < .33, p < .001) and with support for Muslims' freedom (r < .23, p < .001).

Finally, when the respondents were asked how they looked back at the 9/11 attacks on the World Trade Center and the Pentagon, the majority of the respondents indicated that they felt concerned (57 percent) or very concerned (24 percent) about the attacks (Table 9.1). The concern about the attacks of 9/11 was considerably higher than concerns about other, national, events such as the assassination of Pim Fortuyn (May 6, 2002), and the tragic New Year's Eve café fire in Volendam (January 1, 2001), which concerned approximately 75 percent of the respondents. Despite the deep-felt concerns, it did not have an impact on the overall attitude toward Muslims (r = .05, *ns*), nor did it seem to be associated with support for Muslims' freedom (r = .02, *ns*).

Table 9.2 Muslims should not/only slightly have the freedom to perform their activities (percentages within negative, neutral or positive attitude toward Muslims)

	Negative attitude	Neutral attitude	Positive attitude	Total
2000	43.9	20.3	11.6	22.1
2002	65.1	30.2	20.7	36.8
2004	49.3	26.3	14.9	28.7

Explanation

The endorsement of multiculturalism, attitude toward Muslims, age, and (in 2002 and 2004) the endorsement of emancipative values were significant predictors of the level of support (Table 9.3). A stronger endorsement of multiculturalism increased support for the freedom of Muslims to follow their own practices. In line with the expectation that people with a negative attitude toward Muslims rely more on their value orientations, the effect of multiculturalism was stronger among those with a negative attitude toward Muslims (in 2000: $\beta_{negative}$ = .38, $\beta_{positive}$ = .19, ps < .001). Considered independently, a more positive attitude toward Muslims also increased the level of support (β = .30, p < .001). The strength of the effect of multiculturalism and Islamophobia on the level of support did not differ across time.

In 2002 and 2004, more emphasis on emancipative values was related to an increase in support for Muslims' freedom to follow their own practices (β = .12 and β = .13, ps < .001 respectively).[2] Although the effect was not significant in 2000, the 95 percent confidence intervals of the coefficients overlap, indicating that the size of the effect does not significantly differ between the years. In contrast to the expectations, the results of 2002 do not reveal a significant effect between feeling concerned about 9/11 and the level of support for Muslims' freedom to follow their own practices.

To test whether the overall attitude toward Muslims mediated the effect of multicultural and emancipative values on support for the freedom of Muslims, regression analyses were repeated without the attitude toward Muslims as a predictor variable, and additional regression analyses with the attitude toward Muslims as the dependent variable were conducted. Results showed that the attitude toward Muslims was positively affected by a stronger endorsement of multiculturalism and emancipative values (β > .40 and β > .13, ps < .001 respectively). The effects of multicultural and emancipative value orientations on the support for Muslims' freedom were, however, only weakly affected by the removal of the overall attitude from the model. Furthermore, although significant, the indirect effects of multiculturalism and emancipative value orientations via the overall attitude toward Muslims were very weak (β = .06, and β = .02, ps < .001 respectively). This indicates that value orientations mainly have a distinct effect on attitudes and tolerance judgement and further supports the expectation that attitudes and tolerance are different concepts.

Conclusion and discussion

This study examined how support for Muslims' freedom to follow their own practices changed in the years following the attacks of 9/11, and how it was related to Islamophobia, multicultural and emancipative value orientations, and concerns about the attacks of 9/11.

The results show that, on average, there is considerable support for the freedom of Muslims to perform their activities. Nevertheless, in all years, the support for the freedom of Muslims is significantly lower than that for the freedom of Catholics and Protestants. The level of support for Muslims decreased significantly between

Table 9.3 Results of regression analyses support for Muslims' freedom to perform own activities

	2000 (N = 1328)				2002 (N = 1549)				2004 (N = 2146)			
	B	(SE)	Beta	95 % CO.IO. B	B	(SE)	Beta	95 % CO.IO. B	B	(SE)	Beta	95 % CO.IO. B
(Constant)	0.35	(0.05)	—	0.25 −0.46	0.12	(0.06)	—	0.01 −0.23	0.30	(0.05)	—	0.21 −0.39
Gender (male)	0.01	(0.02)	0.01	−0.03 −0.04	0.02	(0.02)	0.03	−0.01 −0.05	0.02	(0.02)	0.03	−0.01 −0.05
Age	0.00	(0.00)	0.12***	0.00 −0.00	0.00	(0.00)	0.07**	0.00 −0.00	0.00	(0.00)	0.06**	0.00 −0.00
Education	0.00	(0.00)	0.00	−0.00 −0.01	0.00	(0.00)	0.02	−0.00 −0.01	−0.00	(0.00)	−0.01	−0.00 −0.00
Income	−0.03	(0.02)	−0.04	−0.07 −0.01	−0.01	(0.02)	−0.01	−0.05 −0.03	−0.01	(0.02)	−0.01	−0.05 −0.03
Religiosity	−0.05	(0.03)	−0.05	−0.10 −0.01	0.02	(0.03)	0.02	−0.03 −0.07	−0.00	(0.02)	−0.00	−0.05 −0.04
Positive attitude	0.30	(0.08)	0.29***	0.16 −0.45	0.33	(0.07)	0.30***	0.19 −0.48	0.31	(0.06)	0.28***	0.19 −0.43
Multiculturalism	0.43	(0.07)	0.38***	0.30 −0.56	0.49	(0.06)	0.40***	0.37 −0.61	0.36	(0.06)	0.27***	0.25 −0.47
Emancipative val.	0.10	(0.08)	0.07	−0.05 −0.26	0.20	(0.07)	0.12**	0.06 −0.33	0.21	(0.06)	0.13***	0.08 −0.33
Concern about 9/11	—	—	—	—	−0.01	(0.04)	−0.01	−0.09 −0.07	—	—	—	—
Multiculturalism positive attitude*	−0.24	(0.10)	−0.19*	−0.44 −0.03	−0.21	(0.11)	−0.15*	−0.42 −0.01	−0.16	(0.09)	−0.12	−0.34 −0.01
Emancipative val. positive attitude*	−0.08	(0.13)	−0.06	−0.34 −0.18	−0.15	(0.13)	−0.10	−0.41 −0.11	−0.14	(0.11)	−0.09	−0.34 −0.07
R²	0.16				0.21				0.13			

Notes
* $p < .05$;
** $p < .01$;
*** $p < .001$.

2000 and 2002 and there was still significantly less support for Muslims' freedom in 2004 compared with 2000. Unfortunately, the question about support for the freedom of activities for the various religious streams within the Dutch society was no longer included in the surveys after 2004, making a comparison over a longer period of time with these data impossible.

Although the results show that there was a decline in support in 2002 at the aggregate level, which might be due to the attacks of 9/11, results at the individual level do not support this expectation. Feeling concerned about the attacks was not significantly related to support for the freedom of Muslims to perform their activities, nor was it related to Islamophobia. This can be for several reasons. First of all, based on the available data, it is not possible to reveal *why* respondents are concerned about the attacks of 9/11. For some, concerns about the attacks can be based on a concern about Islamic extremism, violence and fear for further attacks, which is likely to be related to negative and intolerant attitudes, whereas others could be concerned about the consequences of the attacks of 9/11 for society and the position of Muslims. It is plausible that the effect of being concerned about 9/11 depends on the reasons why someone is concerned. Second, the debate about Islam and Muslims in Dutch society had already become more prominent before the attacks of 9/11. Pim Fortuyn, who was running for parliament elections before he was assassinated on May 6, 2002, published a book titled *Against the Islamization of our culture* (1997, revised version 2001), called Islam a 'backward religion' in an interview (*Rotterdams Dagblad* August 28, 2001) and claimed that the influx of Muslims threatened the liberal Dutch culture. It is likely that the evolution of this debate also contributed to the decline in support for the freedom of Muslims' to perform their own activities between 2000 and 2002. Finally, the lack of results could have a technical reason and be due to the small variation in the extent to which people felt concerned at the attacks: a majority of 81 percent indicated that they felt (very) concerned. However, a comparison between respondents who felt 'concerned' and who felt 'very concerned' also failed to reveal significant differences in attitudes or tolerance. This leads to the conclusion that substantial, rather than technical reasons are responsible for the lack of association.

I suggested that the concept of Islamophobia is different from supporting the rights and liberties of Muslims. The results support this assumption; the correlation between the two concepts is weak and they do not share more than 10 percent of their variance. Furthermore, multiculturalism and, to a lesser extent, emancipative values have been shown to have distinct effects on the attitude and the level of support. Nevertheless, the overall attitude toward Muslims is an important predictor; people with a more negative attitude toward Muslims are less likely to support Muslims' freedom. The strongest predictor of support is multiculturalism; a stronger endorsement of multiculturalism is, especially among those with a negative attitude toward Muslims, related to a higher level of support for Muslims' freedom. The hypothesis that people with a more negative attitude rely more on their multicultural value orientations than people with a positive attitude toward Muslims is supported by the results. Finally, a stronger emphasis on equality and liberty – emancipative values – also contributed to the explanation of support for Muslims' freedom, but did not depend on the attitude toward Muslims.

The model developed in this chapter does not explain much of the variance in the support for the freedom of Muslims to follow their own practices and implies that important predictors are missing. The debate about Muslims in western societies is often focused on whether Islam and Muslims are a threat to the Western societies' values and lifestyles. Future studies would benefit from the inclusion of measures that focus on perceived threat as a predictor variable (see for instance Riek *et al.* 2006).

This study shows that the effects of value orientations and Islamophobia on tolerance are strong and stable predictors of support. Despite popular notions, events such as the 9/11 attacks do not seem to have a decisive impact on relations between Muslims and non-Muslims. Furthermore, the study shows that regardless of the overall attitude toward Muslims, the endorsement of values related to cultural diversity, equality and individual freedoms are important predictors of tolerance. This underlines that tolerance is about more than intergroup relations and the prejudice against one outgroup.

Notes

1 The datasets can be obtained from the Data Archiving Networked Services (DANS) from the Netherlands Organization for Scientific Research at http://easy.dans.knaw.nl/dms under identifiers p1525 (2000), p1624 (2002) and p1692 (2004).

2 Regression analyses including the same scale of emancipative values in all years yield similar results; emancipative values have no significant effect in 2000, but there is a positive relation between the endorsement of emancipative values and the support for Muslims' freedom to perform their own activities in 2002 ($\beta = .12, p < .01$) and 2004 ($\beta = .13, p < .001$).

10 Political tolerance for Muslim practices

An intergroup perspective

Maykel Verkuyten and Edwin Poppe

Should Muslim teachers be allowed to refuse to shake hands with children's parents of the opposite sex? Should all images of pigs be banned from pictures in public offices because these might offend Muslims' feelings? Should new mosques and minarets be allowed to be being built and Islamic schools established? Should Islamic holidays be introduced as national public holidays in addition to Christian ones? Should civil servants be permitted to wear a headscarf? In European countries, it is around these concrete questions that cultural and religious diversity is put to the test and ways of life collide. Islam has moved to the center of public and political debates in Europe and is at the heart of what is perceived as a 'crisis of multiculturalism' (Modood and Ahmad 2007). Therefore, it is important to focus on how people respond to these kinds of practices that mark and symbolize Muslim identities within the deeply embedded Christianity and secularism of most European countries.

Historically, the concept of tolerance evolved from efforts to deal with the harmful and violent effects of religious conflicts (Walzer 1997). The presence of an increasing number of Muslims in Western European countries has given a renewed urgency to the idea of tolerance as a mechanism for dealing with diversity. In this chapter we use an intergroup perspective and focus on tolerance of Muslim practices in the context of Western Europe, and the Netherlands in particular. This context is important because the situation of Muslims in Europe is not only quite different from that of, for example, the Muslim population in North America (Pew Research Centre 2005), but there are also clear differences within Europe. For instance, most Muslims in Western Europe came as immigrants, whereas some Eastern and South-Eastern European countries are home to significant numbers of non-immigrant Muslims.

In the Netherlands, leading politicians have taken a strong negative position on Islam, defining it as a backward religion that seriously threatens Dutch society, and national identity and culture (Vasta 2007; Verkuyten and Zaremba 2005). Furthermore, the Dutch media, and in particular the five most frequently read Dutch newspapers, predominantly frame Islam as a threat to Western values (Roggebrand and Vliegenthart 2007). In 2005, the Pew Global Project indicated that 51 percent of Dutch participants had unfavourable opinions about Muslims. This was the highest percentage of all the countries examined. In France, for example, the percentage was 36 and in Great Britain it was 14. Further, the Dutch majority considers particular practices of Muslims morally wrong and a nationwide survey showed that 50 percent of Dutch people consider the Western and Muslim ways of life as opposites that do not go together (Gijsberts 2005).

The intergroup perspective of this chapter entails that political tolerance for Muslim practices is examined in relation to prejudice, group threats and national identity. We will discuss our empirical studies in which we applied insights from major social psychological theories on intergroup relations, such as social identity theory and integrated threat theory, in order to understand tolerance for Muslim practices. First we will discuss the distinction and relationship between tolerance and prejudice. Subsequently we will address the complexity of tolerance by focusing on the social reasoning behind tolerance judgments. Then we will discuss outgroup threat and national identity as two key intergroup factors underlying tolerance of Muslim practices.

Tolerance and prejudice

Tolerance can be conceptualized in various ways, such as valuing and celebrating difference, a generalized positive attitude toward outgroups, the absence of prejudice, the willingness to accept civic rights and cultural practices for disliked groups, or the 'putting up' with others. We are concerned here with the latter meaning of tolerance, which is a key condition for citizenship and democracy (Sullivan and Transue 1999). Tolerance of dissenting practices is a separate construct that emphasizes forbearance and not begrudging other people their civil liberties. Tolerance is an option when one dislikes something or someone and is the opposite of discrimination; when one endures or refrains from action although other's beliefs and practices may be disapproved of or rejected.

Theoretically, the focus on political tolerance allows for an examination of its difference with prejudice. According to Gibson (2006: 26) this is 'one of the most important tasks of future research'. Most often, the expectation is that both are closely connected because they are grounded, for example, in personal attributes such as authoritarianism (Altemeyer 1988) or social dominance (Sidanius and Pratto 1999). However, the conceptual distinction implies that it should be possible that prejudiced attitudes go together with tolerance.

Furthermore, intolerance can have other bases than outgroup dislike. A generalized positive attitude toward Muslims does not have to imply the acceptance of specific practices of Muslims. For example, positive affect toward Muslims does not have to mean that one accepts practices that go against operative public norms that govern civic relations between people (Parekh, 2000), such as civil servants wearing a burka or a niqab, or refusing to shake hands with citizens of the opposite sex. Principled conservatism and humanistic values rather than prejudice can underlie the opposition to specific practices of minority groups (Sniderman and Piazza 1993).

In a survey study of native Dutch adolescents (N = 380) tolerance was examined in terms of the willingness to accept a Muslim teacher and to accept a Muslim giving a public speech at one's school (Van der Noll *et al.* 2010). It turned out that almost a third of the participants had a prejudicial attitude toward Muslims but also accepted the Muslim teacher and the public speech. Furthermore, there were participants (12.5 percent) with a positive attitude toward Muslims and who gave intolerant answers to the two cases (see also Sniderman and Hagendoorn 2007). In another study among Dutch adolescents (N = 322) similar results were found with 36 percent having a prejudicial attitude toward Muslims but also accepting Muslims being actively involved in their school.

These results indicate that prejudice toward Muslims and intolerance of public activities by members of this group are relatively distinct. Generalized negative affect toward Muslims does not necessarily imply the rejection of specific practices, and a neutral or generalized positive affect does not have to imply an unconditional acceptance of actions and behaviors. The empirical distinction between prejudice and political tolerance has also been found in other studies (for example, Gibson and Gouws 2003). It indicates that research on Islamophobia should not only focus on negative evaluations and feelings toward Muslims but should also consider when and why people tolerate specific practices of Muslims.

However, an empirical distinction between prejudice and tolerance does not have to imply that the underlying determinants differ. For example, research has shown that personality characteristics such as dogmatism and authoritarianism underlie intolerance as well as prejudice (Duckitt 1992; Marcus *et al.* 1995; Vogt 1997). However, factors such as political expertise, political participation and commitment to democratic values seem to be more important for tolerance than for prejudice (Sullivan and Transue 1999). In addition, the perception that societal safety is threatened by Muslims is important for intolerance of Muslim practices among prejudiced individuals but not among individuals who do not have negative feelings toward Muslims (Van der Noll *et al.* 2010).

Social reasoning

To tolerate is to allow, but this does not imply a refusal to judge and that nothing can be affirmed. Tolerance is not relativism or an unconditional acceptance of difference. Developmental and political science research has shown that tolerance is not a global construct. Tolerance depends on which people are asked to tolerate dissenting beliefs and practices, and when they are asked to do so (McClosky and Brill 1983; Vogt 2007). For example, Wainryb *et al.* (1998) found that adolescents were more tolerant of beliefs and practices based on dissenting information than dissenting moral values. The same has been found in a study among native Dutch adolescents' tolerant judgments of Muslims' political rights and dissenting beliefs and practices (Verkuyten and Slooter 2007). Participants took into account various aspects of what they were asked to tolerate and the sense in which they should be tolerant. The nature and the social implication of the behavior, and the underlying belief type, all made a difference to the tolerant judgments. For example, the level of tolerance was lower when the social implications were greater, and participants were more tolerant of practices based on dissenting cultural beliefs than on dissenting moral beliefs.

Furthermore, accepting that people hold dissenting beliefs does not have to imply that one tolerates the public expression of such beliefs or the actual practices based on such beliefs (Vogt 1997). These dimensions of tolerance can trigger different levels of acceptance. Wainryb and colleagues (1998) found, for example, that European American children and early adolescents were more tolerant of dissenting speech than practices. Similarly, Verkuyten and Slooter (2007) found that Dutch adolescents were more tolerant of Muslim parents publicly arguing for differential gender treatment of children or for a very light form of female circumcision (sunna) than for the actual acts themselves. This higher acceptance of the public expression of the dissenting beliefs is consistent with the idea of freedom of speech. It can be seen as a stimulating debate, which is important for the democratic process, and as causing less direct harm or injustice than the actual acts.

However, higher acceptance of public expressions of beliefs, compared to the actual practices based upon these beliefs, depends on the intergroup context. Specifically, Muslims trying to persuade co-believers to engage in a dissenting practice can be perceived as a threat to the in-group by the majority group. In one study (Gieling *et al.* 2010), we examined native Dutch adolescents perceptions of four concrete cases of specific practices that are not illegal but that are hotly debated in Dutch society: the wearing of a headscarf by Muslim women; the refusal of female Muslim teachers to shake hands with males; the founding of separate Islamic schools; and the public expression of the view that homosexuals are inferior people by an imam. We focused not only on the participants' tolerance of these practices but also on their acceptance of people trying to mobilize other Muslims. Participants were asked whether it should be allowed that different Muslim actors campaign to try to convince others to do the same thing. This social mobilization of Muslims is typically seen as threatening to Dutch identity and culture (Velasco González *et al.* 2008; Sniderman and Hagendoorn 2007) and therefore the participants were expected to be less tolerant of Muslims campaigning for co-believers' support for the particular practice than of the actual practice itself. The findings clearly showed this to be the case. Campaigning for support and persuading others implies mobilizing Muslims, for example, to start wearing a headscarf, to stop shaking hands with people of the opposite sex, and to found more Islamic schools. Politicians and the media tend to present these practices as 'backward' and as threatening Dutch identity and culture (Roggebrand and Vliegenthart 2007; Vasta 2007). They would undermine the secular and Christian traditions of the Netherlands. Trying to persuade other Muslims to act similarly is seen as contributing to the 'Islamization of Dutch society' and therefore leads to lower acceptance compared to the act itself.

These findings for tolerance show that it is important to examine the social reasoning behind the evaluation of religious practices. Research on Islamophobia in terms of prejudice tends to focus on stereotypes, feelings and evaluations. What is also needed, however, is an understanding of the underlying criteria that people use to determine whether particular acts and practices are acceptable. Social cognitive domain theory (see Smetana 2006; Turiel 2002), for example, proposes that people use moral – for example, fairness, justice; social-conventional – for example, group norms, traditions; and psychological – for example, autonomy, personal preferences – reasoning to evaluate and reason about specific behaviors and situations.

The findings in our research (Gieling *et al.* 2010; Study 1) indicate that the four cases were indeed seen as referring to the three domains. The wearing of a headscarf predominantly was considered to involve the personal domain, the founding of Islamic schools and the refusal to shake hands as triggering more social conventional concerns, and the imam's speech as raising moral issues. This distinction between the three domains was found independently of age, educational level and gender. Furthermore, in agreement with the domain theory it turned out that tolerance was highest in the personal domain and lowest in the moral domain, with the social conventional domain in between (Gieling *et al.* 2010; Study 2). Thus, the participants were found to be most tolerant of Muslim students wearing a headscarf and least tolerant of the imam's speech. The cases of the Islamic school and the refusal to shake hands, both mainly matters of social convention, fell in between. This difference was found for both types of tolerance: for the actual practices and for Muslims trying to persuade others to engage in the same practices.

Outgroup threat

Research on political tolerance has focused on the role of personality characteristics such as dogmatism, insecurity, and adherence to tradition (see Vogt 1997). Additionally, there is work on the role of political expertise, political participation and commitment to democratic values as determinants of tolerance (Sullivan and Transue 1999). However, relatively little attention is given to intergroup factors such as perceived threats and group identification. Tolerance presupposes group differences and implies that one group has the power to suppress the disliked or threatening behavior of the other. In his review, Gibson (2006) argues that research on tolerance needs to examine different types of threat and that the antecedents of threat perception are poorly understood.

In a study among native Dutch adolescents (Van der Noll *et al.* 2010), and in agreement with research on political tolerance, we found that perceived group threat is a key determinant of tolerance. Both symbolic and safety threat were independently and negatively related to tolerance for Muslim practices. Thus, differences in norms, beliefs, and values that threaten one's worldview – symbolic threat – as well as the belief that the presence of Muslims leads to increased violence and vandalism – safety threat – did fuel negative reactions toward practices and rights of Muslims (see also Sniderman and Hagendoorn 2007). In addition, national identification was found to be positively associated with symbolic and safety threat, but did not have a direct effect on tolerance. Participants who identified relatively strongly with the Dutch were more sensitive and concerned about things that might harm Dutch society and culture. In turn, feelings of threat were associated with less tolerance.

The finding for national identification is in agreement with the social identity perspective (Turner and Reynolds 2001). This perspective argues that higher group identifiers will respond more strongly in terms of their group membership than those who are less committed to their group. For example, research has shown that, compared to low identifiers, those with high group identification are more likely to be concerned about their group, especially when the position and value of the group identity is at stake (see Riek *et al.* 2006). However, the social identity perspective also argues that there is not a direct relationship between group identification and outgroup attitude but that this relationship depends on the meaning or content of the group identity.

A central aspect of the content of national identity concerns history. The importance of historical imagery is emphasized in theoretical accounts of nationhood that define the nation as a community that moves together through time (for example, Anderson 1983; Bhabha 1990). History 'provides us with narratives that tell us who we are, where we came from, and where we should be going. It defines a trajectory which helps construct the essence of a group's identity, how it relates to other groups, and ascertains what its options are for facing the present' (Liu and Hilton 2005: 537).

National identity

According to Zolberg and Woon (1999), the focus on Islam in political debates is related to the fact that European societies, despite national variations, remain deeply embedded in the Christian tradition, in relation to which Muslim immigrants constitute a visible 'other' and Islam a 'bright boundary' (Alba 2005). Internal diversity is defined as threatening because Muslims would erode 'the authenticity of the nation from within' (Triandafyllidou 1998: 602). The increasing number of Islamic schools, mosques, veiled women and other visible signs of Islam would undermine the traditional national ways of life (Sleegers 2007). Consequently, different politicians have argued for including phrases like 'the Christian tradition' as defining the nation, in the national constitution. And in 2004, when a new European constitution was discussed, countries like Poland, Lithuania and Slovakia tried to include such phrases in the document (Judt 2005). Sociological research has found that Christianity is more salient to national identity in European countries with larger Muslim populations (Kunovich 2006). Likewise, in the United States, the Christian roots and nature of American identity would make Muslims an 'indigestible' minority (Huntington 2004: 188).

A notable aspect of these initiatives and findings is the historical narrative by which the national identity is defined and which is used to reject Muslim practices. Temporal and historical narratives provide a sense of collective continuity that is central in national self-understandings (see Sani 2008). Research has shown that people tend to pursue collective identities that satisfy a need for self-continuity (Vignoles *et al.* 2006). This means that people are likely to perceive their nation as being an entity that has endurance across time and space (Sani 2008). A sense of continuity is maintained, for example, by constructing a narrative account of the enduring and essential nature of one's nation: the structure of a historical narrative 'invites those in the present to see themselves as participants in an ongoing drama' (Reicher and Hopkins 2001: 150). Historical continuity provides a sense of timelessness and, in general, people are more likely to invest in a national identity that is defined as continuous (Sani *et al.* 2008). Therefore, societal developments that are seen as causing a rupture with the national past are likely to be perceived as a threat to the continuity of one's national identity. Collective continuity threat predominantly derives from feelings of incompatibility, that is, from changes that are perceived as going against the historically defining features of the nation (Iyer *et al.* 2008; Sindic and Reicher 2009). Islam can be presented as threatening the Christian continuity of the nation. Therefore, it can be expected that people will express higher intolerance for Muslim practices when the national or European identity is defined as rooted in Christianity.

We examined this expectation in three experimental studies in which a Christian historical narrative of Dutch identity was compared to a 'control' condition in which the emphasis was on the Dutch history of water management (Smeekes *et al.* 2011). Participants were asked about their tolerance of Muslim practices, such as the establishment of Islamic schools and the wearing of a headscarf. In all three studies it was found that the level of tolerance was significantly lower in the Christian condition compared to the control condition. Thus, participants were less tolerant of Muslims when Dutch identity was defined as rooted in Christianity showing that historical narratives matter for tolerance judgments. However, this finding was qualified by the level of national identification.

When there is intergroup conflict low identifiers tend to psychologically dissociate themselves from their group and thereby divide rather than unite the community (see for example, Ellemers *et al.* 1997). However, low identifiers might be brought 'on board' when conflict is associated with threats to the historical continuity of the national identity. For example, in the context of New Zealand and by using extracts adapted from political speeches, Sibley and colleagues (2008, Study 3) experimentally manipulated negation – versus recognition – of the historical basis of claims for reparation for past injustices suffered by the Maoris. It was found that the low national identifiers expressed low levels of opposition toward pro-bicultural policy in the control and historical recognition condition. However, in the historical negation condition they had increased levels of opposition comparable to those of high identifiers. Furthermore, in a representative survey in the Netherlands, Sniderman and Hagendoorn (2007) found that low national identifiers are equally supportive of immigration restrictions for Muslims as high identifiers when their national identity is made salient. This means that 'bringing considerations of collective identity to the fore enlarges the coalition opposed to immigration – above and beyond those already predisposed to oppose it' (Sniderman and Hagendoorn 2007: 120).

We live in a world of nations where most citizens care about their country's national identity and culture, although not on a continuous basis and not necessarily in the form of patriotic or nationalist sentiments. As argued by Billig (1995), nationalism is an endemic condition that is indicated on a daily basis in the lives of its citizenry and deeply ingrained in contemporary consciousness. As such, even those who do not find their national identity very important will probably have an underlying commitment to the continuity of their nation. Thus, a relatively large portion of the public should be willing to respond to circumstances that are defined as undermining the historical continuity of the nation. Islamic schools, mosques, veiled women, Islamic public holidays, and other visible signs of Islam are typically presented as being difficult to reconcile with a traditional Christian identity and, therefore, might also lead low identifiers to recognize that some form of in-group protection is needed. Thus, we expected that lower national identifiers would show higher opposition toward Muslim practices when Dutch identity was defined as rooted in Christianity – compared to the control condition. For higher identifiers no such effect was expected because they tend to have quite strong negative views about Muslims (Velasco González *et al.* 2008) which leaves little room for the additional historical representation of Christianity to have an effect (Sniderman and Hagendoorn 2007).

The results of our research are in agreement with these expectations. In the Christian condition, lower identifiers' intolerance for Muslim practices was similar to that of higher identifiers, whereas they were more tolerant in the control condition (Smeekes *et al.* 2011). This was found in all three studies and indicates that lower identifiers can be mobilized to protect their national community from influences that are presented as disrupting its continuity (see also Sibley *et al.* 2008; Sniderman and Hagendoorn 2007). Hence, bringing considerations of national continuity to the fore can enlarge the coalition opposed to Muslim practices.

However, the fact that people are responsive to particular historical representations of their national identity may also sway them in the direction of greater tolerance. National history can be formulated in different ways and various traditions can be presented as self-defining. In the Netherlands, the emphasis is not only on Christianity but also on the long liberal tradition of religious tolerance. It can be expected that higher identifiers show less opposition toward Muslim practices when religious tolerance defines the historical essence of Dutch nationhood, whereas the level of opposition of lower identifiers will not be affected. Low identifiers ordinarily tend to think about the issue of Muslim immigrants from a more tolerant perspective and therefore will not be more accepting when religious tolerance is presented as historically defining the nation (Smeekes *et al.* forthcoming). According to social identity theory (Tajfel and Turner 1979) high identifiers are more motivated to act in accordance with norms and beliefs about the nature of the in-group than low identifiers. For example, research has shown that, for high identifiers, the level of prejudice varies with the salient group norm whereby high identifiers tend to be less prejudiced when there is a pro-social norm (for example, Jetten *et al.* 1997). For high identifiers, accepting outgroups is consistent with maintaining a positive identity when this is in accordance with the defining essence of the in-group. Thus, when the national identity is defined as rooted in religious tolerance, high identifiers can be expected to show less opposition toward Muslim practices. We found evidence for this in three survey studies (Smeekes *et al.* forthcoming). Higher national identifiers were more accepting of Muslim practices when they defined national identity as rooted in religious tolerance, whereas there was no relationship for low identifiers who were already more tolerant. These findings show that different historical narratives can have different effects on tolerance of Muslims.

Conclusions

After September 11, 2001, Muslim communities became the target of increased hostility across many countries in Europe (Allen and Nielsen 2002). Terrorist attacks in Madrid and London further increased the population's negative feelings and reactions toward Muslims. In addition, in various countries, and especially in the Netherlands, politicians and opinion makers started to express very strong and negative views about Islam (Vasta 2007). This has led to an increased academic interest in forms of Islamophobia whereby stereotypes, feelings and prejudice are examined. Implicitly, it is argued that the reduction of stereotypes and prejudice is necessary for more equal and harmonious relationships to develop. However, our knowledge and ability to reduce stereotypes and prejudice remains limited. Generalized perceptions and negative feelings do not appear to be easy to change or to reject. The importance of tolerance is that it keeps these beliefs and feelings from becoming negative actions, thereby forming the first crucial step toward equality and civility (Gibson 2006; Vogt 1997).

Political tolerance is a construct that emphasizes forbearance and self-restraint and is thereby foundational for equality and the development of harmonious inter-group relations. Tolerance has predominantly been studied in terms of personality variables and beliefs about democratic institutions and processes. We have tried to show that an intergroup perspective is also useful for understanding tolerance for Muslim practices. Intergroup factors such as feelings of group threat and national identification, but also intergroup contact (Van der Noll *et al.* 2010), have a clear impact on tolerance for Muslim practices.

In addition, we have shown that the historical content of the national identity affects tolerance. When national identity is defined as rooted in Christianity, lower national identifiers tend to become more rejecting toward Muslims, whereas a historical narrative of national tolerance is associated with higher tolerance among higher identifiers. These findings indicate that a sense of national continuity is important for understanding people's reactions toward Muslim practices. One of the critical ways in which people contest future directions of the nation is by arguing over whether it represents continuity with or a rupture from the past. Continuity of national identity is not self-evident but constructed, for example, by political elites who act as 'entrepreneurs of identity' in trying to mobilize the public (Reicher and Hopkins 2005; Rooijackers and Verkuyten 2011). National history is contested between different politicians because historical continuity is an important source of authority. Discourses of national continuity mobilize the past to realize things in the future, like public support for or opposition to Muslims.

We have discussed several studies on political tolerance of Muslim practices and we want to end by discussing four issues. First, we focused on particular practices that symbolize Muslim identities, and which are at the center of current debates about multiculturalism in various European countries. This means that we focused on hotly debated issues. Future studies could examine whether similar processes are involved in tolerance of other practices and other minority groups. For example, it might be interesting to use a comparative perspective by including practices of Roma people or Hindus in the context of Western Europe.

Second, it is important to note that there are always limits to what can and should be tolerated. Tolerance is not the unconditional acceptance of difference. There are Muslim practices and actions that are not acceptable or reconcilable with liberal principles, such as the unequal treatment of women and girls (see for example, Okin 1999) and authoritarian and insular childrearing practices (Reich 2002). Moreover, there are some Muslims who reject democratic rights and freedoms and favour political-religious radicalism and violent actions, with severe repercussions for individuals and societies. Thus, an emphasis on tolerance does not mean relativism and non-interference.

Third, it is important to point out that proponents of multiculturalism have criticized the classical liberal idea that tolerance is sufficient for dealing adequately with religious diversity because it gives individual citizens the freedoms and rights to define and develop their own identities (Modood 2007). Multiculturalists argue, however, that 'mere' tolerance is not enough and that active support for differences is needed. The withholding of public recognition or misrecognition is seen as a form of oppression (Taylor 1992). Toleration would be an act of generosity from the powerful who grudgingly agree to put up with minorities. In doing so, the larger society's disapproval of Muslim identities and practices is implicitly affirmed. For Muslims living in Europe, the end result of toleration would be a poor substitute for the recognition and affirmation that they would deserve and need. However, the importance and benefits of tolerance should not be underestimated. Its emphasis on civic identity and individual's freedom to define and develop their own identities and ways of life offers crucial spaces for religious and cultural diversity.

Fourth, our focus on political tolerance does not mean that we do not find it important to understand the factors that are associated with negative beliefs and feelings toward Muslims. It is clear that this is important for both practical and theoretical reasons. However, tolerance is the most basic level of positive relations between groups. It is crucial because it is the first and necessary step toward civility and is the foundation of a just society (Vogt 1997). A diverse, equal and peaceful society does not require that we all like each other, but it does necessarily mean that people tolerate one another. It is thus important to improve our understanding of the factors and conditions that underlie tolerance judgments and reasoning. This chapter has made a contribution to this in relation to Muslims living in Europe.

11 Revisiting Islamophobia in contemporary Britain, 2007–10

Clive D. Field

Introduction

This chapter addresses the central research question unifying this volume: the attitudes of ordinary citizens toward Muslims and Islam reflected in surveys. It examines the situation in contemporary Britain through 'meta-analysis' of 64 opinion polls conducted in 2007–10, mostly among representative samples of adults. Such a large pool of quantitative data provides a robust evidence base for summarizing what is known about Islamophobia, avoiding over-reliance upon any individual enquiry. Full details of these surveys appear in the appendix, and textual references to them are solely by study number. Nearly all these polls were multi-purpose (omnibus), often commissioned by several – rarely academic – clients, and contained only a handful of Muslim-related questions. Most were ad hoc – including some that were event-driven – with limited time-series potential.

No survey literally focused on defining and measuring Islamophobia, a concept notably absent from the interview schedules. From this perspective, Islamophobia is an umbrella and somewhat imprecise term, encompassing a wide range of negative attitudes toward Muslims and Islam, not necessarily held in a coherent or consistent way, nor bound within a recognizable ideological or theoretical framework, as proposed by Allen (2010). Indeed, one of the virtues of trawling such unsystematic data is that we can begin to identify layers of Islamophobia, showing there is no single absolute level but varying degrees of prejudice informed by the topic enquired about. We shall be particularly examining three opinion clusters: perceptions of Muslim integration; perceptions of Muslim extremism and patriotism; and personal experiences of and prejudices toward Muslims.

This essay complements an earlier analysis for 1988–2006 (Field 2007) and cannot be understood except against a longer-term background. As Ansari (2004) has shown, although there has been a Muslim presence in Britain since the eighth century, it only became quantitatively significant after the Second World War. During the 1950s and 1960s substantial economic immigration occurred, of Muslim men from south Asian Commonwealth countries. Thereafter, the Muslim population rose rapidly, augmented by the influx of dependent women and children of the original male migrants, the arrival of Muslims fleeing ethno-sectarian conflicts in Africa, the Middle East and Europe, and the emergence from the 1970s of British-born second and third generations. Islam's status was decisively confirmed by the

2001 census, which revealed 1,600,000 Muslims, disproportionately young relative to other religions. The probable 2010 total is 2,500,000 (Field 2010a), with a projection of 7,000,000 by 2029 (Kaufmann 2010: 164–83).

Notwithstanding a population of 1,000,000 by that time, Muslims had low visibility in public opinion terms before the late-1980s. Until then, for the average Briton, Muslims were generally defined by ethno-nationality, not religion. It was the furore over Salman Rushdie's *Satanic Verses* in 1988–9 which first brought Islam as a faith into national focus and demonstrated the potential for conflict between Islamic 'radicalism' and Western values and the implications of that conflict for international relations. Hard on its heels, the hostility of some British Muslims to Britain's involvement in the First Gulf War in 1990 led to doubts about their community's patriotism. Low levels of knowledge of, and contact with, Muslims and Islam helped fuel this nascent Islamophobia.

Tensions fell away throughout the 1990s, only to reignite in 2001. Between 2001 and 2006 Islam and Muslims were rarely out of the public opinion spotlight. Major terrorist incidents (9/11 and 7/7), so-called Anglo-American wars on terror in Afghanistan and Iraq, escalation of the Israel–Palestine conflict, controversies over Islamic dress and cartoons of the Prophet Mohammed, Muslim demands for separate treatment and the then Labour government's seeming readiness to accommodate them – these and other developments bred significant negativity toward Muslims in Britain, captured in an explosion of polling effort (Field 2007: 453–63; Field 2010b), as well as extensive media coverage (Moore *et al.* 2008; Meer and Mouritsen 2009; Meer *et al.* 2010).

Summing up trends to 2006, Field (2007: 465–6) estimated that, 'taking a cross-section of attitudinal measures, somewhere between one in five and one in four Britons now exhibits a strong dislike of, and prejudice against, Islam and Muslims.' A stereotypical portrait of Muslims in the eyes of the majority British population had emerged. 'There appears to be an increasing perception that Muslims in Britain are slow to integrate into mainstream society, feel only a qualified sense of patriotism, and are prone to espouse anti-Western values which lead many to condone so-called Islamic terrorism' (Field 2007: 466). These earlier conclusions suggest specific research questions to be examined for 2007–10.

Self-evidently, a primary question is:

- Does the overall level of Islamophobia in Britain in 2007–10 stand higher or lower than in 2001–6?

However, ancillary questions also need to be addressed:

- Are the three stereotypes identified in the earlier research still current?
- Where does Islamophobia sit in the hierarchy of religious prejudice in Britain?
- What demographic variations exist in attitudes to Muslims and Islam?
- Is Britain more Islamophobic than other Western countries?

Finally, we must ask:

- What gaps in our knowledge of Islamophobia remain?

Perceptions of Muslim integration

A majority of Britons feels Muslims have failed to assimilate into mainstream society. In S2009h 21 percent considered that most Muslims in Britain led separate lives, three-fifths said many did so and just 13 percent believed most Muslims were integrated. Asked in S2008a whether the British Muslim community needed to integrate further, 56 percent agreed – higher than 2004 but similar to 2006 (Field 2007: 457, 460) – while 43 percent in S2010m thought Muslims less integrated than five years previously. Opinion was divided about whether they really wanted to fit in (S2008m, S2008q). Forty-eight percent (S2008a, S2010g) were convinced the country would lose its identity if more Muslim immigration occurred, similar to 2003 (Field 2007: 456), and 35 percent that there were no-go areas in Britain too dangerous for non-Muslims to enter (S2008a).

Just one-third were confident Islam would ever be accepted by Western society (S2007e), the same proportion thinking Muslims had little in common with other religions (S2007e), lacked respect for other cultures (S2008q), and were the major cause of community tension (S2009j). One-third likewise resisted compromises to accommodate minority religious customs (S2007c), and attached importance to immigrants coming from 'Christian' countries (S2008q). Two-fifths denied Muslims had a positive impact on Britain (S2008q, S2009j, S2010j), and one-quarter of those upholding the principle of state-funded faith schools opposed government-financed Muslim schools (S2010l). Three-quarters had reservations about *halal* meat (S2010p).

Muslim women's dress has become one symbol of perceived lack of integration. There is an ongoing legacy from the 2006 row sparked by a government minister's criticism of the full face-veil as a barrier to race relations and a mark of segregation (Field 2007: 460; Meer *et al.* 2010), within the context of legislative moves by several Western European countries to proscribe the *burka*. More than one-half of Britons, and rising, view the face-veil as inhibiting integration and want it banned (S2007c, S2008j, S2010c, S2010d, S2010e, S2010i, S2010n), with yet stronger sensitivities about *burkas* in banks, airports (especially), schools and universities (S2010c, S2010d). This is a harder line than in 2006 (Field 2007: 460). Two-thirds in S2010c agreed that garments concealing a woman's face affronted British values, although, paradoxically, 58 percent also said government should not tell individuals what to wear. Even the female headscarf offends a minority (S2007c, S2008j, S2010c), partly because it is seen to oppress women (S2008j). This is symptomatic of a widely held view that Islam treats women as second-class citizens (S2008c, S2009f, S2009j), the proportion reaching seven-tenths in S2008q and S2010j, more than in 2001 and 2006 (Field 2007: 453, 463).

Another specific obstacle to integration is the clamour by some Muslims to introduce elements of Sharia law into the British legal system. The public vehemently opposes this (S2008i), including three-quarters of non-Muslim university students (S2008c). Indeed, only 2 percent of all adults in S2009j were positive about Sharia, with 30 percent negative and 64 percent neutral. When Rowan Williams, Archbishop of Canterbury, suggested in 2008 that the absorption of aspects of Sharia into the British legal framework was inevitable, he was widely condemned, even by 69 percent of churchgoers (S2008n). Three-quarters of white Britons thought such incorporation to be neither inevitable nor desirable (S2008e). Two-thirds of all adults judged the Archbishop damaged by the controversy, with two-fifths wanting him to step down as head of the Anglican communion (S2008d).

Perceptions of Muslim extremism and patriotism

There have been fewer flash-points around perceived Muslim extremism since late 2006, and some lessening of Islamic-related terrorist incidents on mainland Britain. The principal exceptions were the abortive attacks in London and Glasgow in 2007, which provided the backdrop to S2007l. These crimes were deemed by 71 percent to have given Islam a bad name. For 17 percent they exemplified it was a warlike faith sitting uneasily with modern Western culture, while for three-fifths it remained a peaceful religion distorted by fanatics. In S2007d, 15 percent feared violent conflict between Islam and the West was unavoidable, but 77 percent were hopeful common ground would be found. The overwhelming majority blamed global tensions on intolerant minorities on both sides, and twice as many thought politics rather than religion or culture lay at the root of differences.

If anything, public attitudes hardened subsequently. About one-third feared British Muslims threatened national security (S2007m, S2008a, S2008i) and saw Islam as incompatible with Western democracy and British values (S2008i). Even a majority of university students struggled to reconcile Islam with Western democracy or the separation of religion and government (S2008c). By S2009b, 44 percent were convinced that, even in milder forms, Islam seriously endangered Western civilization. Fifty percent of all adults in S2007k and 45 percent in S2008k expected to be personally affected by Islamic fundamentalism during the next decade, up on the pre-7/7 figure of 36 percent (Field 2007: 456). Thirty-two percent in S2010a worried that they or their immediate family might be victims of an Islamic terror attack in Britain.

Sixty-two percent regarded Islamic terrorism as more of a problem for Britain than other Western countries, on account of the Anglo-American alliance, failures to deal with Islamic radicals and high Muslim immigration (S2010a). One-half criticized both government and universities for doing insufficient to combat Islamic extremism, while the Muslim community was perceived to drag its feet over helping the police, three-quarters condemning the Luton Islamic Centre for not reporting Taimour Abdulwahab al-Abdaly, who later became the Stockholm suicide bomber, to the authorities (S2010t). The same proportion wanted Youtube to be made to remove content posted by radical Muslim clerics (S2010q).

S2010j asked which words respondents associated with Islam; the list was headed by extremism (58 percent), terrorism (50 percent), and violence (33 percent), with Osama bin Laden named the most representative Muslim after the Prophet. Hardly anybody linked Islam with peace, social justice or environmentalism. This reprised S2009j in which 37 percent accused Muslims of being terrorists, 32 percent of preaching hatred, 20 percent of law-breaking, and 19 percent of pursuing violence. Fear of terrorist consequences probably explains why two-thirds of Britons condemned the provocation of American pastor Terry Jones in planning an 'International burn a Koran' day (S2010o) and 55 percent wanted him barred from entering Britain (S2010s).

Such apprehensions about links between Islamic elements and extremism or terrorism raised doubts about the patriotism of some British Muslims, in an echo of 7/7 (Field 2007: 458, 462, 465), which one-half blamed on Islam (S2008i). Only a minority (45 percent in S2007c, 36 percent in S2008j and 46 percent in S2010g) viewed Muslims in Britain as inherently loyal to the country. For 29 percent in S2007m and 37 percent in S2008q personal allegiance to Islam and to Britain was incompatible. Disloyalty was especially suspected when Muslim extremists organized protests against British troops returning from overseas service. When in 2009 some Muslims in Luton called British soldiers coming home from Iraq 'butchers' and 'baby-killers', 53 percent in S2009a demanded such protests be outlawed and the protesters prosecuted. On this occasion, 35 percent took the contrary position, upholding the entitlement to dissent openly – in the same way that 32 percent in S2008m supported the right to make a speech defending bin Laden or al-Qaida. However, in 2010, when Islam4UK – a radical Islamist group – planned a march in opposition to the Afghan war through Wootton Bassett, the town to which dead servicemen from Afghanistan were repatriated, 80 percent endorsed the government's decision to ban the group, with just 14 percent defending free speech. Moreover, 81 percent denounced the cynicism of Anjem Choudary, Islam4UK's spokesperson, in claiming state benefits despite being a qualified lawyer (S2010b).

Personal experiences and prejudices

Most non-Muslims lack deep acquaintance with Muslims and their religion or any desire to be closer to them. Three-quarters of adults still have limited or no knowledge of Islam, similar to 2001–3 (Field 2007: 453, 455-6), and much the same proportion have no interest in learning more (S2009j, S2010j). Specifically, acquaintance with the Qur'an is very low (8 percent, only 20 percent having had contact with it, against 95 percent for the Bible), with two-fifths not knowing who Allah and the Prophet are (S2009j).

As in 2006 (Field 2007: 461), slightly more than one-half have no Muslim friends (S2007a, S2007m, S2008i, S2008m), and a significant minority – more than in 2003 (Field 2007: 456) – would be unhappy if a child or close relative married a Muslim (S2007a, S2007m). One-seventh remain reluctant to have Muslim neighbours (S2007c, S2007n), no great improvement on previous years (Field 2007: 451–2, 455, 461). Fifty-five percent would be sorry or angry if a Muslim became British prime minister (S2008f), and 23 percent would not even vote for a Muslim politician (S2008r). Forty-six percent in S2007m held that Muslims already had too much political power – although the proportion in S2008i was lower – a situation related to the Labour Party's perceived pro-Islam stance (S2010f). In S2007i 22 percent of non-Muslims contended that the then Labour government was doing too much to protect the rights of Muslims – with 16 percent claiming it was doing too little; it was a similar story in S2008h.

An interesting test case of the acceptability of the Muslim presence is to be found in attitudes to mosques. In S2008a, 33 percent recoiled at any new mosque being erected in their neighbourhood and, in S2008m, 55 percent at the building of a large mosque, 40 percent more than rejected construction of a large church. These apparent double standards were further highlighted by the controversy in 2010 surrounding the Ministry of Defence's use of replica mosque cut-outs on its Bellerby firing range, to simulate overseas operational environments. This resulted in protests by the Bradford Council for Mosques and a climb-down by the Ministry. Sixty-four percent of the public could find nothing wrong in the Ministry's use of such replicas, and 54 percent wanted them kept, just 29 percent siding with the protesters (S2010h). However, in a separate YouGov poll soon afterwards, two-fifths criticized a hypothetical foreign defence ministry for using models of Christian churches on a firing range. Even in the multi-racial London borough of Newham, the community was divided about plans to build a mega-mosque next to the 2012 Olympics site (S2009d). In the wake of the Swiss referendum banning minarets, 37 percent wanted Britain to follow suit (S2009k).

There was general agreement (89 percent in S2007n) that people were more suspicious of Muslims than a decade before, somewhat higher than in 2002 (Field 2007: 455). In S2008b, 44 percent perceived that Muslims suffered the greatest discrimination of any group in Britain, while in S2007i and S2008h, of those agreeing that religious prejudice had worsened during the previous quinquennium, nine-tenths named Muslims as victims. In the abstract, there was some sympathy for Muslims, with 56 percent in S2007e accepting they were often judged by events outside their control, and 39 percent in S2007m and 52 percent in S2008i that they were criticized unjustly. Three-tenths in S2008i and S2009j alleged media bias against them, and 21 percent in S2009b that they endured discrimination.

On the other hand, 39 percent in S2009b thought Muslims were unfairly advantaged and 56 percent in S2010r that they often enjoyed greater freedom of speech and action than British Christians. Muslims were the most-cited group in S2007i and S2008h to receive – allegedly – preferential treatment by public services. They were viewed unfavorably by 23 percent of Britons in S2008g, and 27 percent in S2009e and S2009j. This compared with 14 percent before 7/7 – which greatly exacerbated negativity, according to S2008i and S2010m – and 20 percent in 2006 (Field 2007: 457–8, 463); just over three-fifths regarded them favorably. On the feelings barometer in S2008m 35 percent were cool to Muslims, 40 percent neutral and only 23 percent warm. Asked in S2008l which religion they would like to join, a mere 1 percent of adults elected for Islam. One-fifth foresaw Islam as the most practiced European religion by 2057 (S2007h) and one-tenth assessed it as the most effective faith at getting its message across (S2007f). For a significant minority, Islam was irrational and outdated (S2009j).

Hierarchy of religious prejudice

It is increasingly recognized that Islamophobia needs to be examined in comparison with the level and nature of other forms of prejudice. Some have investigated it within the context of discrimination against immigrants, for example Strabac and Listhaug (2008). Others have focused on Islamophobia as manifestation of religious prejudice. Thus, Bleich (2009b) demonstrated how, in Britain, negative attitudes to Muslims have increased relative to other religious groups, while noting that Muslims have not yet sunk to the bottom of the ethno-racial hierarchy. In more qualitative and theoretical research, Meer (2008) considered whether Muslims in Britain are best understood as an ethnic, racial or religious minority, comparing especially anti-Semitism and anti-Muslim sentiment (Meer and Noorani 2008). In this section we draw upon 15 of our 64 polls to reveal how far negative views of Islam and Muslims are mirrored for other religions.

In our previous essay (Field 2007: 465; cf. Field 2006), we noted:'Islamophobic views in Britain would appear easily to outstrip anti-Semitic sentiments in terms of frequency (more than double the size of the hard core), intensity and overt-ness.This is despite the greater longevity of anti-Semitism in Britain.' Much the same applied in 2007–10. Those regarding Muslims unfavourably exceeded the equivalent figure for Jews by 14 percent in S2008g (also S2010g) and 21 percent in S2009e, the favorability rating of Jews rising from 73 to 81 percent, whereas the Muslim rating decreased – from 63 to 61 percent. Likewise, in S2008m, almost three times as many Britons were cool toward Muslims as Jews. Twice as many perceived Muslims to suffer unfair discrimination in Britain as did Jews (S2009b, S2009i), and, of those observing an increase in religious prejudice over the previous five years, just 5 percent in S2007i believed it directed against Jews, 84 percent fewer than for Muslims – with the same gap in S2008h. Even the right-wing British National Party (BNP) was deemed 17 percent more of a threat to Muslims than Jews (S2009g). Traditional stereotypes of Jews are not extin-guished in Britain, but they did decline between 2007 and 2009, most contempo-rary anti-Semitism being driven by anti-Zionism (First International Resources 2009; Julius 2010).

The position is similar for other faiths. Twelve (S2009e) and 14 (S2010g) percent fewer adults view Hindus unfavourably than regard Muslims adversely, and 5 percent fewer have concerns about a relative forming a relationship with a Hindu than a Muslim (S2007a). Hardly any feel increasing religious prejudice against Hindus, and the same with Sikhs and Buddhists (S2007i, S2008h). Indeed, although a mere 0.3 percent were professing Buddhists in 2001, Britons have a 'soft spot' for Buddhists, with just 15 percent in S2008m cool toward them – 20 percent less than for Muslims – and 35 percent warm – 12 percent more, similar to the favorability differential of Buddhists over Muslims in S2010g. One in 11 yearn to become Buddhist (S2008l), the Dalai Lama's appeal (Harris Interactive 2010) perhaps being part-explanation.

Although elements in British Christianity have recently complained about the politico-legal discrimination they experience, only marginal substantiation of this grievance is found in these polls – such as S2007i and S2008h. Less than one-tenth view Christians unfavourably (S2008g, S2008m, S2009e, S2010g), while twice as many consider Christianity compatible with national life as do Islam (S2010g). Ninety-one percent in S2008r were prepared to vote for a Christian politician, 19 percent more than for a Muslim. Indeed, there was 3 percent greater willingness in S2008r to vote for an atheist than a Muslim, and the prospect of an atheist prime minister was three times more palatable than a Muslim one (S2008f). In S2010g atheists were seen 5 percent more favorably than Muslims.

Demographic variations

Breakdowns of responses by standard demographics are not available for all polls, but five correlations can be identified with reasonable certainty: gender, age, social class, region and party political affiliation.

Men regard Muslims less positively than women (Field 2007: 454, 465). Some of this is a function of greater male antipathy to – or lower interest in – religion generally. Gender differences are often no more than 5 percent except for Muslim extremism and patriotism. Thus, 62 percent of men against 54 percent of women associated Islam with extremism, and 34 and 25 percent with violence (S2010j). Similarly, 45 percent of males versus 32 percent of females considered the British Muslim presence to threaten national security (S2007m); and 68 against 57 percent regarded Islamic terrorism as more problematical for Britain than other Western countries (S2010a). Sharia was another issue dividing the sexes; 13 percent more men than women opposed its spread in Britain (S2008i).

Regarding age, there is generally a steady increase in negativity toward Islam and Muslims from the youngest to the oldest cohorts (as in Field 2007: 454–5, 460, 465), simultaneously tracking decreasing knowledge about Islam (S2010j) and fewer Muslim friendships (S2008i). Margins between the two ends of the age spectrum are typically at least 10 percent, often more, as much as 32 percent – 63 percent of over-60s versus 31 percent of 18–24s – over government failings to combat Islamic extremism (S2010t). The elderly were significantly cooler toward Muslims (S2008m); more likely to see them as undermining national security (S2007m, S2008i), to think they impacted negatively on British society (S2010j) and enjoyed greater freedoms than Christians (S2010r). They were also more uneasy about a mosque being built locally (S2008a, S2008m, S2009d), a close relative forming a relationship with a Muslim (S2007a, S2007m), and Muslims embracing politics (S2007m, S2008f, S2008i, S2008r). The young were more inclined than the elderly to say Muslims are treated unfairly (S2008b, S2009i), and less likely to criticize government for over-protecting Muslim rights (S2007i, S2008h).

In terms of social class, there is a fault-line between non-manual and manual workers, between ABC1s and C2DEs on the British market research classification. The former are less antipathetic to Muslims than the latter, although the differences are mostly under 10 percent. Wider variations are sometimes found between the ABs – upper, professional and higher managerial classes – and DEs – semi- and unskilled workers and long-term dependents on benefits. For instance, 58 percent of ABs but 44 percent of DEs believed Muslims enrich British society (S2008a), while 26 and 43 percent respectively wanted it illegal to wear a *burka* in public (S2010d). The bias of DEs is not new (Field 2007: 454, 465) and is partly attributable to 61 percent having no Muslim friends (S2008i, against 43 percent of ABs).

Regionally, the only consistent pattern is that negative attitudes to Muslims occur less in Greater London and Scotland than elsewhere. Even in the aftermath of the Glasgow attack, only 7 percent of Scots described Islam as warlike, 10 points below the national average (S2007l). Scots have also been most prone to recognize discrimination suffered by Muslims (S2008b) and to regard them as socially integrated (S2010g). This relatively low incidence of Scottish Islamophobia mirrors earlier years (Field 2007: 456, 466) and is probably explained, not by inherent religious toleration – considering Scotland's history of Protestant-Catholic sectarianism – but by the paucity of Muslims in that country. In London, by contrast, there is a heavier concentration of Muslims, increasing their chances of inclusion in samples of the general population – thereby influencing responses in a positive direction; and meaning non-Muslims have greater knowledge about Islam (S2010j) and more opportunity to interact with Muslims, reducing negativity (Field 2007: 453, 464–5). Accordingly, Londoners have been in the vanguard of a pro-Muslim worldview. The only qualification is that, because London is at greater risk of being a target for so-called Islamic terrorism, anxieties on that score are 6 percent higher there than the British mean (S2010a).

As for political allegiance, of the three main parties, the Conservatives have a reputation for being less friendly to Islam than Labour (S2010f). In reality, their supporters have been fairly antipathetic to Muslims (as in Field 2007: 454, 456, 460, 463, 465), typically 5–12 points more than the national average. However, the Conservatives are nowhere near as Islamophobic as the United Kingdom Independence Party or the BNP, 64 and 79 percent of whose voters respectively branded Islam a serious danger, with 61 and 70 percent claiming Muslims were unfairly advantaged (S2009b). Not without reason did three-quarters of Britons (S2009g) think Muslims should be afraid if the BNP strengthened its electoral toehold. At the other end of the spectrum, the Green Party's backers were most pro-Muslim (S2009b), followed not far behind by the Liberal Democrats. For all the measures on which Conservatives exceeded the national mean, Liberal Democrats undershot it, usually by a double-digit margin, one of the most striking examples being reactions to the Luton protests, where the gap between Conservatives and Liberal Democrats was 32 percent (S2009a).

International comparisons

In our earlier essay (Field 2007: 466), it was noted that 'concerns about Islam and Muslims have generally been lower in Britain than in Western Europe as a whole, and notably lower than in France, Germany, The Netherlands and Spain'. Sixteen of our 64 polls are multinational, and the incidence of negative attitudes to Islam and Muslims is shown in Table 11.1 for Britain, five other Western European nations and the United States – corresponding to this volume's geographical focus. On a simple rank-order for each miscellaneous – excluding Turkey-related – statement, no simple picture emerges whereby one or two countries consistently exhibit more Islamophobic tendencies. Everything depends upon the question asked (as in Field 2007: 454). However, examining first and second places, Germany and Spain somewhat edge ahead – as before – although France and The Netherlands show less negativity than previously, while opinions in Italy have hardened. Britain tops the Western European league-table on just three of 25 measures, all from S2007m. So, overall, Britain is still less Islamophobic than its continental partners. Relative to the United States, by contrast, Britain is more negative on two-thirds

Table 11.1 International incidence of negative attitudes to Islam/Muslims

Survey	Statement	GB	FR	GE	IT	NE	SP	US
General								
S2007d	Islam–West tensions caused by cultural differences	9	7	25	23			17
S2007d	Islam–West tensions caused by intolerant Muslim minorities	8	17	20	18			12
S2007d	Violent conflict between Islam and West inevitable	15	23	40	14			31
S2007h	Islam most widely practiced European religion in 2057	20	22	13	11		6	9
S2007k	Likely to be personally affected by Islamic fundamentalism in next decade	50	61	57	65	48	71	59
S2007k	EU should not help establish democracies if they elect Islamic fundamentalist leaders	30	50	50	43	45	49	
S2007m	Muslims threaten national security	38	20	28	30		23	21
S2007m	Impossible to be both Muslim and national citizen	29	14	28	26		18	13
S2007m	Muslims not subject to unjustified criticism/prejudice	44	30	43	38		47	30
S2007m	Object to own child marrying Muslim	31	17	37	28		18	30
S2007m	Muslims have excessive political power	46	19	33	34		23	20
S2007m	Possess no Muslim friends	55	28	61	67		70	60
S2008f	Anger/sorrow at Muslim prime minister/president	55						53
S2008g	Hold unfavorable opinion of Muslims	23	38	50			52	23
S2008k	Likely to be personally affected by Islamic fundamentalism in next decade	45	56	49	56	37	64	53
S2008o	Al-Al-Qaida/Islamic extremists behind 9/11	57	63	64	56			
S2008q	Western and Muslim ways of life irreconcilable	38	30	38	46	42		32
S2008q	Most Muslims not respect other cultures	37	42	48	60	42		27
S2008q	Most Muslim immigrants not want to integrate	42	33	52	51	43		27
S2008q	Muslim immigrants not offer much to national culture	40	40	50	55	54		32
S2008q	Muslim women have lower social standing than men	71	66	74	70	63		51

Survey	Statement	GB	FR	GE	IT	NE	SP	US
S2009e	Hold unfavorable opinion of Muslims	27			69		46	
S2009k	Support ban on minarets in our country	37						21
S2010e	Support ban on *burka* in our country	57	70	50	63		65	33
S2010i	Support ban on full face-veils in public	62	82	71			59	28
Turkey-related								
S2007j	Oppose Turkey's EU membership	33	54	38	37		27	5
S2007k	Feelings toward Turkey (0–100 scale)	49	38	42	38	48	42	49
S2007k	Turkey's EU membership bad thing	23	49	43	29	33	24	10
S2008k	Turkey has different values and not part of West	44	68	76	61	55	46	41
S2008k	Feelings toward Turkey (0–100 scale)	50	37	46	37	50	45	47
S2008k	Turkey's EU membership bad thing	21	45	40	27	27	20	8
S2009c	Turkey has different values and not part of West	49	68	77	63	61	52	34
S2009c	Turkey's EU membership bad thing	26	48	46	32	38	20	7
S2009e	Oppose Turkey's EU membership	39	66	69	63		34	
S2010k	Hold unfavourable attitudes to Turkey	33	60	63	62	43	40	46
S2010k	Turkey has different values and not part of West	52	66	73	57	54	55	46
S2010k	Turkey's EU membership bad thing	27	49	44	28	38	27	18

of statements, somewhat reversing the position to 2006 (Field 2007: 466). This may seem surprising, given that most Britons accept that America is often disrespectful to the Islamic world and has ambiguous motives for supporting democracy in Muslim countries (S2008o).

An interesting test case is Turkey, a predominantly Muslim nation seeking membership of the European Union (EU). Table 11.1 shows Britain views Turkey slightly more positively than its European neighbours but still inclines to neutrality rather than warmth (S2007k, S2008k). It is similarly less likely than France, Germany, Italy and The Netherlands to say Turkey has such different values to the West that it cannot be reckoned part of it; but the gap is closing (S2008k, S2009c, S2010k), a shift since 2005 (Field 2007: 458). One-third of British oppose Turkey's EU membership, a far lower proportion than France, Germany and Italy in S2009e, and one-quarter describe it as a 'bad thing', roughly half the number in France and Germany (S2007k, S2008k, S2009c, S2010k).

Conclusions

Returning to our initial questions, there seems little doubt from these 64 polls that the scale of Islamophobia in 2007–10 was higher than in 2001–6, notwithstanding the relative absence of Britain-based terrorism and other flash-points in the later period. Where comparable measures exist, negativity to Islam and Muslims grew or remained static. Whereas pre-2007 one-fifth to one-quarter of Britons were hostile to Islam and Muslims (Field 2007: 465–6), the position in 2007–10 became multi-layered, emphasizing the correlation between level of prejudice and question-wording and topic. The spread of opinion looks something like this:

- Up to one-fifth of adults are strongly Islamophobic, viewing Islam as warlike, seeing violent conflict with it as inevitable, and fearing it will become dominant; they are likewise unwilling to have Muslim neighbours or to vote for Muslim politicians.
- Up to one-third think Muslims have little in common with other religions, lack respect for other cultures, have established no-go areas, create community tension, have qualified loyalty to Britain, and are associated with violence; this group regards Muslims unfavorably and resists concessions to Muslim agendas.
- Up to two-fifths sense Islam endangers Western civilization, Muslims do not want to fit into British society, have little to offer Britain, and benefit from unfair advantages.
- Up to one-half believe Muslims need to do more to integrate – yet have no Muslim friends themselves – and perceive the face-veil a barrier to assimilation; they fear the loss of British identity through Muslim immigration, consider Muslims have excessive political power, and expect to be personally affected by Islamic fundamentalism.
- Up to three-quarters have limited or no knowledge of Islam, lack interest in finding out about it, oppose the introduction of Sharia and the subordinate status of Muslim women, and press for tough action against Muslim extremists.

Turning to our ancillary questions, it is also clear that:

- The three stereotypes of British Muslims identified in the earlier research are still current; most are seen by the majority population as slow to integrate, many to have only a qualified patriotism, and some to be drawn to extremism and even violence.
- Islamophobia is by far the most pervasive form of religious prejudice in Britain, easily outstripping anti-Semitism but also hostility toward other non-Christian faiths associated with Asia, implying Islamophobia is distinct from racism.
- Negative attitudes to Islam and Muslims are disproportionately concentrated among men, the elderly, the DE group and Conservative voters; positive views are held by women, young people, the AB group, Liberal Democrat and Green voters, and in Greater London and Scotland.
- On a direct comparison of measures, Britain remains less Islamophobic than other Western European countries but, since 2007, has become more Islamophobic than the United States.

These findings will make depressing reading for Britain's politicians, policy-makers, faith and community leaders – and ordinary Muslims. Notwithstanding less of an atmosphere of acute crisis affecting Islam and Muslims throughout 2007–10, Islamophobia has encroached further into British society. While, in the abstract, Britons recognize that Muslims suffer discrimination, at a personal level they appear unable to restrain their own suspicions of and hostility toward them. This may arise partly from anxiety about the rapid growth in the Muslim population and its mounting socio-political influence; partly from a sense that Islam is somehow 'un-British'; and partly from dependence on the media for information about Muslims (S2010j), whose coverage is often negative (Moore *et al.* 2008). These citizens are critical of Muslims for failing to integrate and yet make little effort to bridge the divide between the Muslim and majority communities.

Of course, this is not the last word. These polls do not provide a complete picture of Islamophobia in contemporary Britain. Sample sizes were often relatively small. Only a limited range of breaks by standard demographics was offered, with some key variables – including education, ethnicity and religion – rarely analyzed. Respondents were not psychologically profiled, so motivations and predictors for Islamophobia are hard to gauge. No Islamophobic scale was deployed, such as the index for teenagers devised by Brockett *et al.* (2009). Some Muslim-related topics were not adequately addressed in the 2007–10 polls, notably attitudes to foreign policy, human rights and faith schools. In the final analysis, these disparate data provide a useful snapshot but perhaps remain an imperfect substitute for a more systematic, comprehensive and academically driven survey among a large sample of adult Britons.

Appendix: register of surveys

The sequence of information is: survey number, fieldwork dates, area, population/age, sample size, interview method, survey agency, publications. Websites accessed 18 January 2011. Unpublished data in the author's possession have also been used.

S2007a: 8/2006-1/2007; Scotland; 18+; 1,594; face-to-face/self-completion; Scottish Centre for Social Research; Bromley *et al.* (2007).

S2007b: 9/12/2006-28/1/2007; England; 16+; 1,014; face-to-face; Ipsos-MORI; Commission on Integration and Cohesion (2007).

S2007c: 18/12/2006-9/1/2007; GB; 15+; 1,204; telephone; Gallup; http://www.gallup. com, Mogahed and Nyiri (2007), Rheault and Mogahed (2008).

S2007d: 21/12/2006-9/1/2007; GB; 18+; 1,000; telephone; GlobeScan; http://www. worldpublicopinion.org, Greater London Authority (2007).

S2007e: UK; JWT.

S2007f: 1-5/2/2007; GB; 18+; 2,437; online; YouGov; http://www.yougov.co.uk.

S2007g: 16-18/2/2007; GB; 18+; 1,000; telephone; ICM; http://www.icmresearch.co.uk.

S2007h: 28/2-12/3/2007; GB; 16+; 1,128; online; Harris; http://www.harrisinteractive.fr.

S2007i: 4/2007-3/2008; E&W; 16+; 9,336; face-to-face; NatCen; Ferguson, *et al.* (2009), Connolly (2010).

S2007j: 31/5-12/6/2007; GB; 16+; 1,025; online; Harris; http://www.harrisinteractive.com.

S2007k: 4-23/6/2007; GB; 18+; 1,000; telephone; ICM; http://www.transatlantictrends.org.

S2007l: 6-8/7/2007; GB; 18+; 1,001; telephone; ComRes; http://www.comres.co.uk.

S2007m: 1-13/8/2007; GB; 16-64; 1,111; online; Harris; http://www.harrisinteractive.com, Kuper and Dombey (2007).

S2007n: 21-24/9/2007; GB; 18+; 1,209; online; YouGov; http://www.yougov.co.uk.

S2007o: 26/9-7/10/2007; London; 1,005; telephone; Ipsos-MORI; http://www.ipsos-mori.com.

S2008a: 9-10/1/2008; GB; 18+; 1,011; telephone; ICM; http://www.icmresearch.co.uk, Wynne-Jones and Sawer (2008).

S2008b: 17-21/1/2008; GB; 18+; 1,066; online; YouGov; http://www.yougov.co.uk.

S2008c: 22-29/1/2008; UK; non-Muslim university students 18+; 831; online; YouGov; http://www.yougov.co.uk, Thorne and Stuart (2008).

S2008d: 14-15/2/2008; GB; 18+; 2,469; online; YouGov; http://www.yougov.co.uk.

S2008e: 29/2-2/3/2008; GB; white British 18+; 1,012; telephone; Populus; http://www. populuslimited.com.

S2008f: 7-11/3/2008; GB; 18+; 1,301; online; YouGov; http://www.yougov.co.uk.

S2008g: 17/3-6/4/2008; GB; 18+; 753; telephone; Princeton Survey Research Associates [PSRA]; http://www.pewglobal.org, Kohut and Wike (2008).

S2008h: 4/2008-3/2009; E&W; 16+; 9,335; face-to-face; NatCen; Ferguson and Hussey (2010).

S2008i: 21-22/5/2008; GB; 18+; 1,006; telephone; ICM; http://www.channel4.com.

S2008j: 6/2008; GB; 15+; 1,001; telephone; Gallup; http://www.gallup.com, http://www. muslimwestfacts.com.

S2008k: 4-24/6/2008; GB; 18+; 1,001; telephone; ICM; http://www.transatlantictrends.org.

S2008l: 11-13/6/2008; GB; 18+; 2,000; online; YouGov; http://www.yougov.co.uk.

S2008m: 6-11/2008; GB; 18+; 2,247; face-to-face; NatCen; Voas and Ling (2010), ex inf. D.Voas.

S2008n: 18-24/7/2008; UK; churchgoing Christians 18+; 513; online; ComRes; http:// www.comres.co.uk.

S2008o: 31/7-8/8/2008; GB; 18+; 803; telephone; Chatham House; http://www. worldpublicopinion.org.

S2008p: 11/8-12/9/2008; GB; 16+; 1,010; telephone; GlobeScan; http://www. worldpublicopinion.org.

S2008q: 29/8-29/9/2008; GB; 18+; 1,000; telephone; TNS; http://www.transatlantictrends.org.

S2008r: 17-19/10/2008; GB; 18+; 1,007; telephone; ComRes; http://www.comres.co.uk.

S2009a: 12-13/3/2009; GB; 18+; 1,840; online; YouGov; http://www.yougov.co.uk.

S2009b: 29/5-4/6/2009; GB; 18+; 32,268; online;YouGov; http://www.yougov.co.uk.

S2009c: 9/6-1/7/2009; GB; 18+; 1,001; telephone;TNS; http://www.transatlantictrends.org.

S2009d: 10-11/6/2009; Newham (London); 18+; 300; ComRes; http://www.comres.co.uk.

S2009e: 1-11/9/2009; GB; 18+; 1,000; telephone; PSRA; http://www.pewglobal.org.

S2009f: 23-24/10/2009; GB; 18+; 504; telephone; ICM; http://www.icmresearch.co.uk, Kirby (2009).

S2009g: 27-28/10/2009; GB; 18+; 1,409; online; YouGov; http://www.yougov.co.uk, Toberman (2009).

S2009h: 12-13/11/2009; GB; 18+; 2,026; online;YouGov; http://www.yougov.co.uk.

S2009i: 18-25/11/2009; GB; 14-25; 3,994; online;YouGov; http://www.yougov.co.uk.

S2009j: 11/2009; GB; non-Muslims 16+; 500; face-to-face; DJS Research;Tzortzis (2010).

S2009k: 9-12/12/2009; GB; 18+; 2,002; online;Angus Reid; http://www.visioncritical.com.

S2010a: 5-7/1/2010; GB; 18+; 10,344; online; YouGov; http://www.yougov.co.uk, Dunn (2010).

S2010b: 14-15/1/2010; GB; 18+; 2,033; online;YouGov; http://www.yougov.co.uk.

S2010c: 21-22/1/2010; GB; 18+; 2,001; online;Angus Reid; http://www.visioncritical.com.

S2010d: 27-28/1/2010; GB; 18+; 1,016; telephone; ComRes; http://www.comres.co.uk, Grice (2010).

S2010e: 3-10/2/2010; UK; 16-64; 1,097; online; Harris; http://www.harrisinteractive.com, Blitz (2010).

S2010f: 17-18/2/2010; GB; 18+; 1,085; telephone; ComRes; http://www.comres.co.uk.

S2010g: 18-21/2/2010; Scotland; 18+; 1,006; telephone; Ipsos-MORI; http://www.ipsos-mori.com.

S2010h: 9-12/4/2010; GB; 18+; 2,404; online;YouGov; http://www.yougov.co.uk.

S2010i: 15/4-2/5/2010; GB; 18+; 750; telephone; PSRA; http://www.pewglobal.org.

S2010j: 19-21/5/2010; UK; 18+; 2,152; online;YouGov; http://www.yougov.co.uk.

S2010k: 2-24/6/2010; GB; 18+; 1,000; telephone; ICM; http://www.transatlantictrends.org.

S2010l: 25-27/6/2010; GB; 18+; 1,003; telephone; ICM; http://www.icmresearch.co.uk.

S2010m: 4-5/7/2010; GB; 18+; 1,424; online; YouGov; http://www.yougov.co.uk, Sloan (2010).

S2010n: 14-16/7/2010; GB; 18+; 2,205; online;YouGov; http://www.yougov.co.uk.

S2010o: 9-10/9/2010; GB; 18+; 1,858; online;YouGov; http://www.yougov.co.uk.

S2010p: 20/9/2010; GB; 18+; 772; online;YouGov; http://www.yougov.co.uk.

S2010q: 4-5/11/2010; GB; 18+; 1,954; online;YouGov; http://www.yougov.co.uk.

S2010r: 26-29/11/2010; GB; 18+; 1,006; telephone; ComRes; http://www.comres.co.uk.

S2010s: 13-14/12/2010; GB; 18+; 1,810; online;YouGov; http://www.yougov.co.uk.

S2010t: 16-17/12/2010; GB; 18+; 1,966; online;YouGov; http://www.yougov.co.uk.

Part 4

Are Muslims different from other outgroups?

Ethnocentrism and terrorism

12 Islamophobia and the Band of Others

Kerem Ozan Kalkan and Eric M. Uslaner

The United States has had a conflicted approach toward immigration since its inception. As a nation of immigrants, it has alternatively welcomed and repelled immigrant groups. Thirty percent of the American population is from minority groups. But Bill 109 in Arizona, aimed at illegal immigrants, is seen by many Hispanic groups as racial profiling. And Muslim Americans felt targeted in the wake of the terrorist attacks of September 11, 2001. Many Muslims believe that they have been singled out for discrimination because 'mainstream' white Christians fear them. We argue that this view is misplaced. The roots of favorability of Muslims are the same as attitudes toward other outgroups, 'the Band of Others'. Membership of this band determines mainstream Americans' attitudes toward them, rather than the terrorist attacks or political orientations. The Band of Others shapes people's attitudes toward minorities and its effects are persistent over time.

This general sense of ethnocentrism (Kinder and Kam 2009; Davis 2007) shapes Americans' attitudes toward Muslims. Americans viewed Muslims as part of this Band of Others well before the attacks on 9/11. After the attacks, many Americans admitted that they were prejudiced against Muslims (USA Today/Gallup Poll 2006; Newsweek 2007 Poll; Theiss-Morse 2009). But these views largely reinforced earlier attitudes.

There are two important issues concerning the impact of the September 11 terrorist attacks on Americans' attitudes toward Muslims. First, if the theory of Band of Others holds, we expect to find similar prejudices toward other minorities. The reasons behind these attitudes may be different. Yet, the general tendency to welcome or dislike minorities will hold, as reflected in a Gallup (2010) survey on Muslims in America. Second, negative attitudes toward Muslims predated the 9/11 attacks and did not change much.

We first present our main argument and measurement. Then we examine the impact of this theory of generalized attitude toward minorities on Muslim evaluations in series of multivariate analyses and test whether the September 11 terrorist attacks changed the structure of attitudes toward Muslims. Finally, we focus on the implications of the theory of Band of Others for future intergroup relations in the US, with a particular focus on the relationship between familiarity and affect toward Muslim Americans.

Structure of minority attitudes and ethnocentrism

We need a more comprehensive understanding of intergroup attitudes. The theory of ethnocentrism can provide a more thorough framework for studies of attitudes toward minorities than studying attitudes toward only one minority. Each immigrant group faced has discrimination and was not seen as truly American (Higham 1951). Yet, now most –including African-Americans – are viewed positively in surveys. Ethnocentrism, or 'prejudice broadly defined', is a useful and flexible theory (Kinder and Kam 2009). At the beginning of the twentieth century, William Graham Sumner proposed the term ethnocentrism to explain a mental process that tries to divide people into in-groups and outgroups. It is a habit of assigning all unfavorable qualities to outgroups, and associating all desirable qualities with in-groups. Ethnocentrism is 'a mutually exclusive division into "us" versus "them", we who belong and they who do not, ingroup versus outgroup' (Sniderman *et al.* 2000, Kinder and Kam 2009). It involves exaggerating and intensifying everything related to the in-group members (Sumner [1907]2002). Outgroups may be any group that does not look, believe, talk, or behave like 'us' (Kinder and Kam 2009). The content of that line between in-groups and outgroups does not matter. It may be a religious, ethnic, or behavioral boundary or a racial divide.

Ethnocentric evaluations target all outgroups or minorities. Adorno *et al.* (1950) define ethnocentrism as 'prejudice, broadly conceived'. White Americans' attitudes toward blacks are closely related to their attitudes toward other minorities. Sniderman and Piazza (1993: 53) find that prejudice against blacks is 'a blind and irrational reaction – because it has nothing to do with blacks and may just as well manifest itself against Jews, or Asians, or any of many outgroups.' Kinder and Kam (2009) find that ethnocentrism among white Americans is a strong predictor of approval on policies targeting not only blacks but also Latinos and Asians, as well as same sex marriage and increased levels of immigration. People who have thin boundaries between in-groups and outgroups will be more likely to hold positive attitudes toward Muslims in the United States.

Potential causes of ethnocentrism

Kinder and Kam (2009) propose four theoretical perspectives to understand the causes of ethnocentrism. The first one comes from realistic group conflict (Kinder and Kam 2009). The idea of 'if "they" have more "we" have less' (Sniderman and Hagendoorn 2007: 77) is at the heart of realistic group conflict. Realistic group conflict does not suggest a generalized prejudice toward all outgroups. Rather, it 'takes up pairs of opposing groups' (Kinder and Kam 2009: 11). Muslims do not pose an economic threat to whites. They are mostly middle class, as reported in the 2007 Pew Report on Muslim Americans.

The second theoretical framework for ethnocentrism (Kinder and Kam 2009) is the authoritarian personality, which was first coined by (Adorno *et al.* 1950), who found that people who are anti-Semitic are also likely to think that blacks should be kept in their place, and authorities should control Japanese Americans and foreign ideas. Authoritarians place a high value on conformity, sameness, and convention, and display an aversion to individuals and groups who are different from them. This translates readily into intolerance and hostility toward and distrust of those groups who have not been part of the conventional racial, ethnic, religious, and cultural mainstreams in American society (Stenner 2005). We incorporate individuals' authoritarian tendencies in empirical models to test the structure of Muslim attitudes.

The third theoretical framework comes from social identity theory (Kinder and Kam 2009), first developed by Tajfel (1981a). Tajfel found that a great majority of participants reward their own group in experiments. Social categorizations cause in-group favoritism and outgroup hostility easily without any rational grounds of conflict (Brewer 1979; Hammond and Axelrod 2006). Tajfel (1982b: 22) argues, 'one of the principal features of intergroup behavior and attitudes [is] the tendency shown by the members of an in-group to consider members of outgroups in a relatively uniform manner, as "undifferentiated items in a unified social category"' (cf. Sniderman and Hagendoorn 2007: 56).

If ethnocentrism has a social dimension that leads to a generalized prejudice toward outgroups, attitudes toward Muslims should be part of this syndrome. People will perceive Muslims as another member of the Band of Others. The best predictor of attitudes about Muslims should be feelings about blacks, Asian Americans, Latinos, Jews, illegal immigrants, welfare recipients, gays and lesbians, and other outgroups. The final aspect of ethnocentrism is its potential genetic source (Kinder and Kam 2009: 25). Ethnocentric attachments may have a genetic component that is transmitted from one generation to another. We are not ready to accept a genetic basis for social attitudes, but such an account would be consistent with the persistence of ethnocentric attitudes over time.

Ethnocentrism leads people to categorize individuals into in-group and outgroups. It is readily available, quick and easy (Kinder and Kam 2009). People may favor members of the in-group over those belonging to an outgroup based on a minimal reason.

Measurement of ethnocentrism

Kinder and Kam (2009) addressed this measurement issue by limiting their ethnocentrism measure to negative stereotype questions in the American National Election Studies. While such questions tap ethnocentrism well, they are only available for a small number of groups. We need a broader ethnocentrism measure that can capture prejudice not only toward blacks, Asian Americans, and Latinos, but also other minorities. We employ feeling thermometers in the American National Election Studies and favorability ratings in Pew surveys. We use the 2004 and 2008 American National Election Studies (ANES) to conduct the factor analysis for all available marginalized or minority groups. The available groups do not change that much from one year to another. In both years, the analysis will include blacks, Latinos, Asian Americans, Jews, welfare recipients, gays and lesbians, illegal immigrants, and feminists. The 2008 ANES also asked about Hindus and atheists.

Is there a Band of Others? Or more than one? We conduct our factor analysis among 'mainstream Americans' – non-Latino, non-Asian, and non-Jewish whites who do not belong to any minority religion. We excluded Muslims and non-Judeo

Christian respondents from the sample.[1] The remaining respondents will look approximately the way Theiss-Morse (2009) defines the mainstream American. All of the minority attitudes are measured by feeling thermometers, which are positivity biased-corrected.[2]

We focus on groups that are either ethnic or racial minorities or are widely disliked because they are 'behaviorally different' in American society. Ethnic and racial minorities may be disliked because they look and sound – by their languages and accents – different from mainstream Americans. Over time, most of these groups become accepted as 'Americans'. Jews long faced discrimination but are now the most highly rated minority in surveys. Blacks are have faced the most persistent discrimination. As Theiss-Morse (2009: 61) argues, 'blacks have been frequently been reminded of their marginal status as Americans across U.S. history' so that they 'put some distance between themselves and this national group to which they belong'. African-Americans are now highly rated – on feeling thermometers – as are Asian-Americans and Latinos (Lin *et al.* 2005).

Culturally and behaviorally different groups are defined less by how they look than by what they do or believe. Such groups include illegal immigrants, welfare recipients, feminists, gays and lesbians. Negative attitudes toward these groups are stronger and more resistant to change. Many 'mainstream' Americans see them as rejecting traditional gender roles – and thus behaviorally different. We selected these groups because: 1) they are judged less on their ascriptive traits than by their behavior and attitudes; and 2) details of these groups are available in the ANES data. Other groups would fall into this category – radicals, polygamists, etc. – but they are not included in the surveys. In 2008 Hindus were included in the ANES and are part of the cultural/behavioral outgroup.

Muslims are both ethnically and behaviorally different from the mainstream. Both differences will lead 'mainstream' Americans – white Christians – to see Muslims negatively. e expect that belonging to the cultural/behavioral Band of Others will play a larger role in shaping attitudes toward Muslims. It is likely that 'looking different' – as African-Americans, Asians, and many Hispanics do – matters less than having religious practices that seem strange and outside the Judeo-Christian traditions.

Muslims are one of the least liked groups in the United States (Gibson 2008; Kalkan *et al.* 2009; Sides and Gross 2007). Many Americans are not sure whether Muslims agree with their vision of American society (Edgell *et al.* 2006). Muslims are thus seen as culturally and behaviorally different, not just another religious group, in the way that Jews are seen. People may see Muslims as following strange religious practices – the state of Oklahoma banned Sharia law in the 2010 elections. Many Muslims dress distinctively and Americans read about practices in some Muslim countries – such as not permitting women to drive – that they mistakenly believe are followed in the West.

Attitudes toward Muslims should cluster with other disliked groups that are culturally or behaviorally different such as gays and lesbians (Wilcox and Norrander 2002), atheists, and illegal immigrants (Hood and Morris 1997). We include feminists in this outgroup, since many 'mainstream' Americans see them as rejecting traditional gender roles – and thus as being behaviorally different.

We used the method of principal components factor analysis to estimate the loadings and score, with oblique rotation to get a simpler structure. As shown in Figure 12.1, American attitudes toward minorities in 2004 were indeed two-dimensional, meaning that there are 'bands of others', rather than a single monolithic cluster that explains everything. The correlation between these two factors is .38. The first factor includes ethnic and racial minorities that have been in the United States for a long time –blacks and Asian Americans – or highly salient – Latinos. Feelings toward behaviorally or culturally distinct outgroups cluster together. Muslims, gays and lesbians, and illegal immigrants are the most disliked minorities. Muslims – by belonging to a non-Judeo Christian tradition; gays and lesbians – by challenging the 'traditional' definitions of sexual relationships; and illegal immigrants – by not respecting the immigration laws – are behavioral or cultural strangers in the land. Welfare recipients are included in the Band of Others as a proxy for African-Americans, since many – if not most – Americans associate receiving welfare with blacks (Gilens 1999).

We see a similar picture in the 2008 analysis in Figure 12.2. This analysis includes attitudes toward Hindus and atheists, in addition to the groups included in the 2004 survey. Again, we observe three main clusters, with Christian Fundamentalists being clearly distinctive as we saw in 2004. The racial and ethnic minority attitudes are very closely related to each other. People tend to form their evaluations of Asian Americans, Latinos, and blacks within a single band. Unlike 2004, the 2008 cluster includes evaluations of Jews as well.

More consistently than these two structures, the band of culturally or behaviorally 'different' minorities includes the same groups in 2008. Prejudice toward

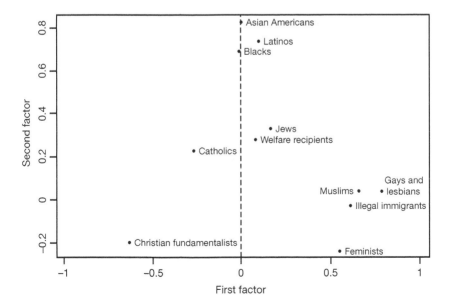

Figure 12.1 Structure of minority attitudes in 2004 (NES 2004)

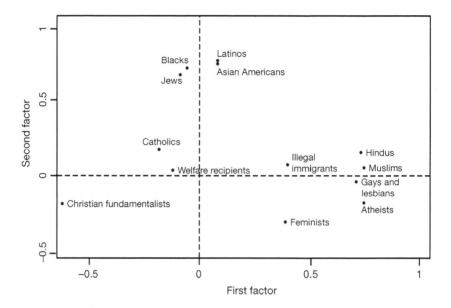

Figure 12.2 Structure of minority attitudes in 2008 (NES 2008)

Muslims, illegal immigrants, gays and lesbians, and feminists tend to go together, along with dislike of Hindus and atheists. The structure persists from 2004 to 2008 without almost no change.

Band of Others and attitudes toward Muslims

What is the most important factor that makes people dislike Muslims? If it is this ethnocentric attachment, or Band of Others, then is the effect independent of other competing explanations, such as political orientations, religious traditionalism, or perceived threat from terrorism after the September 11 terrorist attacks? These are the key questions we pose.

We expect to find that these two measures of Band of Others will be the most important determinant of attitudes toward Muslims both in 2004 and 2008. Those who have positive attitudes toward blacks, Jews, Asian Americans, and Latinos will also have positive feelings toward Muslims. Similarly, if a person is not prejudiced toward cultural/behavioral outgroups, she will welcome Muslims as well.

We posit that there will likely be other factors that also shape attitudes toward Muslims. The theory of the authoritarian personality suggests that people may have strong attachments to conformity, conventional life styles, and sameness, and this attachment translates into intolerance of marginalized groups like Muslims – who may threaten traditional conventions and threaten the dominance of 'mainstream' values (Adorno 1950; Altemeyer 1996). Hetherington and Weiler (2009) argue that authoritarian attitudes have led to increased polarization in American politics.

We follow conventional measurement of authoritarian attitudes by examining questions about desirable traits for children. Respondents pick one of the two, or voluntarily express 'both', options: independence or respect for elders; obedience or self-reliance; curiosity or good manners; being considerate or well behaved. In both the 2004 and 2008 datasets, we coded the authoritarian responses as 1, the democratic choices as 0, and voluntarily expressed responses of 'both' as 0.5. For each respondent, we take the average of her responses to these questions. The higher the rating, the more authoritarian a person is, and, in turn, the more prejudiced toward Muslims she should be.

Negative stereotypes about minorities should also translate into anti-Muslim attitudes (Sniderman and Piazza 1993; Kuklinski *et al.* 1997). Kinder and Kam (2009) also use these negative stereotype questions to construct an ethnocentrism scale for all respondents. It may seem problematic to have both feeling thermometers and negative stereotypes in the same model. However, several researchers have documented that prejudice and stereotypes are two different processes. The former refers to more affect or emotional based evaluations of minorities, whereas the latter is more of cognitive attribution of certain features – like laziness, violence, being disgusting etc. – to minorities (Stangor 2004; Cuddy *et al.* 2007). Gilens (1999) shows that stereotypes about blacks have much stronger effect on welfare attitudes than affective feeling thermometers.

Negative stereotype questions were asked about three minority groups – blacks, Asian Americans, and Latinos. In both datasets, respondents are asked to rate each of these groups on three scales, ranging from lazy to hardworking, from unintelligent to intelligent, and from untrustworthy to trustworthy. We created an index of negative stereotypes by taking the average of these variables for each respondent. The scale reliability coefficient is .86. The more a person has negative stereotypes against African-Americans, Asian-Americans, and Latinos, the more prejudiced we expect he will be toward Muslims.

The September 11 terrorist attacks by radical Muslims heightened the sense of threat from terrorism in American public opinion. People became willing to restrict the civil liberties of Muslims after the attacks (Davis 2007), and their ethnocentric evaluations determined the level of support for anti-terrorism policies (Kam and Kinder 2007). We constructed an index of threat from two variables in the 2004 and 2008 ANES datasets The first asks about the level of federal spending on fighting terrorism and the second concerns the importance of combating international terrorism as a foreign policy goal. These may not be ideal questions, but they are the best measures available in the ANES surveys. However, as Davis (2007: 207) finds: 'whites were fairly uniform in their negative feelings toward Islamic fundamentalists and Arabs, regardless of threat'. Therefore, we do not expect a statistically significant effect of perceived threat on Muslim attitudes. Since it may be related to the level of perceived threat, we also take the level of patriotism into account. This variable was included only in the 2004 ANES. It is a composite score of five variables: how much the US flag makes the respondent feel good, how much she loves her country, how important it is to be an American, whether being an American makes her ashamed or angry. The index score is the average ratings of responses to these questions, and the scale reliability coefficient is .67. Much of the political rhetoric in the United States after 9/11 pitted America versus radical Islam. Americans flew the flag as a symbol of solidarity with each other – and against Islam – following 9/11. Support for political institutions, most notably the military, skyrocketed as Americans invoked the language of 'us versus them'. If Muslims are not 'good Americans', patriotic attachments may lead to anti-Muslim feelings. We do not expect significant effects for patriotism since we believe that the Band of Others will capture such sentiments. We also expect that people who are more religious or traditionalist may hold negative attitudes toward Muslims. Religious traditionalists hold negative attitudes toward groups with unfamiliar characteristics, behaviors, or cultural practices (Altemeyer 2003). We create a scale from four variables with a reliability coefficient averaging .84 for the two datasets: the frequency of church attendance and prayer, the view of the Bible as the literal word of God, and the level of guidance from religion. We also include a dummy for Evangelical Christians (see Layman and Green (2006) for the coding scheme).

Probably the most important alternative explanation of Americans' attitudes toward Muslims focuses on the political orientations of individuals. A common perception is that conservatives or Republicans will be more likely than liberals or Democrats to hold prejudiced views of Muslims. Several scholars have found a significant relationship between ideology and affect toward minority groups (Huddy *et al.* 2005; McClosky and Zaller 1984; Sidanius *et al.* 1996). Edgell *et al.* (2006) and Sniderman *et al.* (1989) found that ideology has little or no impact on minority attitudes. After the September 11 terrorist attacks, neither Democratic nor Republican elites put blame on Muslims or Islam. President Bush made efforts to distinguish radical terrorists from ordinary Muslim citizens who have been living in this country peacefully.

Some Republican politicians – notably former Representatives Virgil Goode (VA) and Tom Tancredo (CO) have been associated with anti-Muslim comments. Democratic elites also mostly supported the war on terrorism, and initially approved the war in Iraq. There was not a clear demarcation between Democratic and Republican elites foreign policy preferences at that time. Elites gave mixed cues, making cues difficult to interpret (Zaller 1992). We measured political orientations by combining the seven point party identification and ideological placement variables. It ranges from strong Democratic/extremely liberal to strong Republican/extremely conservative.[3] Finally, the models included several socio-demographic controls such as age, education, region of residence, and personal income. Party identification and ideology are so highly correlated that including both in the same model may obscure any results. We have estimated such models – and each measure separately – and obtain similar results.

Since the dependent variable – positivity bias corrected Muslim feeling thermometer – is a continuous measure, we estimated an Ordinary Least Squares regression among mainstream Americans – non-Latino, non-Asian, and non-Jewish whites who do not belong to any minority religion – in both the 2004 and 2008 ANES. All of the independent variables were coded to range from 0 to 1 so that we could compare the relative effect of each variable on attitudes toward Muslims. The results for the 2004 and 2008 models are depicted in Figures 12.3 and 12.4, respectively.

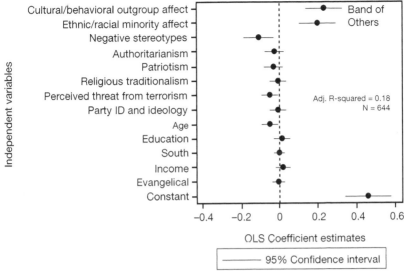

Source: 2004 ANES

Note: The dependent variable is Muslim feeling thermometer. All variables in the model are coded to range from 0 to 1. The model is estimated among non-Latino, non-Jewish and non-Muslim white respondents

Figure 12.3 Band of Others and Muslim attitudes in 2004

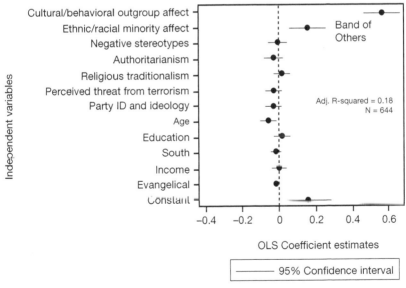

Source: 2008 ANES

Note: The dependent variable is Muslim feeling thermometer. All variables in the model are coded to range from 0 to 1. The model is estimated among non-Latino, non-Jewish and non-Muslim white respondents

Figure 12.3 Band of Others and Muslim attitudes in 2008

Both models suggest that Muslims are perceived as members of two bands of others. The impact of both ethnic/racial minority affect and cultural/behavioral outgroup attitudes are statistically significant. Ethnocentric evaluations of Americans toward minorities have the strongest effect on Muslim evaluations. If we increase these Band of Others variables from their minimum to maximum levels, the increase in Muslim feeling thermometer will be around .2 or .3 units in 2004, and .2 and .6 units in 2008. Under both scenarios, the increase in warmer feelings is large on a 0 to 1 scale.

Negative stereotypes about blacks, Asian Americans, and Latinos had some influence on Muslim attitudes in 2004, but not in 2008. Authoritarian values are not significant, nor is religious traditionalism. There was a significant, although substantively very small, association between perceived threat from terrorism and Muslim attitudes in 2004. The link disappears in 2008. People's attitudes toward Muslims are no longer a function of their sense of threat seven years after the terrorist attacks. Religious traditionalism also shapes cultural/outgroup orientations.

Political orientations do not have statistically significant effect on prejudice toward Muslims. Conservatives and Republicans are no more or less likely than liberals or Democrats to hold prejudice toward Muslims, on average. Dislike of minorities is more of a psychological than a political process. Among socio-demographic variables, only the age of respondents have some effect on Muslim evaluations in both years. The older the person, the more likely she is to be prejudiced. Southern residents are barely more negative than non-Southerners toward Muslims in 2008 but not in 2004. Evangelicals' attitudes are negative but not distinguishable from zero.

There are two important implications of these multivariate models. First, Americans perceive minorities as members of a Band of Others, in a multi-dimensional way. Outgroups that are more familiar to mainstream society are in one dimension, and minorities that are less familiar and behaviorally more different from prototypical Americans are in another dimension. No matter how these bands are constructed, people's level of prejudice toward them is the major determinant of attitudes toward Muslims.

Second, the obvious explanations, such as political orientations or level of threat, have either very small or no effect on attitudes toward Muslims. Individuals' attachments to ethnocentric evaluations are relatively independent of political events or predispositions. The level of perceived threat in the post-September 11 era does not play that important a role in terms of attitudes toward Muslims. Nevertheless, our analysis, so far, has not answered an important question concerning whether the terrorist attacks changed this ethnocentric structure of Muslim attitudes. Is the Band of Others persistent over time? Does its structure change after an important even that is closely related to a minority?

Persistence of the Band of Others

Prejudice toward the Band of Others is a psychological outcome, which is unlikely to change quickly. There may be ups and downs for some minorities at certain times but the general pattern, the ethnocentric structure, should stay the same. People may have held much more negative attitudes toward Muslims right after the terrorist attacks. However, the most crucial determinant of this dislike may still be dislike of blacks, Asians, Latinos, Jews, feminists, gays and lesbians, atheists, and illegal immigrants. One way to test this claim is through comparing similar models in the pre- and post-September 11 datasets. We expected to find that the influence of generalized outgroup affect has always been the strongest predictor of Muslim attitudes. Even before the attacks, Muslims were perceived as members of this persistent ethnocentric structure.

We use four datasets, two of which were conducted before September 11, 2001: the 2000 Pew Campaign Typology and the 2001, 2002, and 2007 Pew Religion in American Public Life Surveys. The dependent variable for all of these models is a four-category Muslim favorability rating that ranges from 'very unfavorable' to 'very favorable'. There are four main independent variables. The first one is the religious outgroup affect, which is similar to the Band of Others variables in the ANES models. It is an average rating of all of the non-Muslim religious minority groups that the respondent evaluated. All of these groups include favorability of Jews and atheists – the wording is 'non-religious people' in 2001 – in all years, with Buddhists added in 2001 and Mormons added in 2007. These Band of Others variables should have the strongest effects on attitudes toward Muslims.

We controled for political orientations – mean rating of party identification and ideology – a dichotomous variable for born-again Evangelicals, and church attendance, along with socio-demographic controls such as age, education, and region of residence. The evangelical dummy variable and the frequency of church attendance are proxies for religious traditionalism. All of these variables follow the same coding scheme as in the ANES models, and the model variables are coded to range from 0 to 1.

Since the dependent variable is categorical, we used ordered logit to estimate the coefficients. The estimation sample includes only mainstream Americans. The results of the models are presented in Table 12.1. Since it is a non-linear model, there is no straightforward substantive interpretation of the coefficients. However, we can still interpret the direction and statistical significance. The positive and statistically significant coefficient estimates on religious outgroup affect clearly support our expectations. Both pre- and post-September 11, the most important mechanism that explains attitudes toward Muslims is people's dislike of other religious minorities. Prejudice toward these religious minorities goes hand in hand with dislike of Muslims regardless of the time frame we use, before or after the attacks. Political predispositions may pick up their effects. Born-again Christians are less likely to evaluate Muslims positively. The level of church attendance has no statistically significant relationship on anti-Muslim prejudice.

We computed the change in predicted probabilities of having 'very favorable' ratings of Muslims when we move from the minimum to maximum value on the independent variables. We assigned the observed sample values to all variables other than the variable of interest. While calculating the influence of religious outgroup affect, we used observed values for the other predictors. The predicted probabilities reflect the average effect of a change in one independent variable across the whole sample (Hanmer and Kalkan 2009).

The biggest substantive change in the predicted probabilities of having a 'very favorable' rating of Muslims comes from people's favorability toward religious minorities.

Table 12.1 Structure of attitudes toward Muslims before and after September 11, 2001

	Pre 9/11		Post 9/11	
	2000	2001	2002	2007
Religious outgroup affect	50.75 (0.51)	80.21 (0.50)	40.80 (0.54)	50.86 (0.48)
Political orientations	-0.31 (0.37)	-0.70 (0.28)	-0.89 (0.34)	-10.61 (0.30)
Born again Christians	-0.10 (0.21)	-0.50 (0.18)	-0.45 (0.20)	-0.51 (0.17)
Worship attendance	0.46 (0.36)	0.29 (0.31)	-0.05 (0.36)	-0.32 (0.30)
South	-0.28 (0.20)	-0.03 (0.16)	-0.46 (0.19)	-0.11 (0.16)
Age	-10.40 (0.46)	-10.47 (0.35)	-0.61 (0.41)	-10.48 (0.36)
Education	0.23 (0.37)	-0.49 (0.32)	10.17 (0.38)	0.44 (0.29)
Cut 1	-0.09 (0.49)	-0.11 (0.38)	0.01 (0.49)	-0.72 (0.41)
Cut 2	10.74 (0.48)	20.07 (0.38)	10.60 (0.48)	10.45 (0.41)
Cut 3	50.26 (0.54)	60.49 (0.45)	50.51 (0.55)	50.06 (0.45)
N	472	782	529	743
Pseudo R2	0.16	0.26	0.11	0.18
EPCP	0.13	0.14	0.10	0.18

Source: 2000 Pew Campaign Typology; 2001, 2002, and 2007 Pew Religion in American Public Life Surveys.

Notes
The cell entries are ordered logit coefficients with standard errors in parentheses. The models are estimated among non-Latino whites who are Christians. The dependent variable is a four-category favorability rating of Muslims, ranging from very unfavorable to very favorable. All independent variables are coded to range from 0 to 1.

A move from true dislike of Jews, atheists, Buddhists, and Mormons to the warmest evaluations of them, increased the predicted probability of having very favorable opinions about Muslims by 52, 61, 25, and 29 percentage points in 2000, 2001, 2002, and 2007, respectively. The other independent variables have much less pronounced effects on attitudes toward Muslims. The effect of the Band of Others is immune to dramatic events such as terrorist attacks. While the changes in probabilities for the Band of Others drops significantly after 9/11, it is still by far the most powerful determinant of attitudes toward Muslims and no other predictor came close to these effects.

Muslims, familiarity, and Band of Others

The racial/ethnic minorities have clearly higher favorability ratings than the cultural/behavioral outgroups in 2004 and 2008. Blacks, Asian-Americans, Jews, and Latinos are rated above the average feeling thermometer. Other minorities, such as Muslims, are consistently rated below the average.

In 2004, Muslim attitudes load both on the racial/ethnic minority and cultural/behavioral minority factors. Muslim Americans are mostly foreign-born, and the American public associates Muslims with Arab-Americans perceptually. In addition to a behaviorally 'different' religion, Muslim Americans may seem to be ethnically 'different' from whites.

Given the relatively more positive ratings of ethnic/racial minorities and the multi-dimensional nature of attitudes toward Muslims, can we say that people's attitudes toward Muslims might grow more favorable as mainstream Americans' familiarity with them increases? Will we observe Muslim attitudes becoming more and more aligned with attitudes toward blacks, Asian-Americans, Latinos, and Jews after 2004?

Adorno *et al.* (1950: 149) argued that an ethnocentric person 'is prepared to reject groups with which he has never had contact' so that a 'new group can easily become an outgroup'. The contact hypothesis suggests increased contact between social groups may lead to a decline in the level of prejudice against outgroups. Contact between different social categories will eventually reduce negative attitudes and stereotypes about the groups that are contacted (Stangor 2004). The contacting groups must hold equal status, the prejudiced outgroup must show signs of acceptable behavior to the in-group, both parties must be in an interdependent environment, broader culture must promote norms concerning tolerance, and finally, 'it is important that enough time be allowed for the changes to take effect' (Stangor 2004: 324). Learning about others can combat stereotypes of outgroups (Kawakami *et al.* 2000), eliminate uncertainty about outgroups (Crosby *et al.* 1980), and increase cultural sensitivity (Dovidio *et al.* 2002).

Since, Muslims introduce 'strange', or at least *not-widely known*, religious preferences and teachings into mainstream American culture (Jamal and Naber 2008: 120–1), attitudes toward Muslims can arise from a lack of familiarity or contact. If people get to know Muslims, this behavioral or cultural 'strangeness' may fade away.

We used the 2007 Pew Religion in Public Life dataset, which has a question about whether the respondents had contact with Muslims. We could not test the 'equal status' aspect of contact theory because the questions are not sufficiently detailed. So we had to focus on simple contact. Forty-one percent of mainstream Americans know someone who is Muslim (see Table 12.2). Those who do not know any Muslims tend to hold unfavorable ratings of Muslims. Among people who know Muslims, the favorability ratings are much higher. Contact leads to less prejudice. The strong chi-squared test statistics (37.06, df=3) also verifies this association.

Table 12.2 The impact of familiarity on Muslim favorability

	Know anyone who is Muslim?	
Muslim favorability	No	Yes
Very unfavorable	22%	13%
Somewhat unfavorable	39	26
Somewhat favorable	34	54
Very favorable	5	7
Total	100 % (N = 413)	100 % (N = 370)
	Chi-squared = 37.06 (df = 3)	

Source: 2007 Pew Religion in American Public Life Survey.

Notes
Among mainstream Americans.

Conclusion

The visibility and salience of Muslims is very recent (see Jamal and Naber 2008). Hence, knowing someone Muslim may still work to reduce prejudice toward them. The perceived differences between the mainstream American culture and Islamic practices may erode over time, and Muslims may become one of mostly liked minorities in the same way as blacks, Jews, Asian Americans, and Latinos. Yet, the 2008 ANES data do not suggest a very promising story in terms of Muslims' place in the multi-dimensional picture of the Band of Others. They are aligned more with the mostly disliked cultural/behavioral outgroups. On the other hand, the 2007 Pew data tell a more positive story. As the familiarity between mainstream Americans and Muslims increases, the likelihood of having more favorable ratings of Muslims may increase. Muslims may experience what Jews, Irish and Italian Americans experienced in the past. Initially disliked, they became an integral part of mainstream society. The links of Muslims with behavioral outgroups suggest that there is a considerable distance to go.

It is unclear as to whether casual contact can lead to less prejudice. Contact, especially the strong friendship ties that Allport found to be critical (Allport 1954), may not develop in the face of prejudice. People who don't like Muslims – or members of other groups – may simply stay away from them in the first place (Forbes 1997). While contact is critical, it may be just as important to focus on reducing negative stereotypes.

Notes

1   We also exclude Christian fundamentalists since they do not load on any factor.
2   Following Wilcox *et al.* (1989), we computed a mean rating out of responses given to all feeling thermometer questions. Then, we subtracted this mean feeling thermometer rating from the minority feeling thermometers for each respondent. We applied this to all of the feeling thermometers we used in this and the following chapters using the ANES datasets.
3   Item non-responses – 'don't know' or 'haven't thought much about it' – are coded to 'the middle of the road' category in the ideological orientation variable before creating the composite score.

13 Think 'terrorist', think 'Muslim'?

Social-psychological mechanisms explaining anti-Islamic prejudice

Marco Cinnirella

Background: Islamophobia – a generic prejudice or a special case?

In this chapter I explore some psychological factors that may help explain the apparent rise in anti-Muslim prejudice – so-called Islamophobia – that has been noted in many countries over the past ten years or so. In particular, I will deploy selected theoretical approaches from social psychology to explore Islamophobic prejudice in the United Kingdom. I will present data from two studies with young people in the UK, and consider the broader implications of the findings from this research. While the data are from a UK sample, and the focus is on Islamophobia, the issues under investigation in fact resonate with broader theoretical questions in the social sciences about the interplay between identity and prejudice.

For the purposes of this chapter, Islamophobia will be conceptualized as a prejudice toward all – or at least, most – members of the Muslim faith, and toward Islam as a religion, which can be manifested both attitudinally via negative attitudes and negative stereotyping – for example, a perception that Muslims are dangerous – and behaviorally via discrimination and related actions – for example, support for new immigration measures perceived to act to the detriment of Muslims, or the act of sitting as far away as possible from a Muslim passenger on public transport. In essence then, the phenomenon in question is a tendency toward perceiving people of a Muslim faith in a negative manner, and to act accordingly. In social psychology – unlike, in contrast, sociology or social anthropology – there is a tendency toward preferring general models of prejudice and discrimination, rather than specific theorizing about particular prejudices. Thus, individual difference approaches such as social dominance orientation (SDO; see Sidanius and Pratto 1999), or intergroup approaches such as social identity theory (SIT; Tajfel and Turner 1986) seek to identify relatively universal socio-psychological mechanisms which can explain most, or perhaps all, prejudices – or so it is claimed. In contrast, I argue in this chapter that due to historical circumstances and the convergence of different socio-psychological forces, there is something special about Islamophobic prejudice which deserves attention and which cannot be fully explained by simply deploying one of these generic theories of prejudice. Instead, I propose an eclectic combination of different theoretical approaches, each of which appears to offer something useful when attempting to understand the social-psychological underpinnings of Islamophobia in the UK – and globally.

Social representations

The first theoretical tradition I will draw upon is that of social representations theory (SR; Moscovici 1981). In particular, what concerns us here are social representations of Muslims and Islam present in the mass media. Social representations are socially shared and constructed representations that act as a fundamental backdrop for the construction of individual attitudes and beliefs. It has been noted many times that individuals often hold stereotypical beliefs about members of social groups with whom they have little or no contact. One way in which they are able to do this is because they are exposed to social representations of the target group in question, and I postulate that these are endorsed less critically if the individual has little direct knowledge of, or contact with, members of the group in question. In the USA Altareb (2008), for example, argued that American citizens usually hold beliefs about Muslims –particularly of Arab descent – and Islam, even though many have no frequent contact with Muslims.

How has the British mass media portrayed Islam and Muslims? Since the Rushdie affair in the late 1980s, and the two Gulf wars, the British mass media have often run news and editorial items asking questions about the compatibility of Islam with so-called Western and/or specifically British values. Since the terrorist attacks on the US in 2001, the frequency of stories focusing on Islam and/or Muslims increased dramatically, and since that time content analytic studies are reasonably equivocal in claiming that the British tabloid press have disseminated social representations of Muslims and of Islam which are noticeable for themes of threat, terrorism and deviance (Moore *et al.* 2008; see also the work of Poole 2002; 2006). Recently, Rusi Jaspal and I argued that the British mass media, and in particular the national press, have disseminated social representations of Muslims in Britain which position Muslims as what we call a 'hybrid' threat to majority – non-Muslim – Britons (Jaspal and Cinnirella 2010). Specifically, we argue that the British tabloid press frequently disseminates social representations of Muslims in which Islam and Muslims are represented as posing a 'symbolic' threat to British cultural practices and values on the one hand, and a 'realistic' threat to perceived security on the other. Together, this positions Muslims and Islam as threatening beliefs, values, cultural practices, and the physical well-being of non-Muslim British people. Furthermore, these social representations of Muslims and Islam are partly anchored into existing social representations of war and conflict, so that Muslims are sometimes positioned as an 'enemy', encouraging dehumanization and negative attitudes toward them (Jaspal and Cinnirella 2010).

It is of particular concern that the theme of terrorism is often present in tabloid newspaper stories that identify individuals as Muslim (Moore *et al.* 2008). There is a danger that, for some British citizens, the perception of the two constructs may become intertwined so that they assume terrorism is disproportionately associated with Islam and Muslims. In the US, for example, there is already some empirical evidence for this perceived association – Park *et al.* (2007) report that when invited to say what first comes to mind when thinking about Muslims, their US college student sample primarily thought about terrorism. This tendency to think 'terrorist', and almost automatically think 'Muslim', is a potential recipe for intergroup tension, prejudice and discrimination, the blame for which must lie squarely at the feet of the mass media.

Fear of terrorism and Islamophobic prejudice

Although the subject of ongoing debate, one of the most important theories of media effects is based on the idea that an important effect of media on attitudes and beliefs is through flagging certain issues as warranting attention – the so-called agenda-setting effect. Here, of interest is the frequent occurrence of terrorism-related news stories in the British mass media, which is likely to have a so-called first-level agenda setting effect of making the issue salient in the minds of media consumers (McCombs and Shaw 1993). This is important, because with thinking about terrorism comes fear (Goodwin *et al.* 2005) and associated perceptions of threat and negativity toward the perceived source of the terrorist threat (Argyrides *et al.* 2002; Bar-Tal and Labin 2001; Huddy, Khatib and Capelos 2002; Perrin, 2005). Despite the fact that in an average year not a single British civilian dies from an act of terrorism on British soil, terrorism is seldom out of the pages of the tabloid press or off the television news screens. Most of this coverage is specifically about terrorism associated with Muslim perpetrators. Thus, words such as Islamist, *jihad* and radicalization seem to have slipped into everyday usage in the UK to such an extent that everyone is assumed to understand them. The message, therefore, that appears to be communicated from a reading of the British mass media, is that further terrorist attacks in the UK are likely, and that Muslims will almost certainly be the perpetrators.

In the USA, following 9/11, empirical research determined that prejudice toward those of a Muslim faith increased, as did support for tougher immigration and national security policies (Argyrides *et al.* 2002; Schildkraut 2002). Since the 9/11 attacks, many British Muslim groups have reported increases in anti-Islamic prejudice and abuse (Islamic Human Rights Commission 2004). In fact, after 9/11, anti-Islamic reactions were recorded across all member states of the European Union (Allen and Nielsen 2002), matching data from the US. Public opinion data are supported by academic research findings – for example, Sheridan and Gillett (2005) and Sheridan (2006) report empirical studies amongst ethnic minorities in the UK, comparing levels of self-reported experiences of prejudice and discrimination before and after 9/11. Participants of a Bangladeshi or Pakistani background – who were predominantly of Muslim faith – reported the largest increases in discrimination of any ethnic groups. Abrams and Houston (2006) have also reported a large population survey in the UK, and found Muslims to be the least accepted minority group in Britain. They were stereotyped as incapable and unfriendly, and perceived as the greatest cultural, physical and economic threat.

How exactly might terrorism be associated with Islamophobic prejudice? As outlined above, there is evidence that the general public in the UK fear terrorism and, furthermore, that there might be a perceived association between Muslims and terrorism in the public's perceptions. Since terrorism is evaluated by most citizens as undesirable, fear-inducing, and destructive, the association of Islam and Muslims with such a construct is almost guaranteed to make perceptions of Muslims more negative. Furthermore, since terrorism is associated with fear, this adds an additional complexity, since negative emotional states are known to affect intergroup attitudes, with negative emotions resulting in more negative evaluations and perceptions of outgroups – these are so-called *mood congruence effects* (see, for example, Bower 1981; Forgas and Moylan 1991; Lerner *et al.* 2003; Powell and Self 2004).

Another reason why fear of terrorism might exacerbate Islamophobic prejudice is offered by terror management theory (TMT; Pyszcynski *et al.* 2003; see also Greenberg *et al.* 2001). TMT suggests that anything that raises an individual's awareness of his or her own mortality creates an aversive psychological state that can trigger defensive reactions. In as much as fear of terrorism makes individuals aware of their own mortality, this, according to TMT, is enough to make individuals react harshly to the perceived cause of such a threat – in this case, potentially, Islam and Muslims. Furthermore, according to TMT, one way in which individuals deal with existential terror caused by awareness of mortality is to value long-standing cultural and traditional practices, such as those associated with national identity. Thus, fear of terrorism might also trigger reactionary responses that encourage an individual to revere national culture and tradition. In the UK case, this may be another facilitator of Islamophobic prejudice, since, as outlined earlier, media representations in the UK have positioned Muslims as threatening to traditional cultural practices and values in the UK – this is what in TMT research is called worldview defence (see McGregor *et al.* 1998; Pyszcynski *et al.* 2003; Yum and Schenk-Hamlin 2005).

Threatened national identity as a cause of Islamophobic prejudice

In the mass media, terrorism is often construed as a threat to the very fabric of a nation – whether it be the nation's infrastructure – such as power grid, transport network – or elements of what are construed to be the values and worldview of a nation and its people. Research in the social identity theory (SIT) and self-categorization theory (SCT) traditions speaks to the issue of how individuals respond when they believe that groups they identify with are under threat from one or more outgroups. I argue that for individuals who have a strong national identity, the perceived threat to the nation posed by terrorism will lead to more extreme reactions against the perceived source of the threat than for individuals who have a relatively low national identity. This proposed mechanism draws upon ideas from Tajfel's research on social stereotyping and social identity (Tajfel 1981b) – in particular, the notion that in-group members look to explain negative events – for example, a terrorist attack – through the scapegoating and subsequent demonising of one or more outgroups, and that in-group members will rally to the support of an in-group when it is threatened. Furthermore, one consistent finding in SIT/SCT studies of threatened social identity (including national identity – see Branscombe and Wann 1994) is that an individual's level of in-group identification moderates reactions to threatened social identity, such that high identifiers will often respond to threat with increased identification and in-group favoritism, and greater out-group derogation. There is also some evidence to suggest that strong identifiers are more susceptible to threat (Maass *et al.* 2003) and react with more anger when group members are victimized, than low identifiers (Yzerbyt *et al.* 2003).

In previous SIT and SCT studies on threat, numerous definitions of threat have been employed and operationalized (Branscombe *et al.*, 1999), none of which assess directly the kind of threat of interest here. The present focus is on terrorist threats to the nation and national identity. Such threats are often portrayed by the mass media as threats to the stability, security and long-term existence of a nation. As yet, SIT and SCT research on threats has tended not to look at threats of this type. Furthermore, much of the existing research has focused on threats posed by majority groups to minority groups, yet in the current chapter I explore the reverse – in examining reactions to Islamic terrorism I am exploring how members of a majority group – in this case white British citizens not of a Muslim faith – react to threatened national identity where the source of the threat is a minority group – Islamic terrorists.

I would argue that one of the reasons why this issue of threatened national identity is particularly important in discussions of Islamophobia is because national identity, arguably, is not like other social identities. I agree with scholars who have argued that there is something special about national identity – because it is: often instilled early in life; an ascribed identity; an identity that is inexorably linked to a citizen's survival; and an identity which offers the promise of psychological attachment to an undying, eternal group (Albert 1977; Druckman 1994; Salazar 1998; Smith 1991). As such, I argue that citizens are likely to react particularly forcefully to perceived threats to national identity, especially when the source of such threats is easily identifiable. There is strong evidence to suggest that the perception of threat to cultural and national homogeneity, or to the nation more generally, can trigger anti-minority attitudes (see also Esses *et al.* 2001), and many studies have demonstrated that threat increases ethnocentrism and xenophobia (Herrmann 1984; Levine and Campbell 1972; Seago 1947; Struch and Schwarz 1989), as well as 'collective emotions', such as anger (Mackie *et al.* 2000).

Media social representations of Muslims and Islam in the UK at times appear to challenge the compatibility of Islam with British traditions and values and, in doing so, position Islam and Muslims as a cultural/symbolic threat to the nation and national identity (Jaspal and Cinnirella 2010). One possible outcome of this is that some non-Muslim British citizens may seek to ostracize British Muslims and view them as in-group black sheep (Marques *et al.* 1988) for whom membership of the in-group is effectively denied, in an effort to re-define in-group membership such that it excludes the deviant black sheep. This phenomenon plays out on an almost weekly basis in the pages of the tabloid press in the UK, where the apparent conflict of interest that Muslims in Britain face, between Islam and being British, is regularly deliberated, particularly in relation to protests over British military action in Iraq and Afghanistan.

One theory that attempts to synthesize research on the implications of perceived threat for intergroup relations is intergroup threat theory (ITT; Stephan *et al.* 2008). ITT adopts a social-psychological approach to threat that argues that whether or not threats have any basis in reality, the perception of threat in and of itself has consequences at both the intergroup and intra-individual levels. The theory posits that there are two basic types of threat, both of which revolve around potential harm that an outgroup could inflict on the in-group. Realistic threats are posed by factors that could cause the in-group physical harm or loss of resources, and can also be represented as individual-level threats causing potential physical or material harm to individual group members as a result of their membership. Symbolic threats represent threats to the meaning system(s) of the in-group, such as challenges to valued in-group norms and values, and at the individual level of analysis may be associated with loss of face, challenges to self-identity and potential threats to self-esteem. As outlined above, the prevailing social representations of terrorism, Islam and Muslims in the UK appear to construe Muslims as an intergroup threat to British non-Muslims on both realistic – for example, the physical threat of harm from terrorism – and symbolic – for example, the threat to national culture and belief systems – dimensions (Jaspal and Cinnirella 2010). As such, ITT would predict negative stereotyping and hostility toward Muslims, especially since the potential threat perceived to come from Muslims is likely to be perceived as both a personal one – for example, terrorism poses a threat to personal safety – and a collective one – for example, the perception that Muslims seek to change established belief systems and cultural practices.

Overview of theoretical approach

The theoretical perspective developed in this chapter is summarized in Figure 13.1. As outlined above, I argue that a number of theoretical traditions within social and applied psychology are required to fully understand the intricacies of Islamophobic prejudice and discrimination. To summarize: media social representations in the UK tend to construe Islam and Muslims as a hybrid threat to both culture and national security, thus constituting both a realistic and symbolic threat, to use the terminology of integrated threat theory. These social representations form the backdrop from which individuals come to form their own attitudes and stereotypes of Muslims. In addition, the association in the mass media between terrorism and Islam/Muslims, serves to activate additional psychological mechanisms of fear of terrorism and defensive responses to mortality salience, as described in previous research on public reactions to terrorism and in terror management theory. Since national identity is, for many, an important social identity, these perceived threats to the nation and its culture and security from Muslims will be responded to, especially by high identifiers, with prejudice and discrimination against Muslims and Islam. While the model described here is eclectic and draws upon multiple theoretical perspectives, I do not claim it is complete – it represents work in progress, and deliberately focuses on identity as a key theme. Other approaches, such as those focusing on individual difference factors that might affect the degree to which prejudice is manifested, and how it manifests, may well also be important – in time I hope to integrate into this model some of these perspectives, such as social dominance theory (Sidanius and Pratto 1999).

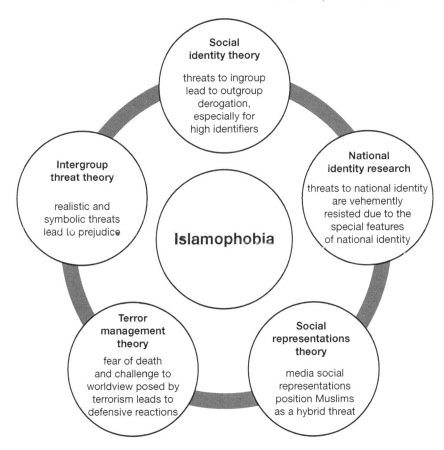

Figure 13.1 Theoretical perspectives drawn upon in the chapter

A programme of empirical research

Taking forward the theoretical approach outlined above, I have been developing a programme of empirical research based on both experimental and survey methodologies, a summary of which is provided here.

Testing for an effect of media exposure on attitudes toward Muslims

Above I argued that media social representations are likely to be an important causal factor leading to Islamophobic prejudice. An interesting question, however, is whether this can be demonstrated. Sceptics might argue that media consumers are sophisticated and can see through negative stereotyping without being affected by it, or else that individuals are sophisticated enough not to stereotype all Muslims negatively, but might instead only view Muslim terrorists or extremists negatively.

A study I conducted with colleagues (Cinnirella 2007; Cinnirella *et al.* under review) in 2006 explored this issue using an experimental approach. Groups of British university students volunteered to take part in what they believed to be two separate research studies – one about attitudes toward the media, and another about 'life in Britain today'. All of the participants were British citizens – 64 female and 56 male, with a mean age of 20 years – and Muslims were excluded from participation –since this was a study of Islamophobia. Participants were randomly allocated to one of three conditions. Across all conditions, participants read a bogus newspaper article they believed to be from the British press, and then completed some measures of their media exposure and reactions to the article. They then proceeded on to what they thought was a separate study, in which they completed counter-balanced scale measures of: British national identity – for example, 'Being British is important to me' (items taken from Cinnirella 1997); attitudes toward Muslims – for example, 'There are many Muslims living in the UK who are too extreme about their religion'; and support for hypothetical policies that would target the civil liberties of Muslims in the UK – for example, 'It is acceptable for the intelligence services to intercept phone calls made by Muslim citizens in Britain' (the latter two scales were custom-written for the study). In the first condition – the control – participants read a newspaper article about crime on university campuses. In the second condition – low threat – the newspaper article argued that the threat from Islamic terrorism to the UK was low, and in the final condition – high threat – participants read an article that suggested the threat to the UK from Islamic terrorism was high.

Our findings were in line with our theoretically driven hypothesis that exposure to media social representations of Muslims is likely to be a causal factor in Islamophobia. Attitudes toward Muslims were significantly more negative in the high threat condition than in the control condition, and support for policies targeting Muslims significantly stronger in this high threat condition (both tested using ANOVA – F tests for effect of manipulation were significant at $p<.001$ in both cases – see Cinnirella *et al.* under review, for detailed findings).

A survey exploring the role of perceived threat

In 2008, working with Catherine Blackwell, I followed up the media effects experiment with a survey study of young non-Muslim British students studying at a college in south-east England (Cinnirella and Blackwell 2009). In this study we aimed to explore in more detail the degree to which perceived threat was a driver of Islamophobic prejudice. Theoretically, our aim was to draw upon integrated threat theory, and the idea that there are two broad forms of threat that an outgroup might pose: symbolic – that is, threats to beliefs and values – and realistic – for example, economic competition, threats to physical existence. In addition, we wanted to explore Huddy and associates' proposal that personal and collective threats might have different outcomes (Huddy *et al.* 2002). Specifically, their argument and findings that collective threat is a better predictor of support for policies – for example, immigration strategies and political ideologies – than personal threat. This notion of different levels of threat is compatible with ITT, since the latter theory also states that intergroup threats might be perceived at individual, group or both levels, with potentially different consequences (Stephan *et al.* 2008).

In this study our participants were 196 16–24 year olds – 139 females and 57 males – from a college in south-east England. Participants volunteered to take part in two unrelated studies, one about national identity, and one about 'life in the UK'. This deception was necessary to prevent demand characteristics and expectancy effects. Each was given a single questionnaire pack. We deployed a number of balanced Likert-type scales in the questionnaire – all manifested good Cronbach alpha levels, indicating internal reliability – including:

1   The same British identity scale as the media effects study described above (from Cinnirella 1997; example item: 'To what extent do you feel pleased to be British?')

2   Islamophobic attitudes, as measured by three custom-written scales – (1) support for new policies targeting Muslims (four items, for example, 'The British government should tighten immigration laws so that fewer Muslims are allowed into this country'); General attitudes toward Muslims scale (12 items; for example, 'British Muslims should be accepted as British citizens just like everyone else who holds a British passport'); Desire for contact with Muslims scale (four items; for example, 'I don't think I would want to share a flat or house with a Muslim person'). We also used a scale measure of Cultural Threat from Muslims (four items, for example, 'Muslims respect British values and traditions' – a sample reverse-scored item).

3   Attitudes toward different groups in society (five point scale, four items, derived from Abrams and Houston 2006). This scale asked 'In general, how negative or positive do you feel toward each of the following groups in Britain?' and participants then rated 'People over 70', 'Muslims', 'Black people (for example, African or Caribbean)', and 'Lesbian women or gay men'.

4   Stereotype trait ratings of Muslims and 'Blacks' (five point scale, 12 items, adapted from Abrams and Houston 2006). Here participants rated how they thought most people in the UK perceived each group on three positive (for example, 'friendly') and three negative traits (for example, 'disgust').

5   Realistic threat posed by Islamic terrorism/terrorists, broken down into personal threat and collective threat (8 point scale, two items, for example, 'I sometimes worry about dying or being injured in a terrorist attack by Muslims').

A detailed discussion of the findings from this study can be found in Cinnirella *et al.* (under review), however a summary of findings relating to the issue of threat is presented here. First, it is worth noting that this young British sample of college students held significantly more negative views about Muslims than they did about the other example social groups we asked them to evaluate (all comparisons p<.001). A similar picture emerged on the stereotype trait task, where participants stated they believed the British public viewed Muslims more negatively – on the three negative traits – and less positively – on the three positive traits – than Black Africans or Caribbeans.

Multiple regression was employed to explore the degree to which our measures of identity and perceived threat predicted the measures of Islamophobia (for full details of these analyses see Cinnirella *et al.* under review). Together, these regressions showed that:

- Perceived symbolic – that is, cultural – threat was important: respondents who felt culturally threatened by Muslims expressed negativity toward them, which supports intergroup threat theory.
- Realistic threat from terrorism, however, was also important, correlating with multiple indices of Islamophobia. This included our measure of personal realistic threat. In fact, in contrast to the results reported by Huddy *et al.* (2002), personal threat was as important a predictor of Islamophobia and support for hypothetical immigration and policing policies that would target Muslims, as collective realistic threat.
- British identity correlated positively with multiple measures of Islamophobia. Thus, the stronger a participant identified themselves with Britain and being British, the more negative their attitudes toward Muslims, the less they wanted contact with Muslims, the more they supported policies that would target Muslims, and the more they perceived Muslims as a symbolic threat to British culture.
- Overall, symbolic threat was the most important/powerful predictor of Islamophobia. However, realistic threat and national identity were also significant predictors of most Islamophobia measures.

Our findings are important for a number of reasons. Like the previous study we report above, this is further evidence that for young British people, national identity appears to be an important predictor of attitudes toward Muslims, and, importantly, also a predictor of willingness to support policies that would restrict the civil liberties of Muslims. This study also demonstrates the utility of integrated threat theory for the study of Islamophobia and, in particular, the distinction between personal and collective threats, and between symbolic versus realistic intergroup threats. However, at the same time our findings both support and contrast with previous research using the ITT framework to explore Islamophobia. For example, both Hitlan *et al.* (2007) and Gonzalez *et al.* (2008) report that perceived symbolic threat from Muslims was associated with Islamophobic attitudes, as we found in this study. However, they also report that realistic threat was a weaker predictor of Islamophobia or not significant as a predictor, unlike our findings indicating that it was an important predictor. Digging below the surface of these differences there is one important methodological difference between these previous studies and the work I report here. Hitlan *et al.* (2007) and Gonzalez *et al.* (2008) both operationalize realistic threat in terms of perceived economic and employment threats – in keeping with, for example, the traditional realistic conflict theory approach of Sherif *et al.* 1961. In contrast, I argue that, in the British context, it is far more appropriate to operationalize the realistic threat associated with Muslims in terms of the perceived threat to national security and personal safety posed by Islamic terrorists and acts of terrorism – a definition of realistic threat which is still in keeping with current formulations of ITT (Stephan *et al.* 2008). This is much more in line with our observations about the content of media portrayals of Muslims within the British press (Jaspal and Cinnirella 2010), which indicate that the press do not position Muslims as an economic threat, but rather as a symbolic/cultural threat to British values and traditions, and as a realistic threat to national security through their involvement in terrorism. Thus, our findings are probably divergent to previous researchers because we chose to operationalize realistic threat differently, although it is possible that there are differences in the nature and antecedents of Islamophobic prejudice across different national contexts.

Conclusions

The research reported in this chapter draws upon an eclectic mix of different theoretical traditions from social psychology. In doing so, I have particularly focused on the relationship between perceived threat and social identity, arguing that in the UK context media social representations often position Muslims as a threat to the majority of Britons. The empirical studies summarized here demonstrate that exposure to media social representations does seem to affect attitudes toward Muslims, and also that both symbolic and realistic threats contribute to Islamophobic attitudes and stereotyping of Muslims. This research programme is ongoing and in the future I plan to examine whether perceived threat associated with Muslims can be manipulated in the laboratory. I also plan to explore whether prejudice-reduction interventions can be designed around these issues of perceived threat.

So far, the implications of this research programme are such that they suggest Islamophobic attitudes are present in young British people, and that perceived threats associated with Muslims need to be addressed in any interventions targeted at reducing Islamophobia. The unfortunate conflation of social representations of terrorism with those of Muslims and Islam in the media (Jaspal and Cinnirella 2010) provides a continuing driver for Islamophobic prejudice, and, perhaps more worryingly, appears to increase support for policies that seek to limit the civil liberties of Muslims living in the UK. Since I have identified Islamophobic prejudice in young British adults, it might be prudent to consider how schooling could tackle this head-on. In the research literature on the negative effects of media violence, some success has been associated with training children and young adults to critically read and view media in such a way that they become inoculated against undesirable media effects. It would be worthwhile exploring in future research whether this kind of media awareness training, while also working with parents, could go some way toward ameliorating the apparent effects of exposure to negative media representations of Muslims in the UK. Ultimately, such interventions could hopefully break the apparent tendency for some Britons to think 'Muslim' and automatically think 'terrorist'.

References

Abbas, Tahir (2007) 'Muslim minorities in Britain: integration, multiculturalism and radicalism in the post-7/7 period', *Journal of Intercultural Studies* 28(3): 287–300.

Abdo, Geneive (2006) *Mecca and Main Street: Muslim Life in America after 9/11*, Oxford: Oxford University Press.

Abrams, D. and Hogg, M.A. (eds) (1990) *Social Identity Theory: Constructive and critical advances*, New York, NY: Springer.

Abrams, Dominic and Diane M. Houston (2006) *Equality, Diversity and Prejudice in Britain: Results from the 2005 National Survey*, Canterbury: University of Kent, Centre for the Study of Group Processes.

Adorno, T.W., Fenkel-Brunswik, E., Levinson, D.J. and Sanford, R.N. (1950) *The Authoritarian Personality*, New York: Harper.

Ajzen, Icek and Fishbein, Martin (1980) *Understanding Attitudes and Predicting Social Behaviour*, Englewood-Cliffs, NJ: Prentice-Hall.

Åkesson, J. (2009) 'Muslimerna är vårt största utländska hot', *Aftonbladet* 19 October.

Alba, R. (2005) 'Bright vs. blurred boundaries: Second-generation assimilation and exclusion in France, Germany, and the United States', *Ethnic and Racial Studies* 28(1): 20–49.

Albert, S. (1977) 'Temporal comparison theory', *Psychological Review* 84: 485–503.

Aldeeb, Sami (2009) *Avenir des Musulmans en Occident: Cas de la Suisse*. Saint-Suplice: Centre de droit arabe et musulman.

Allen, Christopher (2004) 'Endemically European or a European Epidemic? Islamophobia in a Post 9/11 Europe', in Theodore Gabriel, Ron Geaves, Yvonne Haddad and Jane Idleman Smith (eds) *Islam in the West: A Post September 11th Perspective*, London, pp.130-146.

—— (2006) 'Was ist Islamophobie? Ein evolutionärer Zeitstrahl', in Urs Altermatt, Mariano Delago and Guido Vergauwen (eds) *Der Islam in Europa: Zwischen Weltpolitik und Alltag*, Stuttgart: Kohlhammer, pp.67–78.

—— (2010) *Islamophobia*, Farnham: Ashgate.

Allen, Christopher and Nielson, Jorgen (2002) *Summary Report on Islamophobia in the EU after 11 September 2001*, Vienna: European Monitoring Centre on Racism and Xenophobia.

—— (2004) *Islamophobia in the EU after 11 September 2001: Summary report*, On behalf of the European Monitoring Centre on Racism and Xenophobia, Luxembourg: Office for Official Publications of the European Communities.

Allport, G.W. (1958[1954]) *The Nature of Prejudice*, Reading, MA: Addison-Wesley.

Altareb, B.Y. (1998) 'Attitudes towards Muslims: Initial scale development', *Dissertation Abstracts International: Section B: the Sciences and Engineering*, 58, 7-B: 3960.

Altemeyer, B. (1981) *Right-Wing Authoritarianism*, Winnipeg: University of Manitoba Press.

—— (1988) *Enemies of Freedom: Understanding Right-Wing Authoritarianism*, San Francisco: Josey-Bass.

—— (1996) *The Authoritarian Specter*, Cambridge, MA: Harvard University Press.

—— (1998) 'The other "authoritarian personality"', in M.P. Zanna (ed.) *Advances in Experimental Social Psychology*, vol. XXX, San Diego: Academic Press, pp.47–92.

Altemeyer, R. (2003), 'Why do Religious Fundamentalists Tend to Be Prejudiced?', *International Journal for the Psychology of Religion*, 13(1): 17–28.

Alvarez-Miranda, B. (2009) 'La acomodación del culto islámico en España. Comparación con Gran Bretaña, Alemania y Francia', in R. Zapata-Barrero (ed.) *Políticas y gobernabilidad de la Inmigración en España*, Barcelona: Ariel, pp.185–205.

Anderson, B. (1983) *Imagined Communities*, London: Verso.

Ansari, Humayun (2004) *The Infidel Within: Muslims in Britain Since 1800*, London: C. Hurst & Co. Publishers.

Anti-Defamation League of B'nai B'rith (2002) Anti-Semitism in America 2002. Online. http://www.adl.org/anti_semitism/2002/as_survey.pdf (accessed 14 October 2011).

Antonsich, Marco and Jones, Phil I. (2010) 'Mapping the Swiss Referendum on the Minaret Ban', *Political Geography* 29:57–62.

Anwar, M., Blaschke J. and Sander, Å. (eds) (2004) *State Policies Toward Muslim Minorities: Sweden, Great Britain and Germany*, Berlin: Edition Parabolis.

Argyrides, M., Downey, J.L. and Huff, W. (2002) 'Aggression and prejudice: measures before and after the World Trade Center and Pentagon attacks'. Paper presentation, Southeastern Psychological Association, Orlando, FL.

Åslund, O. and Rooth, D-O. (2005) 'Shifts in attitudes and labor market discrimination: Swedish experiences after 9-11', *Journal of Population Economics* 18: 603–29. Bader, V. (2008) *Secularism or Democracy? Associational Governance of Religious Diversity*, Amsterdam: Amsterdam University Press – IMISCOE Research.

Balibar, É. (1991) *Race, Nation, Class: Ambiguous Identities*, London: Verso.

Banchoff, Thomas (ed.) (2007) *Democracy and the New Religious Pluralism*, Oxford: Oxford University Press.

Banting, Keith and Kymlicka, Will (eds) (2006) *Multiculturalism and the Welfare State. Recognition and Redistribution in Contemporary Democracies*, Oxford: Oxford University Press.

Barrett, D.B., Kurian, G.T., and Johnson, T.M. (2001) *World Christian Encyclopedia*. (2nd edn), Oxford: Oxford University Press.

Bar-Tal, D. and Labin, D. (2001) 'The Effect of a Major Event on Stereotyping: Terrorist Attacks in Israel and Israeli Adolescents' Perceptions of Palestinians, Jordanians and Arabs', *European Journal of Social Psychology* 31: 265–80.

Bat Ye'or (2005) *Eurabia: The Euro-Arab Axis*, Madison, NJ: Fairleigh Dickinson University Press.

Behloul, Samuel M. (2009) 'Minarett-Initiative: Im Spannungsfeld zwischen Abwehr-Reflex und impliziter Anerkennung neuer gesellschaftlicher Fakten', in Mathias Tanner, *et al.* (eds) *Streit um das Minarett: Zusammenleben in der religiös pluralistischen Gesellschaft*. Zurich: Theologischer Verlag Zürich, pp.103–22.

Bem, D. (1972) 'Self-perception theory', in L. Berkowitz (ed.) *Advances in Social Psychology*, vol. VI, New York: Academic Press, pp.1–52.

Berinsky, Adam J. (2002) 'Political Context and the Survey Response: The Dynamics of Racial Policy Opinion', *The Journal of Politics* 64 (2): 567–84.

Berrens, R.P., Bohara, A.K., Jenkins-Smith, H., Silva, C. and Weimer, D.L. (2003) 'The Advent of Internet Surveys for Political Research: A Comparison of Telephone and Internet Samples', *Political Analysis* 11: 1–22.

Berry, J.W. (2006) 'Mutual attitudes among immigrants and ethnocultural groups in Canada', *International Journal of Intercultural Relations* 30(6): 719–34.

Bevelander, Pieter and Otterbeck, Jonas (2010) 'Young People's Attitudes towards Muslims in Sweden', *Journal of Ethnic and Racial Studies* 33(3): 404–25.

Bhabha, H.K. (ed.) (1990) *Nation and Narration*, London: Routledge.

Biernat, M.,Vescio,T.K.,Theno, S.A. and Crandall, C.S. (1996) 'Values and prejudice:Toward understanding the impact of American values on outgroup attitudes', in C. Seligman, J.M. Olson and M.P. Zanna (eds). *The Psychology of Values*, Mahwah, New Jersey: Lawrence Erlbaum, pp.153–89.

Billig, M. (1995) *Banal Nationalism*, London: Sage.

Blalock, H. (1967) *Toward a Theory of Minority-Group Relations*, New York:Wiley.

Bleich, Erik (2003) *Race politics in Britain and France: ideas and policymaking since the 1960s*, New York: Cambridge University Press.

—— (2009a) 'Muslims and the State in the Post-9/11 West: Introduction', *Journal of Ethnic and Migration Studies* 35(3): 353–60.

—— (2009b) 'Where do Muslims stand on ethno-racial hierarchies in Britain and France? Evidence from public opinion surveys, 1988–2008', *Patterns of Prejudice* 43(3–4): 379–400.

—— (2011) 'What Is Islamophobia and How Much Is There? Theorizing and Measuring an Emerging Comparative Concept', *American Behavioral Scientist,* 55: 1581–1600. Published online 26 September 2011, DOI: 10.1177/0002764211409387 available at: http://abs. sagepub.com/content/early/2011/09/23/0002764211409387

Blitz, J. (2010) 'Majority supports outlawing the burka', *Financial Times*, 2 March.

Bloom, W. (1990) *Personal Identity, National Identity and International Relations*, Cambridge, UK: Cambridge University Press.

Bogardus, Emory Stephen (1928) *Immigration and Race Attitudes*. New York: DC Heath.

Bollen, Kenneth A. (1989) *Structural Equations with Latent Variables*, New York: John Wiley & Sons.

Boomgaarden, H.G. and Vliegenthart, R. (2007) 'Explaining the rise of anti-immigrant parties: the role of news media content', *Electoral Studies* 26(2): 404–17.

Borger, Julian (2006) 'Poll shows Muslims in Britain are the most anti-western in Europe', *The Guardian*, June 23, 2006.

Bowen, John (2007) *Why the French don't like headscarves: Islam, the State and Public Space*, Princeton: Princeton University Press.

Bower, G.H. (1981) 'Mood and Memory', *American Psychologist* 36: 129–48.

Brader T.,Valentino, N.A. and Suhay, E. (2008) 'What triggers public opposition to immigration?; Anxiety, group cues, and immigration threat', *American Journal of Political Science* 52(4): 959–78.

Branscombe, N.R. and Wann, D.L. (1994) 'Collective self-esteem consequences of outgroup derogation when a valued social identity is on trial', *European Journal of Social Psychology* 24(6): 641–57.

Branscombe, N. R., Ellemers, N., Spears, R. and Doosje, B. (1999) 'The Context and Content of Social Identity Threat', in N. Ellemers., R. Spears and B. Doosje (eds) *Social identity: Context, commitment, content*, Oxford, England: Blackwell Science Ltd, pp.35–58.

Brewer, M.B. (1979) 'In-Group Bias in the Minimal Intergroup Situation: A Cognitive-Motivational Analysis', *Psychological Bulletin* 86(2): 307–24.

Brockett,A.,Village,A. and Francis, L.J. (2009) 'Internal consistency reliability and construct validity of the Attitude toward Muslim Proximity Index', *British Journal of Religious Education* 31: 241–9.

Broder, Henryk M. (2008) *Kritik der reinen Toleranz*, Berlin:WJS Verlag.

Bromley, C., Curtice, J. and Given, L. (2007) *Attitudes to Discrimination in Scotland, 2006*, Edinburgh: Scottish Government.

Brown, M.D. (2000) 'Conceptualising Racism and Islamophobia', in J. Ter Wal and M. Verkuyten (eds) *Comparative Perspectives on Racism*,Aldershot:Ashgate, pp.73–90.

Brubaker, Rogers (2004) *Ethnicity without Groups*, Cambridge, MA: Harvard University Press.

BRÅ (2010) *Hatbrott 2009, Statistik över polisanmälningar där det i motivbilden ingår etnisk bakgrund, religiös tro, sexuell läggning eller könsöverskridande identitet eller uttryck*, (2010), BRÅ, Rapport 2010:12.

Buijs, Frank J. and Rath, Jan (2002) *Muslims in Europe: The State of Research*, New York: Russell Sage Foundation.

Bunzl, Matti (2007) *Anti-Semitism and Islamophobia: Hatreds Old and New in Europe*, Chicago: Prickly Paradigm Press.

Campbell, D.T. and Fiske, D.W. (1959) 'Convergent and discriminant validation by the multi-trait-multimethod matrix', *Psychological Bulletin* 56: 81–105.

Campbell, Angus, Converse, Philip E., Miller, Warren E. and Stokes, Donald E. (1960) *The American Voter*, New York: John Wiley.

Casanova, José (2007) 'Immigration and the New Religious Pluralism: A European Union/ United States Comparison', in Thomas Banchoff (ed.) *Democracy and the New Religious Pluralism*, Oxford: Oxford University Press, pp.59–83.

Cashin, S. (2010) 'To be Muslim or 'Muslim-looking' in America: a comparative exploration of racial and religious prejudice in the 21st century', *Duke Forum for Law and Social Change* 2: 125–39.

Cattacin, S., Gerber, B., Sardi, M., and Wegener, R. (2006). *Monitoring rightwing extremist attitudes, xenophobia and misanthropy in Switzerland. An explorative study*. Research report – PNR 40+, Sociograph – Sociological Research. Study No 1 of the Department of sociology. Geneva: University of Geneva.

CBS (Central Bureau voor de Statistiek) (2004, September), Bijna een miljoen Islamieten in Nederland (Almost one million Muslims in the Netherlands), Webmagazine, Retrieved from http://www.cbs.nl/nl-NL/menu/themas/bevolking/publicaties/artikelen/ archief/2004/2004-1543-wm.htm

Central Intelligence Agency (CIA) (2009) *CIA Factbook 2009*, Washington, DC: Central Intelligence Agency. Retrieved August 10, 2010 from: http://www.geographic.org/ wfb2009/norway/norway_people.html

Cesari, Jocelyne (2004) *When Islam and Democracy Meet: Muslims in Europe and in the United States*, New York: Palgrave Macmillan.

—— (2005a) 'Islam, Secularism and Multiculturalism after 9/11: A Transatlantic Comparison', in Jocelyne Cesari and Sean McLoughlin (eds) *European Muslims and the Secular State*, Aldershot: Ashgate, pp.39–51.

—— (2005b) Special Issue on Mosque Conflicts in European Cities, *Journal of Ethnic and Migration Studies* 31(6).

—— (2006) *Securitization and Religious Divides in Europe. Muslims in Western Europe after 9/11 – Why the Term Islamophobia is More a Predicament than an Explanation* A Challenge Research Project funded by the European Commission. http://www.libertysecurity.org/ IMG/pdf_Challenge_Project_report.pdf.

—— (ed.) (2010a) *Muslims in the West after 9/11. Religion, Politics and Law*, London and New York: Routledge.

—— (2010b) 'Securitization of Islam in Europe', in Jocelyne Cesari (ed.) *Muslims in the West after 9/11. Religion, Politics and Law*, London and New York: Routledge, pp.9–27.

Chandler, Charles R. and Tsai, Yung-mei (2001) 'Social factors influencing immigration attitudes: an analysis of data from the General Social Survey', *Social Science Journal* 38: 177–88.

Chiozza, Giacomo (2007) 'Disaggregating Anti-Americanism: An Analysis of Individual Attitudes toward the United States', in Peter J. Katzenstein and Robert O. Keohane (eds) (2007) *Anti-Americanism in World Politics*, Ithaca and London: Cornell University Press, pp.93–126.

Cinnirella, M. (1997) 'Towards a European identity? Interactions between the national and European social identities manifested by university students in Britain and Italy', *British Journal of Social Psychology* 36(1): 19–31.

—— (2007) 'The role of fear of terrorism and threatened identity in Islamophobic prejudice'. Presented at the British Psychological Society (Social Psychology Section) Annual Conference, University of Kent, Canterbury, UK, September 2007.

Cinnirella, M. and Blackwell, C. (2009) 'The effect of national identity and threat on Attitudes towards British Muslims'. Presented at the British Psychological Society Annual Conference, Brighton, UK, April 2009.

Cinnirella, M., Leman, P., Hastings, K. and Whitbread, N. (under review) 'The role of fear of terrorism and threatened identity in Islamophobic prejudice'.

Citrin, Jack and Green, Donald P. (1997) 'Public Opinion Toward Immigration Reform: The Role of Economic Motivations', *Journal of Politics* 59: 858–81.

Clark, Tom, Putnam, Robert D. and Fieldhouse, Edward (2010) *The Age of Obama. The Changing Place of Minorities in British and American Societies*, Manchester: Manchster University Press.

Cole, Mike (2009) 'A Plethora of "Suitable Enemies": British Racism at the Dawn of the Twenty-First Century', *Ethnic and Racial Studies* 32(9): 1671–85.

Commission on Integration and Cohesion (2007) *Public Attitudes towards Cohesion and Integration*, Wetherby: Communities and Local Government [CLG].

Connolly, H. (2010) *Attitudes, Values and Perceptions: Muslims and the General Population in 2007–08*, London: CLG.

Cronbach, L.J. (1946) 'Response sets and test validity', *Educational and Psychological Measurement* 6: 475–94.

Cronbach, L.J. and Meehl, P.E. (1955) 'Construct validity in psychological tests', *Psychological Bulletin* 52: 281–302.

Crosby, F., Bromley, S. and Saxe, L. (1980) 'Recent Unobtrusive Studies of Black and White Discrimination and Prejudice: A Literature Review', *Psychological Bulletin* 87(3): 546–63.

Cuddy, A.J., Fiske, S.T. and Glick, P. (2007) 'The BIAS map: Behaviors from Intergroup Affect and Stereotypes', *Journal of Personality and Social Psychology* 92(94): 631–48.

Cumming-Bruce, Nick. 2007. 'Rightists strengthen hold on Swiss Parliament', *New York Times*, October 21. http://www.nytimes.com/2007/10/21/world/europe/21ihtswiss.5.7986440.html?scp=5&sq=Swiss%20People%27s%20Party%20SVP%202007%20election&st=cse, (accessed November 3, 2011).

Dahl, Robert A. (1956) *A Preface to Democratic Theory*, Chicago and London: The University of Chicago Press.

Davis, D.W. (2007) *Negative Liberty: Public Opinion and the Terrorist Attacks on America*, New York: Russell Sage Foundation.

Dekker, Henk and Van der Noll, Jolanda (2007) 'Islamophobia and its Origins. A Study among Dutch Youth', Paper presented at the fourth ECPR Conference September 6-8, Pisa, Italy.

Dekker, H., Aspeslagh, R. and Meijerink, F. (1998) 'Attitudes toward Germany and other European Union countries among Dutch youth', *Politics, Groups and the Individual*, 7 (1/2): 57–90.

Dekker, H., Malová, D. and Hoogendoorn, S. (2003) 'Nationalism and its explanations', *Political Psychology* 24(2): 345–76.

De la Garza, Rodolfo, Falcon, Angelo and Garcia, F. Chris (1996) 'Will The Real Americans Please Stand Up: Anglo and Mexican-American Support of Core American Political Values', *American Journal of Political Science* 40(2): 335–51.

Díez-Nicolás, J. (2005) *Las Dos Caras de la Inmigración, Ministerio de Trabajo y Asuntos Sociales.* Madrid: Observatorio Permanente de la Inmigración.

—— (2007a) '¿Regreso a los valores materialistas? El dilema entre seguridad y libertad en los países desarrollados', Federación Española De Sociología, IX Congreso Español de Sociología, 'Poder, Cultura y Civilización', Barcelona, 13-15 de Septiembre de 2007.

—— (2007b) 'Percepción de la 'inmigración' y rechazo al 'inmigrante'', *SOS. Racismo. Informe Anual 2007. Sobre el Racismo en el Estado Español*, Barcelona: Editorial Icaria.

—— (2009a) 'Opinión Pública y Políticas de Inmigración', in Ricard Zapata-Barrero (ed.) *Políticas y Gobernabilidad de la Inmigración en España*, Ariel: Barcelona.

—— (2009b) 'Construcción de un Índice de Xenofobia-Racismo', *Migraciones Internacionales. Revista del Ministerio de Trabajo e Inmigración*, N° 80, Madrid.

Díez-Medrano, J. (2005) 'Nation, Citizenship and Immigration in Contemporary Spain', International Journal of Multicultural Societies 7(2): 133-156.

Dolezal, Martin, Helbling, Marc and Hutter, Swen (2010) 'Debates over Islam in Austria, Germany, and Switzerland: Between Ethnic Citizenship, State–Church Relations and Right-Wing Populism', *West European Politics* 33(2): 171–90.

Doty, R.M., Winter, D.G., Peterson, B.E. and Kemmelmeier, M. (1997) 'Authoritarianism and American students' attitudes about the Gulf War, 1990–1996', *Personality and Social Psychology Bulletin* 23: 1133–43.

Dovidio, J.F., Gaertner, S.L., Kawakami, K. and Hodson, G. (2002) 'Why Can't We Just Get Along? Interpersonal Biases and Interracial Distrust', *Cultural Diversity and Ethnic Minority Psychology*, 8(2): 88–102.

Downs, Anthony (1957) *An Economic Theory of Democracy*, New York: Harper & Brothers.

Druckman, D. (1994) 'Nationalism, Patriotism, and Group Loyalty: A Social Psychological Perspective', *Mershon International Studies Review* 38(1): 43–68.

Duckitt, J. (1992) *The Social Psychology of Prejudice*, New York: Praeger.

Duckitt, J. (2003) 'Prejudice and intergroup hostility', in D. Sears, L. Huddy and R. Jervis (eds) *Oxford Handbook of Political Psychology*, Oxford: Oxford University Press.

Dunn, T.N. (2010) 'Forces are not kit for purpose', *The Sun*, 13 January.

Echebarria-Echabe, Augustin and Fernandez Guede, Emilia (2006) 'Effects of Terrorism on Attitudes and Ideological Orientation', *European Journal of Social Psychology* 36(2): 259–65.

—— (2007) 'A New Measure of Anti-Arab Prejudice: Reliability and Validity Evidence', *Journal of Applied Social Psychology* 37(5): 1077–91.

Edgell, P., Gerteis, J. and Hartmann, D. (2006) 'Atheists as Other: Moral Boundaries and Cultural Membership in American Society', *American Sociological Review*, 71(2): 211–34.

Ellemers, N., Spears, R. and Doosje, B. (1997) 'Sticking together or falling apart: In-group identification as a psychological determinant of group commitment versus individual mobility', *Journal of Personality and Social Psychology* 72(3): 617–26

Entzinger, H. (2007) 'Rising demands and growing frustrations; Mutual perception and value change in multi-ethnic Rotterdam since "9/11"', in E. Poppe and M. Verkuyten (eds) *Culture and Conflict*, Amsterdam: Aksant, pp.183–96.

Esses, V.M., Dovidio, J.F., Jackson, L.M. and Armstrong, T.L. (2001) 'The immigration dilemma: the role of perceived group competition, ethnic prejudice, and national identity', *Journal of Social Issues* 57(3): 389–412.

European Monitoring Centre on Racism and Xenophobia (EUMC) (2003) *The fight against Anti-Semitism and Islamophobia: Bringing communities together*, EUMC, Brussels/Vienna.

—— (2006) *Muslims in the European Union: Discrimination and Islamophobia*, EUMC, Vienna.

Federal Bureau of Investigation (2002) Hate Crime Statistics 2001. Online. http://www.fbi.gov/about-us/cjis/ucr/hate-crime/2001 (accessed Oct. 31, 2011)

Fekete, Liz (2004) 'Anti-Muslim Racism and the European Security State', *Race & Class* 46(3): 3–29.

Ferguson, C., Finch, S. and Turczuk, O. (2009) *2007/08 Citizenship Survey: Race, Religion and Equalities Topic Report*, London: CLG.

Ferguson, C. and Hussey, D. (2010) *2008-09 Citizenship Survey: Race, Religion and Equalities Topic Report*, London: CLG.

Festinger, L. and Carlsmith, J. (1959) 'Cognitive consequences of forced compliance', *Journal of Abnormal and Social Psychology* 58: 203–10.

Fetzer, Joel S. (2000) *Public Attitudes toward Immigration in the United States, France, and Germany*. Cambridge: Cambridge University Press.

Fetzer, Joel S. and Soper, Christopher (2003) 'The roots of public attitudes towards state accommodation of European Muslims' religious practices before and after September 11', *Journal for the Scientific Study of Religion* 42: 247–58.

—— (2005) *Muslims and the State in Britain, France and Germany*, Cambridge: Cambridge University Press.

Field, C.D. (2006) 'John Bull's Judeophobia', *Jahrbuch für Antisemitismusforschung*, 15: 259–300.

—— (2007) 'Islamophobia in contemporary Britain', *Islam and Christian-Muslim Relations* 18: 447–77.

—— (2010a) *Integrated Household Survey*, http://www.brin.ac.uk/news/?p=603.

—— (2010b) *Muslim Opinions and Opinions of Muslims*, http://www.brin.ac.uk/figures/documents/Field-Muslim-opinions-and-opinions-of-Muslims-Dec-2010.pdf.

First International Resources (2009) *Attitudes toward Jews in Seven European Countries*, New York: Anti-Defamation League, http://www.adl.org.

Fishbein, M. and Ajzen, I. (1975) *Belief, Attitude, Intention and Behavior: An introduction to theory and research*, Reading, MA: Addison-Wesley.

Flesler, D. and Pérez Melgosa, A. (2003) 'Battles of Identity, or Playing 'Guest' and 'Host': the Festivals of Moors and Christians in the Context of Moroccan Immigration in Spain', *Journal of Spanish Cultural Studies* 4(2): 151-168.

Foner, Nancy and Richard Alba (2008) 'Immigrant Religion in the U.S. and Western Europe: Bridge or Barrier to Inclusion?', *International Migration Review* 42(2): 360–92.

Forbes, H.D. (1997) *Ethnic Conflict: Commerce, Culture, and the Contact Hypothesis*, New Haven, CT: Yale University Press.

Forgas, J.P. and Moylan, S.J. (1991) 'Affective Influences on Stereotype Judgments', *Cognition and Emotion* 5: 379–97.

Fortuyn, W.S.P. (1997) *Tegen de islamisering van onze cultuur: Nederlandse identiteit als fundament*, Utrecht: AW Bruna.

Forum (2010) *De positie van moslims in Nederland. Feiten en cijfers*, Forum. Utrecht: Instituut voor multiculturele vraagstukken.

Foucault, M. (1971/1998) 'Nietzsche, Genealogy, History' in J.D. Faubion (ed.) *Aesthetics, Method, and Epistemology. The Essential Works of Foucault*, vol. two. New York: The New Press.

Fowers, B.J. and Richardson, F.C. (1996) 'Why is multiculturalism good?', *American psychologist* 51: 609–21.

Frauen gegen eine Islamisierung der Schweiz (2009) 'Unsere Freiheiten bewahren – Frauen gegen eine Islamisierung der Schweiz', http://www.minarette.ch/downloads/argumentarium_frauenfreiheit.pdf, (accessed November 3, 2011).

Gardell, M. (2010) *Islamofobi*, Stockholm: Leopard.

Geisser, Vincent (2003) *La nouvelle islamophobie*, Paris: La Découverte.

Gibson, J. L. (2006) 'Enigmas of intolerance: Fifty years after Stouffer's communism, conformity, and civil liberties', *Perspectives on Politics* 4(1): 21–34.

—— (2008) 'Intolerance and Political Repression in the United States: A Half Century after McCarthyism', *American Journal of Political Science* 52(1): 96–108.

Gibson, J. L. and Gouws, A. (2003) *Overcoming Intolerance in South Africa: Experiments in Democratic Persuasion*, New York: Cambridge University Press.

Gieling, M., Thijs, J. and Verkuyten, M. (2010) 'Tolerance of practices by Muslim actors: An integrative social-developmental perspective', *Child Development* 81(5): 1384–99.

Gilens, M. (1999) *Why Americans Hate Welfare*, Chicago, IL: University of Chicago Press.

Girard, Alain (1971) 'Attitudes des Français à l'égard de l'immigration étrangère: Enquête d'opinion publique', *Population* [Paris], 26: 827–75.

Gijsberts, M. (2005). 'Opvattingen van autochtonen en allochtonen over de multi-etnische samenleving' [Beliefs about the multicultural society among authochtonous and alloch-tones people], in *Jaarreportage Integratie*, The Hague: Social Cultural Planning Office.

Gijsberts, M.I.L., Hagendoorn, L. and Scheepers, P. (eds) (2004) *Nationalism and Exclusion of Migrants: Cross-national comparisons*, Aldershot: Ashgate.

Giugni, Marco and Morariu, Miruna (2010) 'Intolerance Begets Intolerance. Explaining Negative Attitudes toward Foreigners and Muslims in Switzerland, 1996–2007', in Simon Hug and Hanspeter Kriesi (eds) *Value Change in Switzerland*, Lanham: Lexington Press, pp.81–97.

Glock, C.Y. and Stark, R. (1966) *Christian Beliefs and Anti-Semitism*, New York: Harper and Row.

Goldberg, David Theo (2006) 'Racial Europeanization', *Ethnic and Racial Studies* 29(2): 331–64.

González, K, Verkuyten, M, Weesie, J, and Poppe, E. (2008) 'Prejudice towards Muslims in The Netherlands: Testing integrated threat theory', *British Journal of Social Psychology* 47(4): 667–85.

Goodwin, R., Willson, M. and Gaines, S. (2005) 'Terror threat perception and its conse-quences in contemporary Britain', *British Journal of Psychology* 96: 389–406.

Gorsuch, R.L. and Aleshire, D. (1974) 'Christian faith and ethnic prejudice: a review and interpretation of research', *Journal for the Scientific Study of Religion* 13: 281–307.

Gottschalk, Peter and Greenberg, Gabriel (2008) *Islamophobia. Making Muslims the Enemy*, Lanham: Rowman and Littlefield.

Greater London Authority (2007) *The Search for Common Ground*, London: Greater London Authority.

Greenberg, J., Schimel, J., Martens, A., Solomon, S. and Pyszcznyski, T. (2001) 'Sympathy for the Devil: Evidence that Reminding Whites of their Own Morality Promotes More Favorable Reactions to White Racists', *Motivation and Emotion* 25: 113–33.

Grice, A. (2010) 'Poll shows Britons back limited curbs on the veil', *The Independent*, 1 February.

GRIS and Institut Religioscope (2009) 'L'Islam en Suisse: quelques chiffres', in Patrick Haenni and Stéphane Lathion (eds) *Les Minarets de la Discorde: Éclairages sur un Débat Suisse et Européen*. Gollion: Infolio, pp.31–2.

Gross, Dominique M. (2006) 'Immigration Policy and Foreign Population in Switzerland.' *World Bank Policy Research Working Paper 3853*, Washington DC, World Bank.

Gusfield, Joseph (1963) *Symbolic Crusade,* Urbana: University of Illinois Press.

Haddad, Yvonne Y. (ed.) (2002) *Muslims in the West: From Sojourners to Citizens*, Oxford: Oxford University Press.

Haddad, Yvonne Y. and Smith, Jane I. (2002) *Muslim Minorities in the West: Visible and Invisible*, Walnut Creek, CA: Altamira Press.

Hagelund, A. (2003) 'A matter of decency? The Progress Party in Norwegian immigration politics', *Journal of Ethnic and Migration Studies* 29(1): 47–65.

Hagendoorn, Louk (1993) 'Ethnic Categorization and Outgroup Exclusion: The Role of Cultural Values and Social Stereotypes in the Construction of Ethnic Hierarchies', *Ethnic and Racial Studies* 16(1): 26–51.

—— (1995) 'Intergroup Biases in Multiple Group Systems: The Perception of Ethnic Hierarchies', *European Review of Social Psychology* 6: 199–228.

Hainmueller, Jens and Hiscox, Michael (2007) 'Educated Preferences: Explaining Individual Attitudes toward International Trade', *International Organization* 61(2): 399–442.

—— (2010) 'Attitudes toward Highly Skilled and Low Skilled Immigration: Evidence from a Survey Experiment', *American Political Science Review* 104(1): 61–84.

Halliday, Fred (1999) "Islamophobia' reconsidered', *Ethnic and Racial Studies* 22(5): 892–902.

Hammond, R.A. and Axelrod, R. (2006) 'The Evolution of Ethnocentrism', *Journal of Conflict Resolution* 50(6): 926–36.

Hanmer, M.J. and Kalkan, K.O. (2009) 'Behind the Curve: Clarifying the Best Approach to Calculating Predicted Probabilities and Marginal Effects from Limited Dependent Variable Models', Paper presented at the Annual Meeting of the American Political Science Association, September 3–6, 2009, Toronto, ON, Canada.

Hansen, Randall (2011) 'The two faces of liberalism: Islam in contemporary Europe', *Journal of Ethnic and Migration Studies* 3796): 881–97.

Harris Interactive (2010) Barack Obama and the Dalai Lama sit on top of World Leaders Barometer, http://www.harrisinteractive.com.

Harris, M. (1994) 'Mohammed and the Virgin, Folk Dramatizations of Battles Between Moors and Christians in Modern Spain', *The Drama Review* 38(1): 45–61.

Hawthorne, Christopher (2009) 'The Swiss minaret ban: Anxieties unveiled.' *Los Angeles Times*, December 1. http://latimesblogs.latimes.com/culturemonster/2009/12/the-swiss-minaret-ban-islamophobia-lightly-veiled.html, October 6, 2010.

Hayes, Bernadette C. and Dowds, Lizanne (2006) 'Social Contact, Cultural Marginality or Economic Self-Interest? Attitudes Towards Immigrants in Northern Ireland', *Journal of Ethnic and Migration Studies* 32: 455–76.

Heath, Anthony F. and Tilley, James R. (2005) 'British National Identity and Attitudes towards Immigration.' *International Journal on Multicultural Societies* 7: 119–32.

Heaven, P. and St. Quintin, D. (2003) 'Personality factors predict racial prejudice', *Personality and Individual Differences* 34: 625–34.

Helbling, Marc (2008) *Practicing Citizenship and Heterogeneous Nationhood: Naturalization in Swiss Municipalities*, Amsterdam: Amsterdam University Press.

—— (2010) 'Islamophobia in Switzerland: A New Phenomenon or a New Name for Xenophobia', in Simon Hug and Hanspeter Kriesi (eds) *Value Change in Switzerland*, Lanham: Lexington Press, pp.65–80.

—— (2011) 'Why Swiss Germans dislike Germans: Opposition to culturally similar and highly skilled immigrants', *European Societies* 13(1): 5–27.

Helbling, Marc and Kriesi, Hanspeter (2004) 'Staatsbürgerverständnis und politische Mobilisierung: Einbürgerungen in Schweizer Gemeinden', *Swiss Political Science Review* 10 (4): 33–58.

Hello, E., Scheepers, P., Vermulst, A. and Gerris, J.R.M. (2004) 'Association between educational attainment and ethnic distance in young adults; Socialisation by schools or parents?', *Acta Sociologica* 47(3): 253–75.

Henry, P. and Sears, D. (2002) 'The symbolic racism 2000 scale', *Poltical Psychology* 23: 253–83.

Herrmann, R.K. (1984) 'Foreign policy decision making: Perceptions, cognition and artificial intelligence', in D. A. Sylvan and S. Chan (eds) *Foreign policy decision making*, New York: Praeger.

Hetherington, M. and Weiler, J. (2009) *Authoritarianism and Polarization in American Politics*, New York, NY: Cambridge University Press.

Higham, J. (1951) *Strangers in the Land: Patterns of American Nativism, 1860–1925*, New York, NY: Atheneum.

Hirter, Hans and Vatter, Adrian (2010) 'Analyse der eidgenössichen Abstimmungenen vom 29. November 2009', *VOX Survey Report*. Bern: Gfs.bern/Universität Bern.

Hitlan, R., Carrillo, K., Aikman, S.N. and Zárate, M.A. (2007) 'Attitudes toward immigrant groups and the September 11 terrorist attacks', *Peace and Conflict Studies* 13(2): 135–52.

Hitlin, S. and Piliavin, J.A. (2004) 'Values: Reviving a Dormant Concept', *Annual Review of Sociology* 30: 359–93.

Hollifield, James F. (1992) *Immigrants, Markets and States: The Political Economy of Postwar Europe*, Cambridge, MA: Harvard University Press.

Holzer, Werner and Münz, Rainer (1995) 'Wissen und Einstellungen zu Migration, ausländischer Bevölkerung und staatlicher Ausländerpolitik in Österreich', *ÖZS, Österreichische Zeitschrift für Soziologie* 20:69–78.

Hood, M.V., Morris, I.L. (1997) 'Amigo o enemigo? Context, Attitudes and Anglo Public Opinion Toward Immigration', *Social Science Quarterly*, 78(2): 309–23.

Hopkins, Peter and Gale, Richard (eds) (2009) *Muslims in Britain: Race, Place, and Identities*, New York: Columbia University Press.

Hoskin, Marilyn (1991) *New Immigrants and Democratic Society: Minority Integration in Western Democracies*, Westport, CT: Praeger.

Huddy, L., Feldman, S., Taber, C. and Lahav, G. (2005) 'Threat, Anxiety, and Support of Antiterrorism Policies', *American Journal of Political Science* 49(3): 593–608.

Huddy, L., Feldman, S., Capelos, T. and Provost, C. (2002) 'The consequences of terrorism: disentangling the effects of personal and national threat', *Political Psychology* 23(3): 485–509.

Huddy, L., Khatib, N. and Capelos, T. (2002) 'The polls-trends: Reactions to the terrorist attacks of September 11, 2001', *Public Opinion Quarterly* 66: 418–450.

Hughes, D., Hagelskamp, C, Way, N. and Foust, M.D. (2009) 'The role of mothers' and adolescents' perceptions of ethnic-racial socialisation in shaping ethnic-racial identity among early adolescent boys and girls', *Journal of Youth and Adolescence* 38: 605–26.

Hunsberger, B. and Jackson, L.M. (2005) 'Religion, meaning, and prejudice', *Journal of Social Issues* 61: 807–26.

Hunter, Shireen T. (ed.) (2002) *Islam, Europe's Second Religion: The New Social, Cultural and Political Landscape*, Westport, CT: Praeger.

Huntington, S. (2004) *Who we are: The Challenges to American National Identity*, New York: Simon and Schuster.

Hvitfelt, Håkan (1991) 'Svenska attityder till islam', in S. Holmberg and L. Weibull (eds) *Politiska opinioner, SOM-undersökningen 1990*, SOM-rapport 6, GothenburgUniversity.

—— (1998) 'Den muslimska faran – om mediabilden av islam', in Y. Brune (ed.) *Mörk magi i vita medier – svensk nyhetsjournalistik om invandrare, flyktingar och rasism*, Stockholm: Carlssons.

Hådell, S. (1997) Images of Islam in the Swedish Media, University of Wales, College of Cardiff. Master thesis in European Journalism Studies.

Ilias, Shayerah, Fennelly, Katherine and Federico, Christopher M. (2008) 'American Attitudes toward Guest Worker Policies', *International Migration Review* 42: 741–66.

IMDi (2009) *Innvandrere i norske medier: Medieskapt islamfrykt og usynlig hverdagsliv. Årsrapport 2009*, Oslo: Integrerings- og mangfoldsdirektoratet.

Inglehart, R. (1977) *The Silent Revolution: Changing Values and Political Styles Among Western Publics*, Princeton: Princeton University Press.

Inglehart, R. (1990) *Culture shift in advanced industrial society*, Princeton: Princeton University Press.

—— (1997) *Modernization and post modernization*, Princeton: Princeton University Press.

—— (2008) 'Changing Values among Western Publics from 1970 to 2006', *West European Politics*, 31(1–2): 130–146.

Inglehart, R. and Welzel, C. (2005) *Modernization, Cultural Change and Democracy*, New York, NY: Cambridge University Press.

Integrationsbarometer (2005) *Integrationsbarometer 2004: En rapport om allmänhetens inställning till integration, mångfald och diskriminering 2003 och 2004*. Integrationsverkets skriftserie V. Norrköping: Integrationsverket.

—— (2006) *Integrationsbarometer 2005: En rapport om allmänhetens attityder, erfarenheter och kunskaper inom områdena integration, mångfald och diskriminering*. Integrationsverkets rapportserie 2006:05. Norrköping: Integrationsverket.

Ireland, Patrick (1994) *The Policy Challenge of Ethnic Diversity: Immigration Politics in France and Switzerland*, Cambridge, MA: Harvard University Press.

Iseni, Bashkim (2009) 'Les diasporas musulmanes des Balkans en Suisse', in Mallory Schneuwly Purdie, Matteo Gianni and Magali Jenny (eds) *Musulmans d'aujourd'hui: Identités plurielles en Suisse*. Geneva: Labor et Fides, pp.37–52.

Isernia, Pierangelo (2007) 'Anti-Americanism in Europe during the Cold War', in Peter J. Katzenstein and Robert O. Keohane (eds) (2007) *Anti-Americanism in World Politics*, Ithaca and London: Cornell University Press, pp.57–92.

Islam, I. (2005) *The Political Economy of Islamophobia and the Global Discourse on Islam*, The Griffith Asia Institute, Regional Outlook Paper No. 3.

Islamic Human Rights Commission. (2004) *Social Discrimination: Across the Muslim Divide*, London: Islamic Human Rights Commission

Iyer, A., Jetten, J. and Tsivrikos, D. (2008) 'Torn between identities: Predictors of adjustment to identity', in F. Sani (ed.) *Self Continuity: Individual and Collective Perspectives*, Hove: Psychology Press.

Izzett, R.R. (1971) 'Authoritarianism and attitudes toward the Vietnam war as reflected in behavioral and self-report measures', *Journal of Personality and Social Psychology* 17: 145–48.

Jackman, Mary R. (1973) 'Education and Prejudice or Education and Response-Set?' *American Sociological Review* 38(3): 327–39.

Jamal, A.A. and Naber, N.C. (2008) *Race and Arab Americans Before and After 9/11: From Invisible Citizens to Visible Subjects*, Syracuse, NY: Syracuse University Press.

Jaspal, R. and Cinnirella, M. (2010) 'Media representations of British Muslims and hybridised threats to identity', *Contemporary Islam: Dynamics of Muslim Life* 4(3): 289–310.

Jefatura de Estado (1992) 'Ley 26/1992, de 10 Noviembre, por la que se aprueba el acuerdo de cooperación del estado con la comisión islámica de España', *Boletín Oficial del Estado* 272, 12 noviembre (Available at: www.boe.es/g/es/bases_datos/ doc.php?coleccion= iberlex&id=1992/24855)

Jennings, M. K. (2007) 'Political socialization', in: R.J. Dalton and H.-D. Klingemann (eds) *The Oxford Handbook of Political Behavior*, New York, NY: Oxford University Press, pp.29–44.

Jennings, M.K., Stoker, L. and Bowers, J. (2009) 'Politics across generations: Family transmission reconsidered', *The Journal of Politics* 71 (3): 782–99.

Jetten, J., Spears, R. and Manstead, A. S. R. (1997) 'Strength of identification and intergroup differentiation: The influence of group norms', *European Journal of Social Psychology* 27(5): 603–9.

Jones, Frank E. and Lambert, Wallace E. (1965) 'Occupational Rank and Attitudes Toward Immigrants', *Public Opinion Quarterly* 29:137–44.

Joppke, Christian (2007) 'State Neutrality and Islamic Headscarf Laws in France and Germany', *Theory and Society* 36(4): 313–42.

—— (2009a) *Veil: Mirrors of Identity*, Cambridge: Polity Press.

—— (2009b) 'Limits of Integration Policy: Britain and Her Muslims', *Journal of Ethnic and Migration Studies* 35(3): 453–72.

Judt, T. (2005) *Postwar: A History of Europe since 1945*, New York: Penguin.

Julius, A. (2010) *Trials of the Diaspora*, Oxford: Oxford University Press.

Kalkan, Kerem Ozan, Layman, Geoffrey C. and Uslaner, Eric M. (2009) "Bands of Others?" Attitudes toward Muslims in Contemporary American Society', *The Journal of Politics* 71(3): 847–62.

Kam, C.D. and Kinder, D.R. (2007) 'Terror and Ethnocentrism: Foundations of American Support for the War on Terrorism', *Journal of Politics* 69(2): 320–38.

Kao, Grace and Tienda, Marta (1995) 'Optimism and Achievement: The Educational Performance of Immigrant Youth', *Social Science Quarterly* 76(1): 1–19.

Kaplan, Jeffrey (2006) 'Islamophobia in America? September 11 and Islamophobic Hate Crime', *Terrorism and Political Violence* 18(1): 1–33.

Karlsson Minganti, P. (2007) *Muslima: Islamisk väckelse och unga muslimska kvinnors förhandlingar om genus i det samtida Sverige*, Stockholm: Carlsson

Kassim, Azizah (1987) 'The Unwelcome Guests: Indonesian Immigrants and Malaysian Public Responses', *Tō⁻nan Ajia kenkyu⁻ /Southeast Asian Studies* 25:265–78.

Katzenstein, Peter J. and Keohane, Robert O. (eds) (2007) *Anti-Americanism in World Politics*, Ithaca and London: Cornell University Press.

Kaufmann, E. (2010) *Shall the Religious Inherit the Earth?*, London: Profile Books.

Kawakami, K., Dovidio, J.F., Moll, J., Hermsen, S. and Russin, A. (2000) 'Just Say No (to Stereotyping): Effects of Training in the Negation of Stereotypic Associations on Stereotype Activation', *Journal of Personality and Social Psychology* 78(5): 871–88.

Kinder, Donald R. and Sears, David O. (1981) 'Prejudice and Politics: Symbolic Racism Versus Racial Threats to the Good Life', *Journal of Personality and Social Psychology* 40(3):414–31.

Kinder, D.R. and Kam, C. (2009) *Us against Them: Ethnocentric Foundations of American Public Opinion*, Chicago, IL: University of Chicago Press.

King, Gary (1997) *The Solution to the Ecological Inference Problem: Reconstructing Individual Behavior from Aggregate Data*, Princeton: Princeton University Press.

Kirby, I. (2009) 'Now will you listen', *News of the World*, 25 October.

Kitschelt, Herbert, in collaboration with Anthony J. McGann (1995) *Radical Right in Western Europe: A Comparative Analysis*, Ann Arbor, MI: University of Michigan Press.

Klausen, Jytte (2005) *The Islamic Challenge: Politics and Religion in Western Europe*, Oxford: Oxford University Press.

Kleinpenning, G. and Hagendoorn, L. (1993) 'Forms of racism and the cumulative dimension of ethnic attitudes', *Social Psychology Quarterly* 56 (1): 21–36.

Kohut, A. and Wike, R. (2008) 'Xenophobia on the continent', *National Interest*, 30 October.

Koopmans, Ruud, Statham, Paul, Giugni, Marco and Passy, Florence (2005) *Contested Citizenship: Immigration and Cultural Diversity in Europe*, Minneapolis and London: University of Minnesota Press.

Konig, R., Scheepers, P and Felling, A. (2001) 'Research on antisemitism: a review of previous findings and the case of the Netherlands in the 1990s', in K. Phalet and A. Örkény (eds) *Ethnic Minorities and Inter-Ethnic Relations in Context: a Dutch–Hungarian comparison*, Aldershot: Ashgate, pp.179–99.

Kühnel, Steffen and Leibold, Jürgen (2007) 'Islamophobie in der deutschen Bevölkerung: Ein neues Phänomen oder nur ein neuer Namen? Ergebnisse von Bevölkerungsumfragen zur Gruppenbezogenen Menschenfeindlichkeit 2003 bis 2005', in Monika Wohlrab-Sahr and Levent Tezcan (eds) *Konfliktfeld Islam in Europa*, Baden-Baden: Nomos, pp.135–54.

Kuklinski, J.H., Sniderman, P.M., Knight, K., Piazza, T., Tetlock, P.E., Lawrence, G.R. and Mellers, B. (1997) 'Racial Prejudice and Attitudes Toward Affirmative Action', *American Journal of Political Science* 41(2): 402–19.

Kunovich, Robert M. (2002) 'Social Structural Sources of Anti-immigrant Prejudice in Europe', *International Journal of Sociology* 32: 39–57.

—— (2006) 'An exploration of the salience of Christianity for national identity in Europe', *Sociological Perspectives* 49(4): 435–60.

Kuper, S. and Dombey, D. (2007) 'Faith inspires continental divide', *Financial Times*, 20 August.

Lagerlöf, D. (2006) 'Bland judiska konspiratörer och muslimska kolonisatörer – antisemitism och islamofobi på nätet' in *Rasism och främlingsfientlighet i Sverige – Antisemitism och islamofobi 2005. Integrationsverkets rapportserie 2006:02*. Norrköping: Integrationsverket.

Lange, A. (1995) *Den svårfångade opinionen: Förhållningssätt till invandring och invandrare 1995*. Stockholm: CEIFO.

Larsson, G. (2005) 'The impact of global conflicts on local contexts: Muslims in Sweden after 9/11. The rise of Islamophobia, or new possibilities?', *Islam and Christian-Muslim Relations*, 16(1): 29–42.

—— (2007) 'Cyber-Islamophobia?; The case of WikiIslam', *Contemporary Islam* 1: 53–67.

Lasswell, H.D. (1977) 'Political socialisation as a policy science', in S.A. Renshon (ed.) *Handbook of Political Socialisation*, New York, NY: The Free Press, pp.445–67.

Laurence, Jonathan (2012) *The Emancipation of Europe's Muslims: The State's Role in Minority Integration*, Princeton, NJ: Princeton University Press.

Layman, G.C. and Green, J.C. (2006) 'Wars and Rumours of Wars: The Contexts of Cultural Conflict in American Political Behaviour', *British Journal of Political Science* 36(1): 61–89.

Lee, Sherman A., Gibbson, Jeffrey A., Thompson, John M. and Timani, Hussam S. (2009) 'The Islamophobia Scale: Instrument Development and Initial Validation', *International Journal for the Psychology of Religion* 19(2): 92–105.

Leibold, Jürgen and Kühnel, Steffen (2003) 'Islamophobie. Sensible Aufmerksamkeit für spannungsreiche Anzeichen', in Wilhelm Heitmeyer (eds) *Deutsche Zustände. Folge 2*, Frankfurt am Main: Suhrkamp, pp.100–19.

—— (2006) 'Islamophobie. Differenzierung tut not', in Wilhelm Heitmeyer (eds) *Deutsche Zustände. Folge 4*, Frankfurt am Main: Suhrkamp, pp.135–55.

Lerner, J.S., Gonzalez, R.M. Small, D.A. and Fischoff, B. (2003) 'Effects of fear and anger on perceived risks of terrorism: a national field experiment', *Psychological Science* 14(2): 144–50.

Levey, Geoffrey Brahm and Modood, Tariq (2009) 'Liberal democracy, multicultural citizenship and the Danish cartoon affair', in Geoffrey Brahm Levey and Tariq Modood (eds) *Secularism, Religion and Multicultural Citizenship*, New York: Cambridge University Press, pp.216–42.

Levine, R. A. and Campbell, D.T. (1972) *Ethnocentrism: Theories of conflict, ethnic attitudes and behavior*, New York: Wiley.

Lin, M., Kwan, V.S.Y., Cheung, A. and Fiske, S. (2005) 'Stereotype Content Model Explains Prejudice for an Envied Outgroup: Scale of Anti Asian American Stereotypes', *Personality and Social Psychology Bulletin* 31(1): 34–47.

Lindstad, M. and Fjeldstad, Ø. (2005) *Av utenlandsk opprinnelse. Nye nordmenn i avisspaltene*, Kristiansand: IJ Forlaget.

Lindkilde, L. E., Mouritsen, P. and Zapata-Barrero, R. (eds) (2009) The Muhammad Cartoons controversy in comparative perspective, Special issue *Ethnicities* 9(3).

Liu, J.H. and Hilton, D.J. (2005) 'How the past weighs on the present: Social representations of history and their role in identity politics', *British Journal of Social Psychology* 44(4): 537–56.

Love, Erik (2009) 'Confronting Islamophobia in the United States: Framing Civil Rights Activism among Middle Eastern Americans', *Patterns of Prejudice* 43(3–4): 401–25.

Maass, A., Cadinu, M., Guarnieri, G. and Grasselli, A. (2003) 'Sexual Harassment Under Social Identity Threat: The Computer Harassment Paradigm', *Journal of Personality and Social Psychology* 85: 853–70.

McClosky, H. and Brill, A. (1983) *Dimensions of Tolerance: What Americans Believe about Civil Liberties*, New York: Basic Books.

McClosky, H. and Zaller, J.R. (1984) *The American Ethos: Public Attitudes Toward Capitalism and Democracy*, Cambridge, MA: Harvard University Press.

McCombs, M.E. and Shaw, D.L. (1993) 'The Evolution of Agenda-Setting Research: Twenty-Five Years in the Marketplace of Ideas', *Journal of Communication* 43(2): 58–67.

McConahay, J. (1986) 'Modern racism, ambivalence and the modern racism scale', in J.F. Dovidio and L. Gaertner (eds) *Prejudice, Discrimination, and Racism*, San Diego: Academic Press, pp.91–125.

McFarland, S., Ageyev, V. and Abalakina, M. (1990) 'The authoritarian personality in Russia and North America', symposium held at the annual meeting of the International Society of Political Psychology, Washington, DC, July 1990.

McGann, Anthony J. and Kitschelt, Herbert (2005) 'The Radical Right in the Alps: Evolution of Support for the Swiss SVP and the Austrian FPÖ', *Party Politics* 11 (2): 147–71.

McGregor, H. A., Lieberman, J. D., Greenberg, J., Solomon, S., Arndt, J., Simon, L. and Pyszcznyski, T. (1998) 'Terror management and aggression: Evidence that mortality salience promotes aggression against worldview threatening others', *Journal of Personality and Social Psychology* 74: 590–605.

McIntosh, M.E., Mac Iver, M.A., Abele, D.G. and Nolle, D.B. (1995) 'Minority Rights and Majority Rule: Ethnic Tolerance in Romania and Bulgaria', *Social Forces* 73 (3): 939–67.

Mackie, D.M., Devos, T. and Smith, E.R. (2000) 'Intergroup emotions: Explaining offensive action tendencies in an intergroup context', *Journal of Personality and Social Psychology* 79: 602–16.

Mackie, D. and Smith, E. (eds) (2003) *From prejudice to intergroup emotions*, New York, NY: Psychology Press.

McLaren, L. (2003) 'Anti-immigrant prejudice in Europe: contact, threat perception, and preferences for the exclusion of migrants', *Social Forces* 81(3) 909–36.

MacMaster, Neil (2003) 'Islamophobia in France and the 'Algerian Problem'', in Emran Qureshi and Michael A. Sells (eds) *The New Crusades: Constructing the Muslim Enemy*, New York: Columbia University Press, pp.288–313.

Maher, D., Knox, D. and DeCuzzi, A. (2008) 'College student attitudes towards Buddhism and Islam', *Journal of College & Character* 10(2): 1–23.

Malik, Kenan (2005) 'The Islamophobia Myth', *Prospect*, 20 February.

Malm A. (2009) *Hatet mot muslimer*, Stockholm: Atlas.

Mamdani, Mahmood (2004) *Good Muslims, Bad Muslims. America, the Cold War, and the Roots of Terror*, New York: Pantheon.

Marcus, G.E., Sullivan, J.L., Theiss-Morse, E. and Wood, S.L. (1995) *With malice toward some: How people make civil liberties judgments*, Cambridge: Cambridge University Press.

Matar, Nabil (2009) 'Britons and Muslims in the early modern period: from prejudice to (a theory of) toleration', *Patterns of Prejudice* 43(3–4): 213–31.

Marques, J.M., Yzerbyt, V.Y. and Leyens, J.P. (1988) 'The black sheep effect: extremity of judgements towards in-group members as a function of group identification', *European Journal of Social Psychology* 18: 1–16.

Marquis, Lionel and Bergman, Manfred Max (2009) 'Development and Consequences of Referendum Campaigns in Switzerland, 1981–1999', *Swiss Political Science Review* 15(1): 63–97.

Mathwig, Frank (2009) 'Das Kreuz mit den Minaretten: Theologische Bemerkungen zur Rolle der Kirchen in der Minarett-Diskussion', in Mathias Tanner, *et al.* (eds) *Streit um das Minarett: Zusammenleben in der religiös pluralistischen Gesellschaft.* Zurich: Theologischer Verlag Zürich, pp.141–87.

Maussen, Marcel (2006) 'Anti-Muslim Sentiments and Mobilization in the Netherlands. Discourse, Policies and Violence', in Jocelyne Cesari (eds) *Securitization and Religious Divides in Europe. Muslims in Western Europe after 9/11 – Why the Term Islamophobia Is More a Predicament than an Explanation.* A Challenge Research Project funded by the European Commission, pp.100-142. http://www.libertysecurity.org/IMG/pdf_Challenge_Project_report.pdf

—— (2007) The Governance of Islam in Western Europe: A State of the Art Report. Imiscoe Working Paper no.16.

Maxwell, Rahsaan (2006) 'Muslims, South Asians, and the British mainstream: a national identity crisis?', *West European Politics* 29(4): 736–56.

—— (2008) 'Assimilation, Expectations, and Attitudes: How Ethnic Minority Migrant Groups Feel About Mainstream Society', *Du Bois Review* 5(2): 387–412.

—— (2009) 'Caribbean and South Asian identification with British society: The importance of perceived discrimination', *Ethnic and Racial Studies* 32(8): 1449–69.

—— (2010a) 'Trust in Government among British Muslims: The Importance of Migration Status', *Political Behavior* 32(1): 89–109.

—— (2010b) 'Embedded Communities: National Identification among British Muslims', Presented at the American Political Science Association conference, September 2–5, Washington DC

—— (2010c) 'Evaluating Integration: Political Attitudes Across Migrant Generations in Europe', *International Migration Review* 25(1): 25–52.

Mayda, Anna Maria (2006) 'Who is against Immigration? A Cross-Country Investigation of Individual Attitudes Toward Immigrants', *Review of Economics and Statistics* 88: 510–30.

Mayer, Jean-François (2009) 'L'ombre du minaret: genèse et enjeux d'une initiative', in Patrick Haenni and Stéphane Lathion (eds) *Les Minarets de la Discorde: Éclairages sur un Débat Suisse et Européen.* Gollion: Infolio, pp.12–22.

Mazzoleni, Oscar (2008) *Nationlisme et populisme en Suisse: La radicalisation de la 'nouvelle' UDC.* Lausannne: Presses polytechniques et univeritaires romandes.

Meer, N. (2008) 'The politics of voluntary and involuntary identities', *Patterns of Prejudice* 42: 61–81.

Meer, N. and Mouritsen, P. (2009) 'Political cultures compared', *Ethnicities* 9: 334–60.

Meer, N. and Noorani, T. (2008) 'A sociological comparison of anti-Semitism and anti-Muslim sentiment in Britain', *Sociological Review* 56: 195–219.

Meer, N., Dwyer, C. and Modood, T. (2010) 'Embodying nationhood?', *Sociological Review* 58: 84–111.

Mella, O and Palm, I. (2010) *Mångfaldsbarometern (Diversity barometer),* Sociologiska Institutionen, Uppsala Universitet.

Michelson, Melissa (2003) 'The corrosive effect of acculturation: How Mexican Americans lose political trust', *Social Science Quarterly* 84(4): 918–933.

Minarette.ch. (2010) 'Eidgenenössische Volksinitiative für ein Bauverbot von Minaretten', http://www.minarette.ch/index.html, October 8, 2010.

Modood, Tariq (2003) 'Muslims and the Politics of Difference', *The Political Quarterly* 74(1): 100–15.

—— (2005) *Multicultural Politics: Racism, Ethnicity and Muslims in Britain,* Minneapolis: University of Minnesota Press.

—— (2007) *Multiculturalism,* Cambridge: Polity Press.

Modood, T. and Ahmad, F. (2007) 'British Muslim perspectives on multiculturalism', *Theory, Culture and Society* 24(2): 187–213.

Modood, Tariq and Berthoud, Richard (1997) *Ethnic Minorities in Britain: Diversity and Disadvantage*, London: Policy Studies Institute.

Mogahed, D. and Nyiri, Z. (2007) 'Reinventing integration', *Harvard International Review* 29/2: 14–18.

Moore, K., Mason, P. and Lewis, J. (2008) *Images of Islam in the UK*, Cardiff: Cardiff School of Journalism, Media and Cultural Studies.

Moreras, J. (2003) 'Limits and contradictions in the legal recognition of Muslims in Spain', in W. Shadid and P.S. Von Koningsveld (eds) *Religious Freedom and the Neutrality of the State: The Position of Islam in the European Union*, Leiden: Peeters, pp.52–64.

Moscovici, S. (1981) 'On social representations', in J.P. Forgas (ed.) *Social Cognition: Perspectives on everyday understanding*, London: Academic Press, pp.181–209.

Mudde, Cas (2007) *Populist Radical Right Parties*, Cambridge: Cambridge University Press,

Müller, Felix (2009) 'Rechtliche und politische Aspekte der eidgenössischen Volksinitiave 'Gegen den Bau von Minaretten', in Mathias Tanner, *et al.* (eds) *Streit um das Minarett: Zusammenleben in der religiös pluralistischen Gesellschaft*. Zurich: Theologischer Verlag Zürich, pp.61–86.

Müller, Felix and Tanner, Mathias (2009) 'Muslime Minarette und de Minarett- Initiative in der Schweiz: Grundlagen', in Mathias Tanner, *et al.* (eds) *Streit um das Minarett: Zusammenleben in der religiös pluralistischen Gesellschaft*. Zurich: Theologischer Verlag Zürich, pp.21–43.

Nacos, B.L. and Torres-Reyna, O. (2006) *Fuelling Our Fears: Stereotyping, media coverage, and public opinion of Muslim Americans*, Lanham: Rowman & Littlefield.

Nielsson, G.P. (1985) 'States and 'Nation-Groups' a Global Taxonomy', in Tiryakian, Edward A. and Rogowski, Ronald (eds) *New Nationalisms of the Developed West*, Boston: Allen & Unwin.

Nielsen, Jørgen S. (1992) *Muslims in Western Europe*, Edinburgh: University of Edinburgh Press.

—— (1999) *Toward a European Islam*, London: Macmillan.

Nieuwenhuizen, E. and Visser, J. (2005) *Publieke Opinie*. Available: http://www.art1.nl/artikel/1242-Publieke_opinie [2008, 09/24].

Nisbet, E.C., Ostman, R. and Shanahan J. (2009) 'Public opinion towards Muslim Americans: Civil liberties and the role of religiosity, ideology and media use', in A.H. Sinno (ed.) *Muslims In Western Politics*, Bloomington, IN: Indiana University Press, pp.161–99.

Norris, Pippa (2005) *Radical Right: Voters and Parties in the Electoral Market*, Cambridge: Cambridge University Press.

Oborne, Peter and Jones, James (2008) *Muslims Under Siege: Alienating Vulnerable Communities*, Colchester: University of Essex.

Offe, Claus and Preuss, Ulrich K. (1991) 'Democratic Institutions and Moral Resources', in David Held (ed.) *Political Theory Today*, Cambridge: Polity, pp.143–71.

Okin, S. M. (1999) 'Is multiculturalism bad for women?', in J. Cohen, M. Howard and M. Nussbaum (eds) *Is Multiculturalism Bad for Women?*, Princeton, NJ: Princeton University Press.

Open Society Institute (2010a) *Muslims in Europe: A Report on 11 EU Cities*, New York, London, Budapest: Open Society Institute.

—— (2010b) *Muslims in Leicester*, New York, London, Budapest: Open Society Institute.

Oswald, D. (2005) 'Understanding anti-Arab reactions post-9/11: the role of threats, social categories, and personal ideologies', *Journal of Applied Social Psychology* 25: 1775–99.

Otterbeck, J. (2002) 'The Depiction of Islam in Sweden', *The Muslim World* 92(1–2).

Otterbeck, J. (2010a) *Samtidsislam: Unga muslimer i Malmö och Köpenhamn*, Stockholm: Carlsson.

—— (2010b) 'Sweden: Cooperation and Conflict' in A. Triandafyllidou (ed.) *Muslims in 21st Century Europe: Structural and Cultural Perspectives*, London: Routledge.

Otterbeck, Jonas and Bevelander, Pieter (2006) *Islamofobi: En studie av begreppet, ungdomars attityder och unga muslimers utsatthet*, Stockholm: Forum för levande historia.

Ouis, Pernilla and Roald, Anne Sofie (2003) *Muslim i Sverige*. Stockholm: Wahlström & Widstrand.

Panagopoulos, Costas (2006) 'The Polls-Trends. Arab and Muslim Americans and Islam in the Aftermath of 9/11', *Public Opinion Quarterly* 70(4): 608–24.

Parekh, B. (2000) *Rethinking Multiculturalism: Cultural Diversity and Political Theory*, London: MacMillan.

Park, Jaihuyn, Felix, Karla and Lee, Grace (2007) 'Implicit attitudes towards arab-muslims and the moderating effects of social information', *Basic and Applied Social Psychology* 29(1): 35–45.

Pauly, Robert J. (2004) *Islam in Europe. Integration or Marginalization?* Aldershot: Ashgate.

Pedhazur, E. J. and Pedhazur-Schmelkin, L. (1991) *'Selected topics', in Measurement, Design, and Analysis: an integrated approach*, Hillsdale, NJ: Erlbaum, pp.109–114.

Perrin, A.J. (2005) 'National Threat and Political Culture: Authoritarianism, Antiauthoritarianism, and the September 11 Attacks', *Political Psychology* 26(2): 167–94.

Persson, Anna V. and Musher-Eizenman, Dara R. (2005) 'College Students' Attitudes toward Blacks and Arabs following a Terrorist Attack as a Function of Varying Levels of Media Exposure', *Journal of Applied Social Psychology* 35(9): 1879–93.

Peter, Frank (2006) 'Individualization and Religious Authority in Western European Islam. Review Essay', *Islam and Christian-Muslim Relations* 17(1): 105–18.

Peterson, S. (1981) 'International News Selection by the Elite Press: A Case Study', *Public Opinion Quarterly* 45(2): 143–63.

Pettigrew, T.F. (1998) 'Reactions toward the new minorities of Western Europe', *Annual Review of Sociology* 24: 77–103.

Pettigrew, T.F. (1998b) 'Intergroup contact theory', *Annual Review Psychology* 49: 65–85.

Pettigrew, T.F. and Tropp, L.R. (2006) 'A meta-analytic test of intergroup contact theory', *Journal of Personality and Social Psychology* 90(5): 751–83.

Pew Research Center (2005) *Islamic Extremism: Common Concern for Muslim and Western Publics*, Washington, DC: Pew Research Center for the People & the Press. http://pewglobal.org/files/pdf/248.pdf (Accessed 1 August 2010).

—— (2006) *The Great Divide: How Westerners and Muslims View Each Other*, Washington, DC: The Pew Global Attitudes Project.

—— (2007) *Public Expresses Mixed Views of Islam, Mormonism*, Washington, DC: Pew Research Center for the People & the Press.

—— (2008) *Unfavourable Views of Jews and Muslims On The Increase in Europe*, Washington, DC: Pew Research Center for the People & the Press.

—— (2009a) *Mapping the Global Muslim Population: A Report on the Size and Distribution of the World's Muslim Population*, Washington, DC: The Pew Global Attitudes Project.

Pew Research Center (2009b) *Muslims Widely Seen As Facing Discrimination; Views of religious similarities and differences*, Washington, DC: Pew Research Center for the People & the Press.

Policy Exchange (2007) *Living apart together: British Muslims and the paradox of multiculturalism*, London: Policy Exchange.

Poole, E. (2002) *Reporting Islam*, London: Tauris.

—— (2006) 'The effects of September 11 and the war in Iraq on British newspaper coverage', in E. Poole and J.E. Richardson (eds) *Muslims in the News Media*, London: I.B Tauris, pp.89–102.

Poole, E. and Richardson, J.E. (eds) (2006) *Muslims and the News Media*, London: Tauris.

Powell, L. and Self, W.R. (2004) 'Personalized Fear, Personalized Control, and Reactions to the September 11 Attacks', *North American Journal of Psychology* 6(1): 55–70.

Poynting, Scott and Mason, Victoria (2007) 'The resistible rise of Islamophobia', *Journal of Sociology* 43(1): 61–86.

Pratto, F., Sidanius, J., Stallworth, L.M. and Malle, B.F. (1994) 'Social dominance orientation: a personality variable predicting social and political attitudes', *Journal of Personality and Social Psychology* 67: 741–63.

Pratto, F., Liu, J., Levin, S., Sidanius, J., Shih, M., Bachrach, H. and Hegarty, P. (2000) 'Social dominance orientation and the legitimization of inequality across cultures', *Journal of Cross-Cultural Psychology* 31: 369–409.

Pyszcynski, T., Solomon, S., and Greenberg, J. (2003) *In the Wake of 9/11: The Psychology of Terror*, Washington, D.C.: American Psychological Association.

Quillian, L. (1995) 'Prejudice As a Response to Perceived Group Threat: Population Composition and Anti-Immigrant and Racial Prejudice in Europe', *American Sociological Review* 60(4): 586–611.

Quist, R. and Resendez, M. (2002) 'Social dominance threat: examining social dominance theory's explanation of prejudice as legitimizing myths', *Basic and Applied Social Psychology* 24(4): 287–93.

Rasinski, K.A., Smith, T. and Díez-Nicolás, J. (2005) 'When the Trains Exploded in Madrid: Fear, Anger, Public Opinion, and Government Change', *Public Opinion Pros* (Available at: www.publicopinionpros.com/), December.

Reich, R. (2002) *Bridging Liberalism and Multiculturalism in American Education*, Chicago: University Chicago Press.

Reicher, S. and Hopkins, N. (2001) *Self and Nation, Categorisation, Contestation and Mobilization*, London: Sage.

Reynolds, W. (1982) 'Development of reliable and valid short forms of the Marlowe-Crowne Social Desirability Scale', *Journal of Clinical Psychology* 38: 119–25.

Rheault, M. and Mogahed, D. (2008) 'Cartoons and controversy', *Harvard International Review* 30/2: 68–71.

Richardson, J.E. (2004) *(Mis)Representing Islam: The Racism and Rhetoric of British Broadsheet Newspapers*, Philadelphia PA: John Benjamins Publishing Company.

Rickert, E. (1998) 'Authoritarianism and economic threat: implications for political behavior', *Political Psychology* 19: 707–20.

Riek, B.M., Mania, E.W. and Gaertner, S.L. (2006) 'Intergroup threat and out-group attitudes: A meta-analytic review', *Personality and Social Psychology Review* 10(4): 336–53.

Ring, J. and Morgentau, S. (2004) *Intolerans: Antisemitiska, homofobiska och invandrarfientliga tendenser bland unga*, Stockholm: Forum för levande historia.

Robinson, William S. (1950) 'Ecological Correlation and the Behavior of Individuals', *American Political Science* Review 15: 351–7.

Robinson, J., Witenberg, R. and Sanson, A. (2001) 'The socialization of tolerance', in M. Augoustinos (ed.) *Understanding Prejudice, Racism, and Social Conflict*, London: Sage.

Röder, Antje and Mühlau, Peter (2010) 'Discrimination, exclusion and immigrants' confidence in public institutions in Europe', *Institute for International Integration Studies Discussion Paper No. 320*, March 2010.

Roggebrand, C. and Vliegenthart, R. (2007) 'Divergent framing: The public debate on migration in the Dutch parliament and media, 1995–2004', *West European Politics* 30(3): 524–48.

Rokeach, M. (1973) *The nature of human values*, Free Press, New York.

Rooijackers, I. and Verkuyten, M. (2011) 'Mobilizing support for the extreme right: A discursive analysis of minority leadership', *British Journal of Social Psychology* DOI: 10.1111/j.2044-8309.2010.02008.x

Rosenberg, M. (1965) *Society And The Adolescent Self-image*, Princeton, NJ: Princeton University Press.

Runnymede Trust (1997) *Islamophobia: A Challenge for us all*, London: The Runnymede Trust.

Russell, D. (2002) 'In search of underlying dimensions: the use (and abuse) of factor analysis in Personality and Social Psychology Bulletin', *Personality and Social Psychology Bulletin* 28: 1629–46.

Said, Edward W. (2003[1978]) *Orientalism*, London: Penguin Books.

Said, E. (1985) 'Orientalism Reconsidered', *Race & Class* 27(2).

Said, E. (1997) Covering Islam: *How the Media and the Experts Determine how We See the Rest of the World*, 2nd edn New York: Vintage.

Salazar, J. M. (1998) 'Social identity and national identity', in S. Worchel, J. F. Morales, D. Páez and J.-C. Deschamps (eds) *Social identity: International perspectives*, London: Sage, pp.114–23.

Samtal med svenska muslimer – Situationen för svenska muslimer efter terroristattacken i USA den 11 september 2001 (2003) *Integrationsverkets rapportserie 2003:3*. Norrköping: Integrationsverket.

Sani, F. (ed.) (2008) *Self Continuity: Individual and Collective Perspectives*, Hove: Psychology Press.

Sani, F., Bowe, M. and Herrera, M. (2008) 'Perceived collective continuity: Seeing groups as temporally enduring entities', in F. Sani (ed.) *Self Continuity: Individual and Collective Perspectives*, Hove: Psychology Press.

Saroglou, V., Lamkaddem, B., Van Pachterbeke, M. and Buxant, C. (2009) 'Host society's dislike of the Islamic veil: The role of subtle prejudice, values, and religion', *International Journal of Intercultural Relations* 33: 419–28.

Scheepers, P., Gijsberts, M. and Coenders, M. (2002a) 'Ethnic Exclusionism in European Countries – Public Opposition to Civil Rights for Legal Migrants as a Response to Perceived Ethnic Threat', *European Sociological Review* 18(1): 17–34.

Scheepers, P., Gijsberts, M. and Hello, E. (2002b) 'Religiosity and prejudice against ethnic minorities in Europe: cross-national tests on a controversial relationship', *Review of Religious Research* 43: 242–265.

Schildkraut, Deborah J. (2002) 'The More Things Change ... American Identity and Mass and Elite Responses to 9/11', *Political Psychology* 23(3): 511–35.

Schissel, Bernard, Wanner, R. and Frideres, James S. (1989) 'Social and Economic Context and Attitudes toward Immigrants in Canadian Cities', *International Migration Review* 23: 289–308.

Schneider, S. L. (2008) 'Anti-Immigrant Attitudes in Europe: Outgroup Size and Perceived Ethnic Threat', *European Sociological Review* 24(1): 53–67.

Schneuwly Purdie, Mallory (2009) 'Sociographie de l'islam en Suisse', in Mallory Schneuwly Purdie, Matteo Gianni and Magali Jenny (eds) *Musulmans d'aujourd'hui: Identités plurielles en Suisse*. Geneva: Labor et Fides, pp.23–36.

Schuman, H., Steeh, C., Bobo, L. and Krysan, M. (1997) *Racial Attitudes in America: Trends and Interpretations*, Revised edn, Cambridge, MA: Harvard University Press.

Schwartz, Shalom H. (1994) 'Are There Universal Aspects in the Structure and Contents of Human Values?', *Journal of Social Issues* 50(4): 19–45.

SCP [The Netherlands Institute for Social Research] (2005) Jaarrapport integratie 2005 (Annual Report Integration 2005), Den Haag: SCP.

Seago, D. W. (1947) 'Stereotypes: Before Pearl Harbor and after', *Journal of Social Psychology* 23: 55–64.

Sears, David O. (2003) 'Childhood and adult political development', in D.O. Sears, L. Huddy and R. Jervis (eds) *Oxford Handbook of Political Psychology*, Oxford: Oxford University Press, pp.60–109.

—— (1998) 'Symbolic Racism', in Katz, P.A. and Taylor, D.A. (eds) *Eliminating Racism: Profiles in Controversy*, New York: Plenum Press, pp.53–84.

Sears, D.O. and Henry, P.J. (2003) 'The origins of symbolic racism', *Journal of Personality and Social Psychology* 85(2): 259–75.

Selznick, G. and Steinberg, S. (1969) *The Tenacity of Prejudice*, New York: Harper and Rowe.

Semyonov, M., Raijman, R., Yom Tov, A. and Schmidt, P. (2004) 'Population size, perceived threat, and exclusion: a multiple-indicators analysis of attitudes toward foreigners in Germany', *Social Science Research* 33: 681–701.

Semyonov, M., Raijman, R. and Gorodzeisky, A. (2006) 'The Rise of Anti-Foreigner Sentiment in European Societies, 1988–2000', *American Sociological Review* 71(3): 426–49.

Shadid, W. (2007) 'Muslims and Islam in Western media: Selective coverage and negative presentation', *The Maghreb Review* 31(3/4): 293–306.

Shaheen, J.G. (1997) *Arab and Muslim Stereotyping in American Popular Culture*, Washington, DC: Georgetown University.

Shaheen, J. (2001) *Reel bad Arabs: How Hollywood vilifies a people*, Northampton, MA: Interlink.

Shaugnessy, J. and Zechmeister, E. (1990) *Research Methods in Psychology*, New York: McGraw-Hill.

Sheridan, Lorraine P. (2006) 'Islamophobia Pre- and Post-September 11th, 2001', *Journal of Interpersonal Violence* 21(3): 317–36.

Sheridan, L.P. and Gillet, R. (2005) 'Major world events and discrimination', *Asian Journal of Social Psychology* 8: 191–197.

Sherif, M., Harvey, O.J., White, B.J., Hood, W.R. and Sherif, C.W. (1961) *Intergroup cooperation and competition: The Robbers Cave Experiment*, Norman, OK: University Book Exchange.

Shooman, Yasemin and Riem Spielhaus (2010) 'The Concept of the Muslim Enemy in the Public Discourse', in Jocelyne Cesari (ed.) *Muslims in the West after 9/11. Religion, Politics and Law*, London and New York: Routledge, pp.198-228.

Shryock, Andrew (2010) *Islamophobia/Islamophilia: Beyond the Politics of Enemy and Friend*, Bloomington, IN: Indiana University Press.

Sibley, C.G., Liu, J.H., Duckitt, J. and Khan, S.S. (2008) 'Social representations of history and the legitimation of social inequality: The form and function of historical negation', *European Journal of Social Psychology* 38(3): 542–65.

Sidanius, J. (1993) 'The psychology of group conflict and the dynamics of oppression: a social dominance perspective', in S. Iyengar and W. McGuire (eds) *Explorations in Political Psychology: Duke Studies in Political Psychology Series*, Durham and London: Duke University Press, pp.113–49.

Sidanius, J. and Pratto, F. (1999) *Social Dominance: An Intergroup Theory of Social Hierarchy and Oppression*, Cambridge: Cambridge University Press.

Sidanius, J., Pratto, F. and Bobo, L. 1996 'Racism, Conservatism, Affirmative Action, and Intellectual Sophistication: A Matter of Principled Conservatism or Group Dominance?', *Journal of Personality and Social Psychology* 70(3): 476–90.

Sides, J. and Gross, K. (2007) Stereotypes of Muslims, Their Causes, and Their Consequences, Paper presented at the Annual Meeting of the American Political Science Association, Chicago, IL.

Sindic, D. and Reicher, S. D. (2009) 'Our way of life is worth defending: Testing a model of attitudes towards superordinate group membership through a study of Scots' attitudes towards Britain', *European Journal of Social Psychology* 39(1): 114–29.

Sixtensson, J. (2009) *Hemma och främmande i staden: Kvinnor med slöja berättar*, Malmö: Malmö University.

Skenderovic, Damir (2006) 'Feindbild Muslime – Islamophobie in der radikalen Rechten', in Urs Altermatt, Mariano Delago and Guido Vergauwen (eds) *Der Islam in Europa: Zwischen Weltpolitik und Alltag*, Stuttgart: Kohlhammer, pp.79–95.

Sleegers, F. (2007) *In debat over Nederland* [In debate about the Netherlands], Amsterdam: Amsterdam University Press.

Sloan, J. (2010) '3 in 4 fear a fresh strike', *The Sun*, 7 July.

Smeekes, A., Verkuyten, M. and Poppe, E. (2011) 'Mobilising opposition towards Muslim immigrants: National identification and the representation of national history', *British Journal of Social Psychology* 50(2): 265–80.

Smeekes, A., Verkuyten, M. and Poppe, E. (forthcoming) Historical tolerance and the acceptance of Muslim expressive rights. (manuscript in preparation).

Smetana, J. G. (2006) 'Social-cognitive domain theory: Consistencies and variations in children's moral and social judgments' in M. Killen and J. Smetana (eds) *Handbook of Moral Development*, Mahwah, NJ: Lawrence Erlbaum.

Smith, A.D. (1991) *National Identity*, London: Penguin.

Smith, Jane I. (2010) 'Islam in America', in Jocelyne Cesari (ed.) *Muslims in the West after 9/11. Religion, Politics and Law*, London and New York: Routledge, pp.28–42.

Sniderman, Paul M. and Hagendoorn, Louk (2007) *When Ways of Life Collide. Multiculturalism and its Discontents in the Netherlands*, Princeton: Princeton University Press.

Sniderman, P.M. and Piazza, T. (1993) *The Scar of Race*, Cambridge, MA: Harvard University Press.

Sniderman, P.M., Hagendoorn, L. and Prior, M. (2004) 'Predispositional Factors and Situational Triggers: Exclusionary Reactions to Immigrant Minorities', *American Political Science Review* 98(1): 35–50.

Sniderman, P.M., Peri, P., de Figueiredo, R.J.P. and Piazza, T. (2000) *The Outsider: Prejudice and Politics in Italy*, Princeton, NJ: Princeton University Press.

Sniderman, P.M., Tetlock, P.E., Glaser, J.E., Green, D.P. and Hout, M. (1989) 'Principled Tolerance and the American Mass Public', *British Journal of Political Science*, 19(1): 25–45.

Spillman, Lyn (1995) 'Culture, Social Structures, and Discursive Fields', in Ben Agger (ed.) *Current Perspectives in Social Theory (15)*, Greenwich and London: JAI Press.

Stangor, C. (2004) *Social Groups in Action and Interaction*, New York, NY: Psychology Press.

Statham, Paul (1999) 'Political Mobilisation by Minorities in Britain: a negative feedback of 'race relations'?', *Journal of Ethnic and Migration Studies* 25(4): 597–626.

Statistics Norway (2009) Samfunnsspeilet 3/2009. Retrieved August 10, 2010 from: http://www.ssb.no/ssp/utg/200903/ssp.pdf

Stenner, K. (2005) *The Authoritarian Dynamic*, New York: Cambridge University Press.

Stephan, W.G. and Stephan, C.W. (2000) 'An integrated threat theory of prejudice', in S. Oskamp (ed.) *Reducing Prejudice and Discrimination*, Mahwah, NJ: Lawrence Erlbaum, pp.23–45.

Stephan, W.G., Renfro, C.L., Esses, V.M., Stephan, C.M. and Martin, T. (2005) 'The effects of feeling threatened on attitudes towards immigrants', *International Journal of Intercultural Relations* 29: 1–19.

Stephan, W.G., Ybarra, O. and Morrison, R.K. (2008) 'Intergroup Threat Theory', in T. Nelson (ed.) *Handbook of Prejudice*, Mahwah, NJ: Lawrence Erlbaum Associates.

Stolz, Jörg (2005) 'Explaining Islamophobia; A test of four theories based on the case of a Swiss city', *Swiss Journal of Sociology* 31(3): 547–66.

Strabac, Zan and Listhaug, Ola (2008) 'Anti-Muslim prejudice in Europe: A multilevel analysis of survey data from 30 countries', *Social Science Research* 37(1): 268–86.

Struch, N. and Schwartz, S. H. (1989) 'Intergroup aggression: Its predictors and distinctness from in-group bias', *Journal of Personality and Social Psychology* 56(3): 364–73.

Sullivan, J.L. and Transue, J.E. (1999) 'The Psychological Underpinnings of Democracy: A Selective Review of Research on Political Tolerance, Interpersonal Trust, and Social Capital', *Annual Review of Psychology* 50: 625–50.

Sumner, W.G. ([1907]2002) *Folkways: A Study of Mores, Manners, Customs and Morals*, Mineola, NY: Dover Publications.

Swiss Parliamentary Commission (2009) http://www.parlament.ch/d/mm/2009/Seiten/mm-spk-s-2009-03-27.aspx, October 15, 2010.

Tajfel, H. (1981a) *Human Groups and Social Categories: Studies in Social Psychology*, New York, NY: Cambridge University Press.

—— (1981b) 'Social Stereotypes and Social Groups', in J.C. Turner and H. Giles (eds) *Intergroup Behaviour*, Oxford: Blackwell, pp.144–67.

—— (1982a) *Social Identity and Intergroup Relations*, Cambridge: Cambrige University Press.

—— (1982b) Social identity of inter-group relations', *Annual Review of Psychology* 33(1): 1–39.

Tajfel, H. and Turner, J C. (1986) 'The social identity theory of intergroup behavior', in S. Worchel and W. G. Austin (eds) *Psychology of intergroup relations*, Chicago: Nelson-Hall, pp.7–17.

Tanner, Erwin (2009) 'Interdire les minarets dans la constitution fédérale', in Patrick Haenni and Stéphane Lathion (eds) *Les Minarets de la Discorde: Éclairages sur un Débat Suisse et Européen*. Gollion: Infolio, pp.69–81.

Tausch, N., Hewstone, M., Kenworthy, J., Cairns, E. and Christ, O. (2007) 'Cross-community contact, perceived status differences, and intergroup attitudes in Northern Ireland: The mediating roles of individual-level versus group-level threats and the moderating role of social identification', *Political Psychology* 28(1): 53–68.

Taylor, C. (1992) 'The politics of recognition', in A. Gutmann (ed.) *Multiculturalism: Examining the Politics of Recognition*, Princeton, NJ.: Princeton University Press.

Theiss-Morse, Elizabeth (2009) *Who Counts as an American? The Boundaries of National Identity*, New York, NY: Cambridge University Press.

Thomas, Elaine R. (2006) 'Keeping Identity at a Distance: Explaining France's New Legal Restrictions on the Islamic Headscarf', *Ethnic and Racial Studies* 29(2): 237–59.

Thorne, J. and Stuart, H. (2008) *Islam on Campus*, London: Centre for Social Cohesion.

Toberman, B. (2009) 'Poll: BNP leader "lied" over Holocaust', *Jewish Chronicle*, 30 October.

Triandafyllidou, Anna (1998) 'National identity and the 'Other'', *Ethnic and Racial Studies* 21(4): 593–612.

—— (ed.) (2010) *Muslims in 21st Century Europe: Structural and Cultural Perspectives*, London: Routledge.

Tribalat, Michèle and Kaltenbach, Jeannette (2002) *La République et l'islam: entre crainte et aveuglement*. Paris: Gallimard.

Turiel, E. (2002) *The Culture of Morality*, Cambridge: Cambridge University Press.

Turner, J.C. and Reynolds, K., (2001) 'The social identity perspective in intergroup relations: Theories, themes, and controversies', in R. Brown and S.L. Gaertner (eds), *Blackwell Handbook of Social Psychology: Intergroup Processes*. Oxford: Blackwell.

Tzortzis, H.A. (2010) *Perceptions on Islam & Muslims*, London: Islamic Education and Research Academy.

United States Department of State (2010) '2009 Country Reports on Human Rights Practices: Switzerland'. http://www.state.gov/g/drl/rls/hrrpt/2009/eur/136061.htm, October 1, 2010.

Van der Noll, J. and Dekker, H. (2010) 'Islamophobia: In search of an explanation of negative attitudes toward Islam and Muslims, testing political socialization theory', *Politics, Culture and Socialization* 1(3): 239–55.

Van der Noll, Jolanda, Poppe, Edwin and Verkuyten, Maykel (2010) 'Political Tolerance and Prejudice: Differential Reactions towards Muslims in the Netherlands', *Basic and Applied Social Psychology* 32(1): 46–56.

Van Oudenhoven, Pieter, Jan, Prins, Karin and Buunk, Bram (1998) 'Attitudes of majority and minority members towards adaptation of immigrants', *European Journal of Social Psychology* 28(6): 995–1013.

Vasta, E. (2007) 'From ethnic minorities to ethnic majority policy: multiculturalism and the shift to assimilation in the Netherlands', *Ethnic and Racial Studies* 30(5): 713–40.

Velasco González, Karina, Verkuyten, Maykel, Weesie, Jeroen and Poppe, Edwin (2008) 'Prejudice towards Muslims in the Netherlands: Testing Integrated Threat Theory', *British Journal of Social Psychology* 47(4): 667–85.

Vercauteren, E. (2005) Islamofobie: een nieuw racisme? Een theoretische inleiding, MA Conflict and Development edn, Ghent University.

Verkuyten, M. (2005) 'Ethnic group identification and group evaluation among minority and majority groups: Testing the multiculturalism hypothesis', *Journal of Personality and Social Psychology*, 88(1): 121–38.

Verkuyten, M. and Slooter, L. (2007) 'Tolerance of Muslim beliefs and practices: Age related differences and context effects', *International Journal of Behavioral Development* 31(5): 467–77.

Verkuyten, M. and Zaremba, L. (2005) 'Interethnic relations in a changing political context', *Social Psychology Quarterly* 68(4): 375–86.

Vertovec, S. and Wessendorf, S. (eds) (2010) *The Multiculturalism Backlash: European discourses, policies and practices*, London: Routledge.

Vignoles, V.L., Regalia, C., Manzi, C., Golledge, J. and Scabini, E. (2006) 'Beyond Self-Esteem: Influence of Multiple Motives on Identity Construction', *Journal of Personality and Social Psychology* 90(2): 308–33.

Voas, D. and Ling, R. (2010) 'Religion in Britain and the United States', in A. Park, J. Curtice, K. Thomson, M. Phillips, E. Clery and S. Butt (eds), *British Social Attitudes: The 26th Report*, London: Sage, pp.65–86.

Vogt, W.P. (1997) *Tolerance and Education. Learning To Live with Diversity and Difference*, Sage Publications Inc, Thousand Oaks, CA.

Wainryb, C., Shaw, L.A. and Maianu, C. (1998) 'Tolerance and intolerance: Children's and adolescents' judgements of dissenting beliefs, speech, persons, and conduct', *Child Development* 69(6): 1541–55.

Wainryb, C., Shaw, L.A., Langley, M., Cottam, K. and Lewis, R. (2004) 'Children's thinking about diversity of belief in the early school years: Judgments of relativism, tolerance, and disagreeing persons', *Child Development* 75(3): 687–703.

Wälti, Carole (2009) 'Poll shows majority against banning minarets'. http://www.swissinfo. ch/eng/Specials/Islam_and_Switzerland/Minaret_vote/Poll_shows_majority_against_ banning_minarets.html?cid=1303148, September 30, 2010.

Walzer, M. (1997) *On Toleration*, New Haven, CT: Yale University Press.

Wanner, Philippe and Piguet, Étienne (2002) 'The Practice of Naturalization in Switzerland: A Statistical Overview', *Population 2002*, 57(6): 917–26.

Ward, C. and Masgoret, A.M. (2006) 'An integrative model of attitudes towards immigrants', *International Journal of Intercultural Relations* 30(6): 671–82.

Weil, F. D. (1985) 'The variable effects of education on liberal attitudes: A comparative-historical analysis of anti-Semitism using public opinion survey data', *American Sociological Review* 50: 458–74.

Welzel, C., Inglehart, R. and Klingemann, H.D. (2003) 'The theory of human development: A cross-cultural analysis', *European Journal of Political Research* 42(3): 341–79.

Wenzel, James (2006) 'Acculturation Effects on Trust in National and Local Government Among Mexican Americans', *Social Science Quarterly* 87(5): 1073–87.

Werbner, Pnina (2005) 'Islamophobia: Incitement to Religious Hatred – Legislating for a New Fear?, *Anthropology Today* 21(1): 5–9.

West, Ed. (2009) 'Vatican deplores Swiss ban on minarets.' *The Catholic Herald*, December 4. http://archive.catholicherald.co.uk/articles/a0000699.shtml, October 1, 2010.

Westin, Charles (1984) *Majoritet om minoritet: En studie i etnisk tolerans i 80-talens Sverige.* Stockholm: LiberFölag.

Whitley, B.E., Jr. (1999) 'Right-wing authoritarianism, social dominance orientation, and prejudice', *Journal of Personality and Social Psychology* 77: 126–34.

Wilcox, C. and Norrander, B. (2002) 'Of Moods and Morals: The Dynamics of Opinion on Abortion and Gay Rights' in B. Norrander and C. Wilcox (eds) *Understanding Public Opinion*, Washington, DC: CQ Press.

Wilcox, C., Sigelman, L. and Cook, E. (1989) 'Some Like it Hot: Individual Differences in Responses to Group Feeling Thermometers', *Public Opinion Quarterly* 53(2): 246–57.

Wille, Klaus (2009) 'Swiss Ban on Minaret Construction May Prompt Legal Challenges.' *Bloomberg News*, November 29. http://www.bloomberg.com/apps/news?pid=newsarchive&sid=an2H0gANoLi8, October 6, 2010.

Wohlrab-Sahr, Monika and Tezcan, Levent (eds) (2007) *Konfliktfeld Islam in Europa*, Baden-Baden: Nomos.

Wynne-Jones, J. and Sawer, P. (2008) 'More than half of Britons believe Muslims must do more to integrate', *Sunday Telegraph*, 13 January.

Yalonios, C., Mogannam, G. and Milton, K. (2005) *Western Perceptions of Islam and Muslims: A Study of Public Opinion and the Role of the Media in the United States and Western Europe*, San Rafael, CA: Communique Partners.

Yum, Y. and Schenck-Hamlin, W. (2005) 'Reactions to 9/11 as a Function of Terror Management and Perspective Taking', *Journal of Social Psychology* 145(3): 265–86.

Yzerbyt, V., Dumont, M. and Wigboldus, D. (2003) 'I feel for us: The impact of categorization and identification on emotions and action tendencies', *British Journal of Social Psychology* 42(4): 533–49.

Zaller, J.R. (1992) *The Nature and Origins of Mass Opinion*, New York: Cambridge University Press.

Zapata-Barrero, R (2006) 'The Muslim community and Spanish tradition: maurophobia as a fact, and impartiality as a desideratum', in T. Modood, A. Triandafyllidou and R. Zapata-Barrero (eds) *Multiculturalism, Muslims and citizenship: a European approach*, New York: Routledge, pp.143–61.

—— (2008) 'Policies and public opinion towards immigrants: the Spanish case', *Journal Ethnic and Racial Studies* 32(7): 1101–20.

—— (ed.) (2009a) *Políticas y gobernabilidad de la Inmigración en España*, Barcelona: Ariel.

—— (2010a) 'Dynamics of diversity in Spain: old questions, new challenges', in S. Vertovec and S. Wessendorf (eds) *The Multiculturalism Backlash: European discourses, policies and practices*, London: Routledge, pp.181–200.

—— (2010b) 'Managing diversity in Spanish Society: a practical approach', *Journal of Intercultural Studies* 31(4): 383–402.

Zapata-Barrero, R. and Qasem, I. (2008) 'The politics of discourse towards Islam and Muslim communities in Europe', in P. Mouritsen and K. E. Jørgensen (eds) *Constituting Communities: Political Solutions to Cultural Conflict*, Hampshire: Palgrave Macmillan, pp.73–93

Zapata-Barrero, R. and Witte, N. de (2010) 'Muslims in Spain: Blurring past and present Moors', in A. Triandafyllidou (ed.) *Muslims in 21st century Europe: Structural and cultural perspectives*, London: Routledge, pp.181–98.

Zick, A., Wolf, C., Küpper, B., Davidov, E., Schmidt, P. and Heitmeyer, W. (2008) 'The syndrome of group-focused enmity: The interrelation of prejudices tested with multiple cross-sectional and panel data', *Journal of Social Issues* 64(2): 363–83.

Zolberg, A.R. and Woon, L.L. (1999) 'Why Islam is like Spanish: Cultural Incorporation in Europe and the United States', *Politics and Society* 27(1): 5–38.

Index